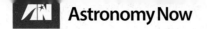
Astronomy Now

SATURN
EXPLORING THE RINGED PLANET

Hundreds of amazing pictures of Saturn, its rings and moons

GW00692131

Written and edited by Keith Cooper
Designed by Steve Kelly
Published by Steven Young

ISBN: 978-0-955-0278-3-3

Astronomy Now
PO Box 175
Tonbridge
Kent
TN10 4ZY

astronomynow.com
Tel: 01732 446111

Foreword

Superlatives are often used in the field of space exploration – sometimes somewhat freely, but in the case of the Cassini–Huygens mission, utterly deserved. This project, which is far from over, has truly re-written the textbooks for the Saturnian system. At the political level, it has shown how international co-operation in space research should be done – the collaboration between the European Space Agency and NASA has been open, generous, efficient and has worked spectacularly well.

This has been the first mission dedicated to studying the Saturnian system from really close quarters – the first to stay in orbit rather than to fly by as with Pioneer 11 and the two Voyager spacecraft. Saturn itself has been revealed in great detail, also its majestic ring system and its complex magnetosphere. Yet the greatest revelations have probably come from Saturn's moons, in particular Titan and Enceladus. Titan, of course, was a special target from the very start with the Huygens probe directed to descend through its atmosphere and to land on its up-to-then mysterious surface. Titan has now been revealed by the combination of in situ measurements from Huygens and remote measurements by Cassini to be a wonderful and complex place – with hydrocarbon seas and lakes of liquid methane and ethane, rivers, dune fields, cryovolcanoes, weather systems, rain and an extremely rich and thick atmosphere. As if that wasn't enough, there is strong evidence that below Titan's icy mantle there lies a global sub-surface ocean of water! Almost as a bonus, Enceladus has been found to be spewing water into space through cracks in the surface as well as being a likely home for organic molecules – highly unexpected discoveries!

For me, it has been a wonderful experience. I was chosen in 1990 to provide one of the six instruments to be carried by the Huygens probe, namely the Surface Science Package. We six PIs (Principal Investigators) had published between us precisely one scientific paper on the subject of Titan, such was the lack of previous research on Titan! For the next 15 years, until the glorious landing day on 14 January 2005, when we descended through Titan's atmosphere and surprisingly gently settled onto the surface, I was privileged to be part of a world-wide team of scientists, engineers and planners from universities, industries and space agencies who, between them, crafted a wonderfully sophisticated space probe in the shape of Huygens. This remarkable craft had to be totally autonomous for its period of glory because from the moment it was released from Cassini on Christmas Day 2004, it was completely 'on its own' – it had no radio receiver so all of its subsequent actions and decisions had to be taken by itself during its 21-day plunge towards Titan, its switch on and perilous two-and-a-half hour descent to the surface. What happened then is now history and I feel so honoured to have been a part of that history.

Let's look forward because, after Cassini–Huygens, we shall go back to Titan, Enceladus and in fact the whole Saturnian system. Because of what Cassini–Huygens has told us, we now know what sort of specialised platforms to go back with – balloons or 'boats' for Titan, deep drillers for Enceladus and whatever more our resourceful space scientists and engineers can dream up. Thinking selfishly, I hope to be part of that, but if not, I shall watch with anticipation!

Professor John Zarnecki
PI, Huygens Surface Science Package
The Open University
August 2015

An artist's impression of Huygens thundering towards Titan, with Saturn in the background. Image: ESA/D Ducros.

An epic
of exploration

Great voyages of exploration are the stuff of legend: Christopher Columbus, Marco Polo, Ferdinand Magellan, Scott of the Antarctic, Apollo 11. Not all our explorers are human, however. To reach the most distant regions of the Solar System, our emissaries are robotic, guided by computer programming and uploaded commands from Earth. Among them is the Cassini–Huygens mission, one of the greatest space missions ever undertaken.

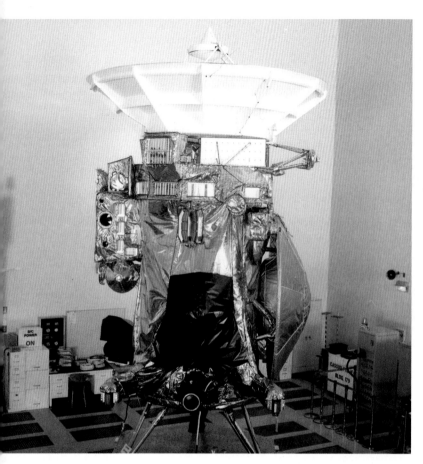

sliver of light that is a band of icy rings seen edge-on, all above a creamy planetary atmosphere wracked by storm clouds?

The sheer artistry that seeps from the pixels of each and every picture contributes to what has been an outstanding mission of discovery. Cassini's role is not simply to investigate just one planet, but to thoroughly explore an entire miniature planetary system composed of Saturn's diverse range of moons. Through studies of Saturn, its moons and its rings, we are learning about not just the ringed planet, but in the grander scheme of things about the birth and evolution of worlds, as well as the possible origins of life. We have been surprised, amazed and mystified, sometimes all at the same time, by what Cassini–Huygens has discovered.

Those discoveries make up the meat of the story, but as every fairy tale teaches us, each story has a beginning. Cassini–Huygens' story began in the year 1982, born of two parents with a complex lineage. One of these parents was science, the nature of which urged us to explore and to return to Saturn and revisit the mysteries that had been thrown up by the previous Pioneer and Voyager excursions to the ringed planet. The other parent was international diplomacy. During the early 1980s the European Space Agency (ESA) was still a fledgling organisation, having established itself in 1975. During ESA's efforts to make its mark on the world stage, European scientists became irritated at an apparent sense that senior figures at NASA were not taking ESA seriously, viewing the Europeans as merely a junior partner rather than as contemporary equals. ESA was ambitious and if NASA was not going to work with them towards those ambitions, Europe would look for a new partner to go to the stars with. The Soviet Union were right on Europe's doorstep and had pedigree in space. Slowly ESA began to make tentative advances towards the Soviets, a move towards the Cold War enemy that sent a wave of mild alarm through Washington.

In an effort to steer the European Space Agency away from working with the Soviet Union, renewed discussions between NASA and ESA scientists led, in 1982, to the concept of the Saturn Orbiter/Titan Probe (SOTP), which initially was to be based on the unbuilt Mariner Mark II spacecraft chassis and which would explore both Saturn and its largest moon, Titan. Various reports and design studies into how the mission could be performed came and went, some of them depicting NASA and ESA working together, others pitching the Cassini mission as a standalone US effort. Ultimately, however, NASA wanted to go to Saturn with Europe and in 1988 both space agencies shook hands and agreed to the mission. NASA would construct and manage the orbiter, named Cassini after Giovanni Domenico (Jean-Dominique) Cassini, whose seventeenth century observations of Saturn revealed four new moons (Iapetus, Rhea, Tethys and Dione) and also discovered the Cassini Division, which is an apparent gap in the ring system. The Italian Space Agency also contributed individually to Cassini, supplying the spacecraft's high-gain radio antenna dish as well as the radar systems that would utilise the antenna. Meanwhile, ESA would build the Titan lander, named Huygens after Christiaan Huygens, the Dutch astronomer who discovered Titan in 1655. The Huygens probe would ride piggyback to Saturn

The story of the Cassini–Huygens spacecraft has been an epic adventure of modern times but, like any true epic, insurmountable odds and vengeful enemies will stop at nothing to thwart the hero. Only, in Cassini–Huygens' case, the seemingly insurmountable odds were the international politics that gave birth to the mission, while the vengeful enemies were the United States Congress and an army of environmental protestors. Yet somehow, defying savage budget cuts and potentially fatal technical faults, Cassini–Huygens triumphed over all, successfully reaching the promised land of Saturn in July 2004.

It took a seven-year voyage across the ocean of space and fifteen years of planning and development prior to blasting off from Cape Canaveral, in October 1997, to get Cassini to its destination. In the decade since its arrival into Saturnian orbit, Cassini has not only transformed what we know about the ringed planet, but in a more general sense has redefined our expectations for planetary exploration. The spectacular images that Cassini has captured of the giant planet, its graceful rings and its myriad moons, each one brimming with character, unique and distinct from each other, are like science fiction made reality. Where else could you watch two moons passing by in the night, skirting the edge of a thin

BATTLESTAR GALACTICA

The Cassini spacecraft, which is about the height of a double-decker bus, waits patiently in a clean room at the Jet Propulsion Laboratory. The shallow cone-shaped objected mounted on its side (right) is the Huygens probe.
Image: NASA/JPL.

THE SPECTACULAR IMAGES THAT CASSINI HAS CAPTURED OF THE GIANT PLANET, ITS GRACEFUL RINGS AND ITS MYRIAD MOONS, ARE LIKE SCIENCE FICTION MADE REALITY

RADIATION LEVELS

One of Cassini's three radioisotopic thermoelectric generators (RTGs) that caused such controversy in the days prior to the spacecraft's launch. Image: NASA/JPL.

on Cassini, then detach at the appropriate moment to dive into the atmosphere of Titan and possibly touch down on its surface. In many ways, Huygens was a far more ambitious concept than even the Cassini orbiter. Although it was officially an atmospheric probe (nobody at the time knew what was on the surface of Titan, so planning a landing was difficult), if Huygens was able to touchdown (or splashdown) on Titan's surface it would have made the most remote landing ever attempted on a Solar System body.

Although the two space agencies had agreed on the joint mission, that did not necessarily make it so. The United States Congress had first to be convinced to part with the cash. It was not an easy pitch; the price tag was hefty. The Cassini orbiter spacecraft would cost $1.4 billion for NASA's contractor, Lockheed Martin, to build, and $422 million to launch, not forgetting the operating costs on top of that. Congress authorised the mission in 1989, yet politicians considered killing Cassini twice, in 1992 and 1995, though to renege on the project at that stage would have resulted in a minor diplomatic incident with Europe, which had already invested half a billion dollars in the Huygens probe, as well as $160 million from the Italian Space Agency for Cassini's antenna dish. To help finance Cassini, another mission built around the same 'Mariner Mark II' chassis, namely the Comet Rendezvous Asteroid Fly-By (CRAF), was scrapped. ESA took up this project themselves and it evolved into the

CASSINI GETS UNDERWAY

Protestors had tried to prevent the launch of Cassini, but on 15 October 1997 it blasted off on one of the greatest voyages of discovery ever undertaken. Image: NASA/JPL/KSC.

highly successful Rosetta mission (which also featured the second most distant landing, in the form of the Philae probe onto the surface of the comet).

Despite its dual stays of execution, Cassini was unloved in many corners during those early days, even finding enemies at the very top of NASA. Dan Goldin, the agency's administrator between 1992 and 2001, deemed the huge expense of the Cassini mission to be utterly wasteful. Goldin's modus operandi was to reduce NASA's costs by making missions "faster, better, cheaper". In comparison, Goldin referred to Cassini as a dollar-guzzling "Battlestar Galactica" mission (fans of the 1978 science fiction series to which Goldin referred may consider the analogy a complement – Goldin's comments came before the 2004–2009 remake – but the original *Battlestar Galactica* was cancelled after just one season, mainly as a result of the spiralling costs to produce the show, mirroring the spiralling costs of Cassini). Goldin publicly stated that if Cassini had been proposed under his watch, the mission never would have happened. In retrospect, Goldin's opinion is extremely short-sighted given Cassini's tremendous success, but fortunately his predecessor, Len Fisk, had taken a less conservative viewpoint. Like the Hubble Space Telescope, Cassini proved extremely expensive but well worth the cost. Goldin's 'faster, better, cheaper' model had one main success – the Mars Pathfinder mission – and a series of failures and lost spacecraft. Cassini outlasted them all.

Yet even with Cassini–Huygens sitting pretty on the launch pad at Cape Canaveral in October 1997, forces were moving in an attempt to make one last-ditch effort to kill Cassini before it ever left Earth.

Radiation warning

Solar energy just does not cut it far beyond the Sun in the outer Solar System, where our star becomes an increasingly anaemic figure the further out a spacecraft travels. So to provide enough power for the spacecraft to operate over many years, Cassini carries on board a trio of radioisotope thermoelectric generators, known as RTGs for short, as well as a bunch of radioisotope heater units that protect the orbiter's instruments from becoming too cold and breaking down.

Cassini's RTGs produce heat from the radioactive decay of plutonium-238. This heat is then converted into

CASSINI ARCED INTO THE NIGHT AIR ON A STREAM OF FIRE DURING THE EARLY MORNING OF 15 OCTOBER 1997.

electricity thanks to the thermoelectric effect, whereby in the simplest terms, a difference in temperature at two junctions between a pair of electrical semi-conductors can generate a voltage and hence an electrical current. Cassini carried at launch 33 kilograms of plutonium – the most that had ever been sent into space before (Galileo before it carried 16 kilograms of plutonium-238 split between two RTGs).

There is nothing inherently dangerous with functioning RTGs, particularly when they are in space, far from life on Earth, but not everybody was convinced that Cassini and its plutonium cargo could get into space safely. Environmental and anti-nuclear protestors, led by such prominent scientists as Dr Michio Kaku and several former NASA engineers, expressed concerns that should the Titan IV rocket carrying Cassini explode on the launch-pad, or in mid-air, it could create an environmental disaster greater than Chernobyl, by spreading the radioactive plutonium across large swathes of land and air, exposing billions of people to radioactive fallout and potentially resulting in at least 5,000 extra deaths from cancer. Even if Cassini made it into space safely, it was set to return in 1999 during a fly-by to gain a gravitational slingshot from Earth towards the outer Solar System. The protestors feared a miscalculation in its orbit could see it enter Earth's atmosphere and break up, spreading the plutonium everywhere, despite NASA insisting that the ceramic casing surrounding the RTGs was tough enough to survive an explosion or re-entry through the atmosphere and a crash landing.

In the protestors' minds it had all the ingredients for a nightmare scenario and they campaigned for the White House Office of Science and Technology Policy to reconsider the launch. It falls to the White House to authorise every launch of an RTG and, satisfied that all safety precautions had been taken, officials rejected the call to cancel the launch. A last-ditch attempt to scupper the launch via an injunction was thrown out of court and Cassini was free to blast off, which it did so, arcing into the night air on a stream of fire during the early morning of 15 October 1997.

Cassini was not on the way to Saturn yet though. It needed to build up speed first, bouncing around between Earth, Venus and Jupiter in a game of gravitational pinball before being thrown onto a faster trajectory towards Saturn. The first encounter with Venus on 26 April 1998 boosted Cassini–Huygen's velocity by seven kilometres per second, enough to send it out beyond the orbit of Earth, almost to the realm of Mars' orbit. Firing its engines to reduce its speed by 0.45 kilometres per second, the spacecraft was able to loop back towards Venus and gain another boost of nearly seven kilometres per second on 24 June 1999, before returning home for a close approach of Earth at an altitude of 1,166 kilometres. Despite the fears of some that Cassini, now travelling at 19 kilometres per second, could re-enter the atmosphere, NASA's mission planners had got their calculations spot on. Cassini,

ONWARDS TO SATURN!

Cassini streaks into the night sky, safely beginning its long voyage to the ringed planet Saturn. Image: NASA/JPL/KSC.

SOLAR SYSTEM ROYALTY

The most detailed image of Jupiter, the king of the planets, ever taken, produced by Cassini in December 2000 while on its way to Saturn. Compare the turbulent visage of Jupiter with the relative calmness of Saturn's atmosphere. Cassini was 10 million kilometres from Jupiter when it took this shot. Image: NASA/JPL/ Space Science Institute.

VIEW OF THE RINGED WORLD

A wide view of Saturn and its rings, captured by Voyager 2. Rhea and Dione are immediately below Saturn. Image: NASA/JPL.

CHEMISTRY IN THE RINGS

This enhanced picture from Voyager 2 shows Saturn's rings in false colour, highlighting chemical differences between the differing ringlets with distance from the planet. Image: NASA/JPL.

SHADOW OF THE MOON

Saturn and two of its moons, Dione and Tethys (closest to Saturn, and its shadow is also cast onto the planet, as seen at bottom right), as imaged from a distance of 13 million kilometres during Voyager 1's fly-by of the planet. Note the gap in the rings through which the planet's atmosphere can be seen. This is the Cassini Division and it is not as empty as it appears. Image: NASA/JPL.

sped up a further 5.5 kilometres per second by Earth's gravity, said goodbye and set sail for the outer Solar System. Its first stop would be a fleeting yet rewarding visit to the giant planet Jupiter.

Jupiter and Saturn are similar in many ways, yet different in others. They are comfortably the biggest planets in the Solar System, both are gaseous, they probably formed in the same way and the moons orbiting each world number in the sixties. However, Jupiter exhibits much starker contrast between its atmospheric bands and greater activity in its turbulent storms, while Saturn's rings are quite unlike anything else in the Solar System. Jupiter, Uranus and Neptune all have rings too, but these are dark, thin imitations of Saturn's crowing glory.

So Jupiter was an excellent way to test Cassini's scientific prowess when it sailed past at a distance of 10 million kilometres on 30 December 2000. It might sound like a rather distant 'close' approach, but it was sufficient for Jupiter's substantial gravity to act on Cassini–Huygens and fling it the rest of the way to Saturn with an additional boost of 2.2 kilometres per second.

The fly-by was a huge success, providing just a preview of what Cassini could do once it reached Saturn. Long-range images of Jupiter taken on 1 October 2000 wowed the imaging team, led by Dr Carolyn Porco of the Space Science Institute, who exclaimed, "The spacecraft is steadier than any I have ever seen – it's so steady the images are unexpectedly sharp and clear, even in the longest exposures taken in the most challenging spectral regions."

Cassini's narrow-angle camera captured the first ever movie sequences of the rotation of clouds near Jupiter's poles, bringing thousands of immense atmospheric storms into clarity. Cassini also produced an iconic image of a quarter-Jupiter, its Great Red Spot glaring angrily at the camera, while the spacecraft was also on hand to witness the aftermath of the merger of three smaller storms into a new, larger storm called 'Oval BA' that subsequently turned red and became known as 'Red Spot Junior' a few years later. Meanwhile, by teaming up with the Galileo spacecraft that was in orbit around Jupiter at the time, Cassini was able to take measurements of the composition of the giant planet's atmosphere, detecting the likes of hydrocarbons such as methane and acetylene, plus water vapour besides the ubiquitous hydrogen gas that makes up the bulk of the planet.

Cassini showed the full extent of the Io Plasma Torus – a fuzzy ring of charged sulphur particles belched out into space by volcanoes on Jupiter's moon Io and

> JUPITER AND SATURN ARE SIMILAR IN MANY WAYS: THEY ARE COMFORTABLY THE BIGGEST PLANETS IN THE SOLAR SYSTEM, BOTH ARE GASEOUS, THEY PROBABLY FORMED IN THE SAME WAY AND THE MOONS ORBITING EACH WORLD NUMBER IN THE SIXTIES.

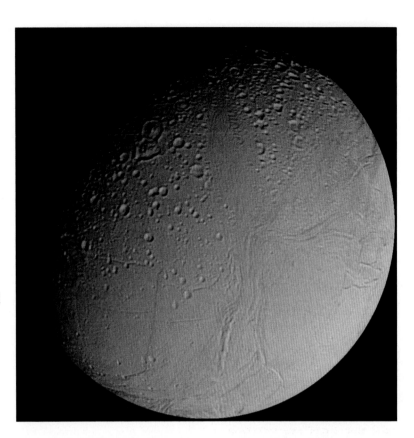

ENCELADUS HOLDS ITS SECRETS CLOSE

Saturn's icy moon Enceladus, pictured by Voyager 2 in 1981. Although there were hints that Enceladus had been geologically active in the past, there was little to prepare for Enceladus' true nature, which would be discovered by Cassini 25 years later. Image: NASA/JPL/USGS.

MYSTERIOUS MOON

With the best images that the Voyagers could produce of Titan showing the surface shrouded in a hydrocarbon smog, Saturn's largest moon remained largely an enigma until the arrival of Cassini. In this image, taken by Voyager 1, you can see the haze layer high above the moon. Image: NASA/JPL.

Gravitational slingshots

Cassini's journey was made more arduous by having to climb away from the pull of the Sun's gravity, which tugged on the spacecraft, trying to keep it in the inner Solar System. In order to achieve escape velocity into the outer Solar System (the region far beyond the Asteroid Belt where Saturn resides), Cassini had to increase its velocity. To do this, it swung past Venus twice and Earth once, increasing its speed as it fell under their gravitational influence. By flying past them along their direction of movement around the Sun, Cassini gained a velocity boost by stealing some of their orbital momentum around the Sun.

This technique was first developed by mathematician Michael Minovitch, while working at the Jet Propulsion Laboratory in 1961. It was used to great effect during the Voyager missions, in particular allowing Voyager 2 to visit Jupiter, Saturn, Uranus and Neptune in the space of a dozen years, using each planet to fling spacecraft on towards the next one.

attached to lines of magnetic field emanating from Jupiter. Cassini witnessed the plumes from some of Io's volcanoes reaching out into space, while Jupiter's extended magnetic field as a whole – known as a magnetosphere, a feature that Saturn also possesses – was mapped by Cassini's Radio and Plasma Wave Spectrometer, providing more information about the specifics of how Jupiter's polar auroral lights are created. Then there were the observations of Himalia, a captured asteroid surrounded by smaller pieces that had fragmented from the main body – the perfect rehearsal for when it was Cassini's time to hunt for tiny moonlets around Saturn. It is astonishing to consider that originally budget cuts were have meant Cassini's instruments would have been switched off during the Jupiter encounter.

As the year 2001 began – the year of Arthur C Clarke's famous 'Space Odyssey' that in the novel centred around a mission to Saturn (and not Jupiter, as seen in

the 1968 film) – Cassini–Huygens began the last leg of its journey. Everyone involved in the mission was on a high following the Jupiter fly-by, but fate it seemed was determined to not let them rest on their laurels. Problems were just around the corner.

The trouble with Huygens

In the long years during which a spacecraft is cruising towards its destination, scientists and engineers behind the mission back on Earth do not just put their feet up and smoke a cigar. Because, despite all the years of work, getting a mission to the launch pad on time can become a bit of a rush and further testing of a spacecraft's components may be required even after it has set sail to the stars.

The Cassini–Huygens mission was no different and, although most of the spacecraft's components had been sufficiently tested before it blasted off into the night sky, two engineers at the European Space Agency, namely Claudio Sollazzo and Boris Smeds, were concerned

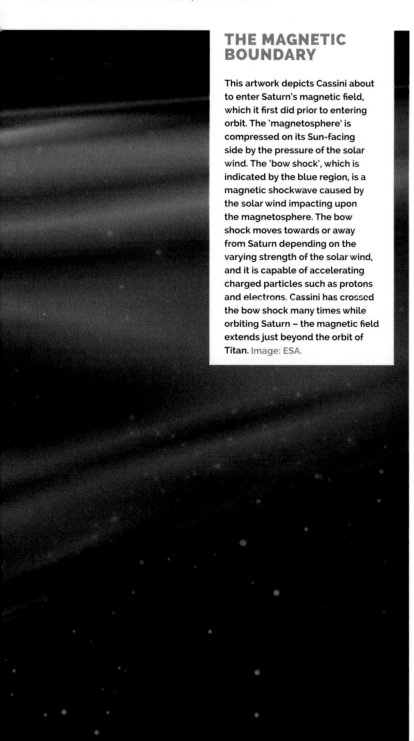

THE MAGNETIC BOUNDARY

This artwork depicts Cassini about to enter Saturn's magnetic field, which it first did prior to entering orbit. The 'magnetosphere' is compressed on its Sun-facing side by the pressure of the solar wind. The 'bow shock', which is indicated by the blue region, is a magnetic shockwave caused by the solar wind impacting upon the magnetosphere. The bow shock moves towards or away from Saturn depending on the varying strength of the solar wind, and it is capable of accelerating charged particles such as protons and electrons. Cassini has crossed the bow shock many times while orbiting Saturn – the magnetic field extends just beyond the orbit of Titan. Image: ESA.

that the communication link between Cassini and the Huygens probe that would enter Titan's atmosphere was not as robust as it should be. Of course, further testing after launch costs more money, and getting permission to continue tests took some persuading, but their persistent testing after the launch paid off.

The plan was for Huygens to drop off the Cassini mothership and plummet into Titan's atmosphere, accelerating relative to Cassini. This acceleration would impart a Doppler shift on Huygens' radio signals back to the spacecraft. A Doppler shift is a common phenomenon: a familiar analogy is a police car speeding towards and then past you. As the car approaches, its siren becomes increasingly high-pitched because the sound waves are being compressed. As the police car then drives away, its sound waves become stretched, reducing the pitch again. Radio waves also experience this when a spacecraft that is transmitting is moving towards or away from the receiver. Cassini's receiver, although operating over a narrow range, had been built to deal with this, but a crucial detail had been overlooked: the frequency shift would also alter the modulation of the bits of data in the signal. In other words, all Cassini would hear would be a high-pitched gibberish, like listening to a recorded voice at fast speed and with the words out of order. All of Huygens' data would be lost. The situation was wryly described by the Open University's Professor John Zarnecki, who headed up the Surface Science Package on Huygens, as "a cock-up."

So what to do? After much head-scratching at multiple workshops convened to tackle the problem, the solution was delightfully simple. The initial plan had Huygens separating from Cassini on 6 November 2004 and entering Titan's atmosphere on 27 November. Instead, Huygens would be released on Christmas Eve and would dive into Titan's atmosphere on 14 January 2005. The change of dates meant that Huygens would approach Titan on a different trajectory that was perpendicular to the motion of Cassini, limiting the Doppler shift in the signals between the two and preserving the modulation. The timeline had changed, but the mission was saved and Huygens could now look forward to a festive farewell.

Aside from a slight problem with Cassini's narrow-angle camera, the lens of which became fogged up by an unknown contaminant but which was eradicated by heating the camera to room temperature (ordinarily the camera was operating at –90 degrees Celsius), the rest of the trip to Saturn was plain sailing. As the date of Cassini–Huygens' July 2004 orbital insertion began to loom, thoughts moved ahead to what we could expect from the mission. Three previous spacecraft had headed out this way – what had they shown us that Cassini could build on?

The race to Saturn

All our previous visits to the ringed planet occurred in a quick spurt over the space of three years. Pioneer 11 was the first to reach Saturn, in 1979. Like its successors Voyager 1 and 2 a few years later, it flew past, destined for

CASSINI'S IMAGES REVEALED A GLORIOUS WORLD, TIPPED SLIGHTLY SO ITS SOUTH POLE WAS ON VIEW, AWAITING IT

interstellar space, rather than enter orbit and spend the rest if its days around Saturn, as Cassini would. Regardless of the fleeting nature of its visit, Pioneer 11 gave us our first close-up look at this mysterious world, the telescopic view of which had beguiled astronomers for centuries. The spacecraft was also very expendable. Scientists wanted to send the expensive Voyagers through the Asteroid Belt and then through the plane of Saturn's rings (in particular to help slingshot Voyager 2 onwards toward the seventh planet, Uranus), but little was known about the Saturn's rings, so Pioneer 11 became the guinea pig, traversing the Asteroid Belt between Mars and Jupiter, then passing 43,000 kilometres above Jupiter itself before heading on towards Saturn and flying through the ring plane just beyond the edge of the bright A-ring, the outermost known ring at the time. It did not look like there was any potentially hazardous ring material beyond the A-ring, but it was impossible to be sure: suppose there existed a belt of dark material into which Pioneer 11 could crash. As it happens there are rings beyond the A-ring, but these are separated by large gaps in space. Pioneer 11 climbed up through the ring plane safely, but only just avoided an unknown and unseen moonlet that was revealed after the fact, through the way Saturn's magnetosphere was wrapped around it. Having survived, Pioneer 11 got some glimpses of Saturn's myriad moons but the resolution was low and surface details were scarce, although one key discovery was that Titan's atmosphere was thick and opaque, leaving what lay below a complete mystery. It also discovered a new ring, the F-ring, beyond the A-ring and found that the dark gaps between the rings, such as the Cassini Division between the A- and B-rings, are not empty at all, but are filled with dark dust.

With Pioneer 11 effectively a test run, bigger and better things were expected from the twin Voyager probes, which made their own fly-bys of Saturn in November 1980 and August 1981. One way of putting it is that, while Pioneer 11 saw Saturn and its moons, the Voyagers learnt about them. Take Saturn's atmosphere, for instance. Its creamy, bland hues are at odds with Jupiter's frenetically churning sky. Observations by the Voyagers indicated that this could be partly caused by greater horizontal mixing of the atmosphere at Saturn, rather than the component of vertical mixing at Jupiter that causes material that turns a browny-red when exposed to solar ultraviolet to well

SATURN ON THE HORIZON

In November 2003, still eight months and 114 million kilometres from Saturn, Cassini's narrow angle camera imaged the planet against the serene blackness of space. Even at this distance details are evident in Saturn's atmosphere and the bright B-ring, while Saturn's own shadow can be seen cutting across the rings. The tip of the northern hemisphere appears blue, a result of it being winter there.
Image: NASA/JPL/ Space Science Institute.

up from below the clouds. Its atmospheric composition was found to be primarily hydrogen and helium, but with less helium than expected, while other gases such as methane, ethane, acetylene and phosphene turned up. The Voyagers also measured the wind speed blowing through Saturn's upper atmosphere as 500 metres per second (1,800 kilometres/1,100 miles per hour) in an easterly direction, with the strongest winds gusting at the equator. Meanwhile, Voyager 2 was able to identify a multitude of tumultuous oval-shaped atmospheric storms similar to those on Jupiter, but smaller and duller. There were even hints of a huge hexagonal structure in the atmosphere at the planet's north pole, a vortex at the south, and auroral lights shining in ultraviolet.

The rings also came into focus. The main rings were found to be made up of dozens of narrow ringlets, and the Cassini Division contained five distinct bright ringlets. Meanwhile strange, shadowy spoke-like shapes shimmered across the B-ring, and tiny moonlets named Pandora and Prometheus were found on either side of the F-ring, with Prometheus shepherding the ring particles into one narrow band. Similarly, a moonlet called Pan was discovered in the Encke Gap, which is a dark band in the A-ring.

For the moons, the Voyager missions proved a revelation. High-resolution images showed Enceladus to be ice-white, Mimas to be scarred by a huge crater called Herschel, the trio of large moons Rhea, Dione and Tethys to be battered with craters but sporting evidence for ancient geological activity that had been frozen into the landscape, and Iapetus' dark and light hemispheres – the cause of its varying brightness when seen through telescopes on Earth – to be confirmed. Titan's surface, alas, largely remained an enigma, its atmosphere proving to be a near-impenetrable shroud, but the Voyagers did at least learn more about that shroud.

In particular, Titan's atmospheric chemistry seemed to hint at all sorts of potential for pre-biotic reactions. One of the Voyagers' major discoveries was that the majority of Titan's atmosphere (95 percent) is molecular nitrogen, which is not detectable from Earth, while most of the rest is methane. Yet the Voyagers found that other atmospheric constituents, in small doses, were complex hydrocarbons (these are molecules that combine atoms of carbon and hydrogen in different quantities, and which are pre-cursors for compounds important for life, because they can form long, complex, molecular chains thanks to the way they are bonded together) produced by ultraviolet light from the Sun acting on methane in Titan's upper atmosphere, breaking it apart so that the bits and pieces can reform as larger molecules.

The Voyagers detected the likes of ethane, acetylene, ethylene and propane filtering down towards the surface from the upper reaches of the atmosphere. Even more intriguing was a measurement of the surface temperature, with the mercury plunging to –179 degrees Celsius, which is very close to the melting point of methane. These discoveries prompted visions of a moon covered in lakes and oceans of methane, enriched in other hydrocarbons too and, recalling that on Earth it is believed that the simplest forms of life began in liquid pools filled with pre-biotic matter, looking somewhat similar to early Earth, but frozen. Some scientists even speculated that there could be life, albeit with biological processes far slower than life on Earth as a result of Titan's low temperature. However, without a radar instrument to penetrate through the thick, hazy atmosphere filled with a smog of hydrocarbon aerosols, it was impossible to be sure about anything on the surface.

Arrival at Saturn

So the scene was set for Cassini, a quarter of a century later. In February 2004 the spacecraft was 69.4 million kilometres from Saturn, having already travelled almost 3.5 billion kilometres through space. Yet its images showed a glorious world awaiting it, tipped slightly so its south pole was on view, and details in the atmosphere and rings began to be resolved (see the image on the opposite page and overleaf. With excitement growing, Saturn loomed larger and larger in Cassini's cameras as the weeks and kilometres passed by. In March, Cassini caught two giant, thousand-kilometre wide storms merging in Saturn's atmosphere, while in April the spacecraft's cameras began surveillance of Titan.

Things really heated up in June, less than a month from orbital insertion. On the eleventh of the month Cassini encountered the sentinel standing guard at the gateway to the realm of Saturn: its outermost moon, named Phoebe.

A dark, lumpen satellite, encrusted with craters and orbiting retrograde (meaning in the opposite, backwards, direction to all the other moons) and at an angle to the plane of the other moons of Saturn, Phoebe is an oddball, believed to be a captured cometary nucleus, 220 kilometres wide, that had wandered in-system from the Kuiper Belt an indeterminate time ago and had been caught and trapped by Saturn's extensive gravitational field. Once thought to be a captured asteroid, its density is now known to be more akin to ice worlds such as Pluto and Neptune's moon Triton, which is also a captured body from the Kuiper Belt. Voyager 2 had succeeded in producing only a single image of Phoebe at large distance; Voyager 1 did not even produce that much. Cassini's fly-by, at 2,071 kilometres, therefore proved to be something of an eye-opener – a unique look at an object from the space beyond Pluto, conveniently placed in orbit around Saturn.

Nineteen days out from entering orbit, Phoebe was a bonus for the mission. Saturn was now impossible to miss and close enough to make new and exciting discoveries. Tiny shepherd moons no larger than five kilometres across, herding the F-ring, were spotted, but Cassini has been unable to recover them since, suggesting that they were merely temporary clumps of ring material. Towards the end of June Cassini ploughed through Saturn's bow shock, which is the turbulent and constantly moving boundary of the planet's giant magnetosphere. Then, on 30 June 2004, the time came: the end of a journey through space that had lasted nearly seven years. Riding up through the ring plane, just as Pioneer 11 and the

SENTINEL

Saturn's outermost moon, Phoebe, cratered and irregularly-shaped, was the first of Saturn's moons to be encountered by Cassini. Phoebe sports an ice-rich composition, evident in the way some of the crater walls have slipped down into the ice, exposing brighter material. Image: NASA/JPL/Space Science Institute.

Voyagers had done all those years ago, Cassini then had to fire its engines, hitting the breaks and putting itself into orbit around Saturn. It was a high-precision manoeuvre – if just one thing went wrong, Cassini would fly past Saturn and become lost to deep space.

"There are three hold-your-breath moments," said Robert Mitchell, the Programme Manager for the mission, just prior to the orbital insertion manoeuvre. "The first is when we see the signal coming back after we cross the ring plane in the ascending direction. The second is an indication that the burn has begun at 7:36pm Pacific time. Finally, the signal showing the burn completion at the right time."

Breath was held as Cassini passed through the ring plane, successfully navigating its way through any unseen debris that may have been lurking there. Hearts beat faster when the signal came back – time delayed of course because of the distance the signal had to travel to reach Earth – that the 96-minute engine burn had begun. And then raucous cheers in mission control when Cassini confirmed it had ended the burn at the allotted time and safely entered orbit around Saturn.

Cassini has proved that the old idiom that says it is not the destination that counts, but rather what you learn on the journey there, can sometimes be a myth. As we will see throughout the rest of this book, Cassini–Huygens' journey to Saturn was simply a necessity. It was the discoveries it made at the end of its journey to Saturn that really counted.

RIDING UP THROUGH THE RING PLANE, CASSINI HAD TO FIRE ITS ENGINES, HITTING THE BREAKS AND PUTTING ITSELF INTO ORBIT – IF JUST ONE THING WENT WRONG, CASSINI WOULD BECOME LOST TO DEEP SPACE

SATURN SUPREME

Taken on 7 May 2004, less than two months away from insertion into orbit around Saturn, Cassini captured this stunning portrait of the ringed world. By this stage, Saturn was looming large enough that this image is composed of two images from the narrow angle camera, stitched together.
Image: NASA/JPL/Space Science Institute.

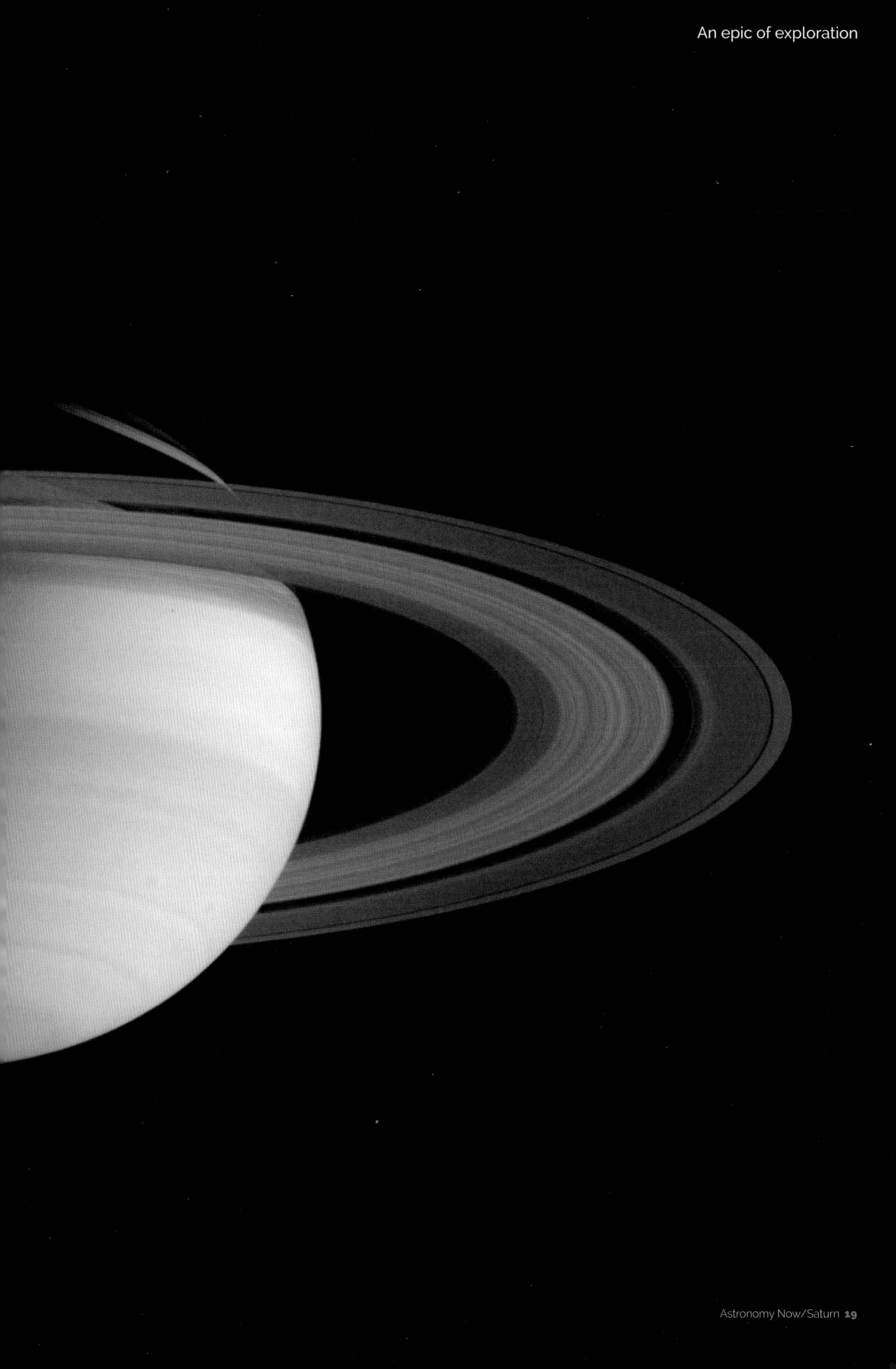

Cassini has not ventured to Saturn unprepared: mounted in various locations upon its chassis are a dozen science instruments that work in isolation or tandem to scrutinise every nook and cranny of the Saturnian system, turning the mysteries of the enigmatic ringed world and its system of moons into matter of fact.

1

REMOTE SENSING PALLET

Composite Infrared Spectrometer (CIRS)

Splitting infrared light into its individual narrow wavelengths, CIRS studies thermal emission from the surfaces of the moons plus Saturn's rings and the atmospheres of Saturn and Titan. Consequently, CIRS is able to measure the temperature of these locations, which is a major factor when studying the weather and atmospheric systems on Saturn and Titan. Furthermore, different materials and gases emit heat differently and CIRS is able to identify what they are and their abundance based on the strength of the infrared light at specific wavelengths.

Imaging Science Subsystem (ISS)

Every stunning vista of moons gliding in front of Saturn, or the rings cutting through the blackness of space, is the product of the ISS. As the spacecraft's visual eyes, the ISS comprises a wide-angle CCD camera and a narrow-angle version. The CCD sensors – analogous to the sensor chips that you find in your digital cameras at home – sport 1,024 × 1,024 pixel arrays. Filters allow the cameras to image in specific wavelengths and combining any three filters creates the colour images. Many images in this book appear in greyscale because they have been taken through only one filter. The ISS is a workhorse, producing approximately 2,700 raw images per month.

Ultraviolet Imaging Spectrograph (UVIS)

Some elements and molecules emit at ultraviolet wavelengths and, like CIRS, the ultraviolet spectrograph is able to split the ultraviolet light into narrow wavelengths to determine what materials have been emitting that light. These materials include gases that are not detectable in visible or infrared light, plus 'night-shine' from the dark hemispheres of the moons. UVIS is also capable of detecting details in the rings, such as clumps of icy material, by watching how the rings block the light of more distant stars. In a similar way, UVIS can watch the limb of Titan's atmosphere moving in front of the Sun, looking for absorption lines in the ultraviolet spectrum that are the signature of gaseous molecules in Titan's atmosphere absorbing sunlight.

Visible and Infrared Mapping Spectrometer (VIMS)

A spectrometer designed to study the surfaces of Saturn's many moons, searching for everything from rock to various ices and organic compounds. VIMS can break light up into 352 narrow wavelength channels (256 in infrared and 96 in visible light). It is able to take images by scanning across a row of pixels, then a row below and so on, to spectroscopically map any object that it targets.

MAGNETOMETER (MAG)

"The magnetosphere instruments are certainly some of the best on Cassini," Dennis Matson, the mission's former Project Scientist, told *Astronomy Now* prior to the spacecraft's arrival at Saturn. "They characterise the magnetic field and the plasma ions that are inside it and the magnetic field is also one of the ways we have for looking inside planets to infer what their internal structure is."

So along with CAPS, INMS, MIMI and RPWS, Cassini's magnetometer instrument, protruding from Cassini on an 11-metre long boom, is a vital tool in revealing the 'unseen' Saturn: the invisible magnetosphere and the dynamo in the planet's core that generates it. It measures the strength and direction of the magnetic field, and also how the moons impinge on the magnetic field.

2

FIELDS, PARTICLES AND WAVES PALLET

Cassini Plasma Spectrometer (CAPS)

The environment around Saturn, particularly within its extended magnetic field, called the magnetosphere, is filled with high-energy charged particles that form a diffuse plasma of ionised gas (i.e. hot gas in which the atoms have been stripped of their electrons). CAPS is able to detect these 'ions' as well as the free electrons and protons that whizz around in the vicinity of Saturn, determining their density, velocity, composition and how they move or flow along the magnetic field lines.

Cosmic Dust Analyser (CDA)

Designed, as the name suggests, to detect tiny grains of dust just a thousandth of a millimetre in size, the CDA found dust grains in interplanetary space during the journey to Saturn, as well as those coming from Saturn's rings. The grains impact the instrument, turning into a puff of hot plasma that the CDA then analyses to determine the composition of the dust, as well as measure its velocity and determine what orbits the dust grains are moving along and where they could originate.

Ion and Neutral Mass Spectrometer (INMS)

INMS is used to study ions and neutral particles trapped in the magnetosphere of Saturn, as well as those present in the upper atmosphere of Titan and those sputtering from Saturn's rings and the surfaces of the icy moons, determining how they interact with the magnetosphere.

Magnetospheric Imaging Instrument (MIMI)

Charged particles such as ions, protons and electrons are an important constituent of the magnetic environment around Saturn, helping to trace out the structure of the magnetosphere and showing where particles are being accelerated to high energies. MIMI is able to show where these charged particles cluster in the magnetosphere and is able to analyse what the ions are made from. MIMI can also study the electrons accelerated as part of the Saturn Kilometric Radiation produced by disturbances in the planet's magnetic field.

Radio and Plasma Wave Science (RPWS)

As the solar wind interacts with Saturn's magnetic field, it produces radio signals that RPWS is able to detect. It can also detect radio pulses from lightning in atmospheric storms. A Langmuir probe measures the density and temperature of free electrons in the magnetic field, while an electric field sensor and magnetic search coils make up the rest of RPWS.

Meet Cassini Huygens!

MICROWAVE REMOTE SENSING

RAdio Detection And Ranging (RADAR)

One of the lessons learned from the Voyager fly-bys of Saturn was that it would be impossible to map the surface of Titan from orbit without using radar to penetrate through the thick atmosphere.

According to Dennis Matson, "RADAR has many operating modes but one particular mode is a synthetic aperture imaging device that will ensure that we have high-resolution images of Titan's surface. On any given pass of Titan that Cassini makes we are only able to image about one percent of the surface."

RADAR uses the high gain antenna on the front of the spacecraft, which is also used for communicating with Earth.

Radio Science (RSS)

By beaming radio signals towards Earth through the atmospheres of Titan or Saturn, or through Saturn's rings, and looking for slight frequency changes, RSS is able to probe those objects to learn more about their composition. The signals from RSS are picked up by the giant antennas in Australia, Spain and the United States that make up NASA'S Deep Space Network, before being passed on to scientists on the ground.

RADIOISOTOPE THERMOELECTRIC GENERATORS (RTGS)

THRUSTERS

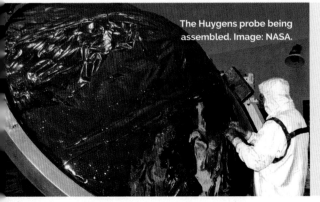

The Huygens probe being assembled. Image: NASA.

HUYGENS PROBE

Huygens is ESA's probe designed to descend into the atmosphere of Titan and try to land on its surface. On board are six different experiments: the Gas Chromatograph and Mass Spectrometer (GCMS) to identify molecules within the atmosphere; the Aerosol Collector and Pyrolyser (ACP) that samples Titan's atmosphere at two points, 40 kilometres and then 23 to 17 kilometres above the surface; the Descent Imager/Spectral Radiometer (DISR) that chronicles the flight through the atmosphere; the Huygens Atmosphere Structure Instrument (HASI) that measures the physical properties of the atmosphere including its thermal and pressure profiles; the Doppler Wind Experiment (DWE) that measures the wind speed at various altitudes; and the Surface Science Package for analysing the ground after landing.

IN THE GRIP OF WINTER

In January 2005, when Cassini took this image, the northern hemisphere of Saturn was still in the grip of winter. The reduced sunlight that the wintertime hemisphere receives reduces the amount of ultraviolet incident upon the atmosphere there. Ultraviolet light normally breaks down methane molecules to produce haze, so without it the atmosphere is clearer, which leads to the preferential scattering of blue light, much like we see in Earth's atmosphere. Against this sea of blue are cast the shadows of individual rings, while 398-kilometre wide moon Mimas drifts serenely across the bottom of the scene. Image: NASA/JPL/ Space Science Institute.

A world of floating diamonds

We see Saturn from the outside, a spinning ball of gas 116,464 kilometres across, with serene hues of golden-cream. Yet it's what is deep inside the planet that really counts, with metallic hydrogen, helium rain and vast chunks of diamond.

A **day** on red Mars lasts 24 hours and 37 minutes. On Jupiter you will find a new day dawns every nine hours and 56 minutes. Venus' days last longer than its year – 243 Earth days. Yet when Cassini arrived at Saturn in 2004, nobody knew the exact length of its day.

A day is, of course, measured by how long it takes a planet to complete one rotation around its axis (the technical jargon for this is a 'sidereal day'). On the solid, rocky planets this is easy to measure: pick a feature on the surface such as a mountain or a crater and watch it rotate around, timing how long it takes to return to its starting position. However, on the gas and ice giant planets, this becomes a little more difficult because there is no solid surface on which to base a measurement of their rotation. The clouds and bands in their atmosphere all rotate at different speeds, often depending upon latitude and the strength of local winds. Instead, scientists measure the precise length of their days based on the rotation of their inherent magnetic fields, which are generated deep within their cores. This works for Jupiter, Uranus and Neptune because their magnetic fields are tilted with respect to their axis of rotation, hence magnetometers can detect the magnetic field bobbing up and down as it rotates. On Saturn, the magnetosphere is perfectly aligned with the planet's spin axis, meaning there is no undulating magnetic field to detect.

So scientists need to be cleverer. When the solar wind – a stream of charged particles emanating from the Sun and moving out radially into the Solar System – impacts Saturn's magnetic field, it drives some of the particles down lines of magnetism, called field lines. These field lines converge onto the magnetic poles of the planet – which, as we have seen, are located in the same place as its rotational poles – and as the charged particles inevitably spiral around a magnetic field, they release powerful bursts of low-frequency radio waves, which we term 'Saturn Kilometric Radiation', or SKR for short. When the Voyagers swung past Saturn in 1980 and 1981 respectively, they timed the rotation of the SKR events to determine the length of Saturn's day as 10 hours, 39 minutes and 24 seconds.

That seemed to be that, but 15 years later the joint NASA/ESA Ulysses spacecraft, which spent its time looping between the Sun and beyond Jupiter's orbit, observed the length of Saturn's day to have increased by six minutes, to 10 hours, 45 minutes and 45 seconds, based on SKR measurements. Cassini verified this with its Radio and Plasma Wave Science (RPWS) experiment in 2004, only for the spacecraft to find later that Saturn changed its mind and that subsequent measurements of SKR showed that the length of day had altered yet again, speeding up to 10 hours, 34 minutes and 13 seconds.

By this stage, perplexed scientists were throwing their hands up in the air in frustration. It seemed as though Saturn had slowed down before speeding up again, which is of course impossible. So if Saturn's rotation is not really changing speed, then that means something else is going on with the radio emission that disconnects it from the true rotation rate of the planet. Scientists have noticed a correlation between variations in the radio emission and the rotation of the Sun, implying that the solar wind is somehow at fault. Emissions of charged particles amidst water vapour vented from beneath the surface of Saturn's moon Enceladus are also under suspicion. Either way, the result remains the same: we still don't know the exact length of Saturn's day.

A PALER SHADE OF BLUE

The blue of winter in Saturn's northern hemisphere, as seen by Cassini on 4 May 2005. The shadows of the rings further chill the empty Saturnian skies, and reveal how tilted Saturn was relative to the Sun at the time the image was taken. Image: NASA/JPL/Space Science Institute.

However, let's not see this as a failure on Cassini's part. The point of the story is to highlight the massive influence that the planet's magnetic field plays in the Saturnian system. Little wonder that Cassini's complement of instruments dedicated to measuring charged particles and magnetic fields are considered so important, even if the Imaging Science Subsystem steals much of the glory.

Dynamic effect

Earth's magnetic field is generated by a spinning sphere of molten iron and nickel surrounding a solid iron core and, as the molten layer sloshes about, it generates an electric current that produces a corresponding magnetic field – a natural dynamo, deep within the planet.

As far as we can tell, despite being 578 times stronger than Earth's magnetic field, Saturn's magnetic field is produced in a similar manner, although the specifics might differ compared to Earth – the interior of Saturn is very much a mysterious location that tests our understanding of physics to the extreme. The temperatures in Saturn's core (11,700 degrees Celsius) are twice the temperature inside Earth's core (5,700 degrees Celsius, which is slightly hotter than the surface of the Sun) and the pressure is similarly twice as great. Under those extreme conditions, the likes of hydrogen and helium are prone to behaving 'exotically'.

At the centre of Saturn there is believed to exist a crushed sphere of rock and iron, rendered molten. If we look back to 4.5 billion years ago, scientists' strongest theory for the formation of Jupiter and Saturn and why they grew to be so huge is that they began life not as gaseous worlds, but as giant rocky worlds, a dozen or so times larger than Earth. Because of their greater gravity these rocky giants were able to gather increasingly more material from the planet-forming disc of gas and dust that surrounded the Sun. They swiftly accumulated bloated gaseous envelopes onto their rocky cores, growing into the behemoths they are today. The remnants of their rocky cores – a memory of what they once were – are now lost underneath a hundred trillion trillion kilograms of gas.

> AT THE CENTRE OF SATURN IS BELIEVED TO EXIST A CRUSHED SPHERE OF ROCK AND IRON, 25,000 KILOMETRES ACROSS AND RENDERED MOLTEN.

Around this core is a dense layer of liquid hydrogen and helium, which is also described as metallic. It's pretty weird stuff. Ordinarily, hydrogen molecules are electrical insulators. Under the intense pressure inside Saturn, however, molecular hydrogen is broken up into individual hydrogen atoms, which swiftly lose their electrons in the forbidding heat. Electrons are negatively charged – the electrical current bringing power to your computer, television, lights and so forth is composed of a flow of electrons. Hence the molecular hydrogen is converted into conducting 'metallic' hydrogen. It no longer remains a gas either, for the intense pressure gives it liquid properties instead. Mixed with helium it can produce helium rain that pours onto the core. The electrically conducting fluid sloshes around the molten core, creating a dynamo effect and a magnetic field. Meanwhile, the phase change from a gas into a liquid that then rains onto the core releases heat energy into the interior of Saturn. This might explain why Saturn looks so 'young'; the older a planet, the cooler its interior should be following the fires of its formation, yet Saturn's thermal emission is that of a planet two billion years younger and warmer. Jérémy Leconte of École Normale Supérieure de Lyon in France and Gilles Chabrier of the University of Exeter have theorised that horizontal layers of gas within Saturn prevent the upwards convection of heat and instead encourage horizontal diffusion, trapping the heat inside the planet rather than allowing it to leak into space at the same rate at which heat loss has occurred on its contemporaries.

Reconnection

Even weirder is what we might find drifting through Saturn's liquid hydrogen 'ocean'. Carbon soot or graphite that is produced in the many lightning strikes that flash violently in the raging storms inhabiting the upper atmosphere, breaking apart hydrocarbons such as methane, can drift down to the lower planetary decks, where it is compressed by the pressure into large chunks of diamond, nicknamed 'diamondbergs', which float through the liquid hydrogen. If they exist then, as they

sink further into Saturn, the diamond eventually melts into a liquid too and can potentially fall onto the planet's core as diamond rain.

The planetary core is an estimated 25,000 kilometres across. If we could imagine rising up from the core and through the layers of Saturn's atmosphere, which in total extends 58,232 kilometres from the very centre of the planet, we next arrive at a thick region of liquid molecular hydrogen that is not metallic – the pressure is not great enough at these altitudes to split the molecules

WINTER ENCROACHES

The gold of summer and the chilled blue of winter clash on Saturn, divided by the thin boundary of the rings in this image taken by Cassini on 22 September 2005. The moon captured in the scene is called Dione. Image: NASA/JPL–Caltech/ Space Science Institute.

into atomic nuclei and electrons. This layer takes us all the way to the upper atmosphere, above which are the creamy-hued cloud tops that cast such an enchanting spell for Cassini's cameras. The magnetic field generated by the internal dynamo rises up too, through the poles before looping around the planet.

In Earth's magnetosphere a mechanism known as 'reconnection', whereby magnetic field lines break and then reconnect to release energy that had been stored in the initially taut field lines, channels charged particles, blown here on the solar wind, down into the atmosphere where they cause atoms of oxygen and nitrogen to glow in the sky, a phenomenon we know better as the northern or southern lights, or more generally as aurorae. Saturn too has aurorae and they have been a source of attention not just for Cassini, but also for astronomers back on Earth utilising the Hubble Space Telescope. They want to know how Saturn generates its polar lights and whether this mechanism is different to how the aurorae are created in Earth's atmosphere, or whether it is the same process, which would help inform us about our own magnetosphere as well as highlight that, despite the differences in size and composition, the planets are not always all that different in the way they do things. Now, thanks to Cassini, we know Saturn's aurorae are created through exactly the same process as Earth's.

Saturn's magnetospheric bubble is flattened in the face of the inrushing solar wind and sculpted into a teardrop shape as the wind flows past. The stretched-out part is known as the magnetotail and is always directed opposite the Sun. Sometimes, under a particularly strong gust of the solar wind, the magnetotail can break, causing blobs of plasma trapped in the field lines to drift away with the wind. A three-year campaign by astronomers at the University of Leicester using the Hubble Space Telescope showed that such breakages cause the magnetotail to

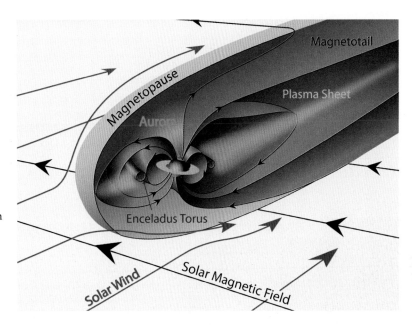

PLANETARY MAGNETISM

A diagrammatic depiction of Saturn's magnetosphere, which is formed by the magnetic field generated by Saturn's internal dynamo. The magnetosphere is flattened facing the Sun, and streamlined into a 'tail' by the solar wind, which flows around the magnetosphere. The Enceladus torus is a doughnut shaped belt of plasma vented into space by the geysers on the moon Enceladus and trapped in the magnetosphere. The plasma sheet shows where plasma is leaking out from the magnetosphere, to be carried away by the magnetotail and eventually the solar wind. Image: Fran Bagenal and Steve Bartlett (University of Colorado, Boulder).

RADIO GA GA

The pattern of radio waves from Saturn's kilometric radiation, as controlled by the planet's rotation. Red indicates the most powerful radio bursts. They are associated with the planet's aurorae and are displayed here over a time frame spanning from 2004 to 2011. The observations were made with Cassini's RPWS instrument. You can see how the rotational variations swapped over following the equinox in 2009. Image: NASA/JPL–Caltech/University of Iowa.

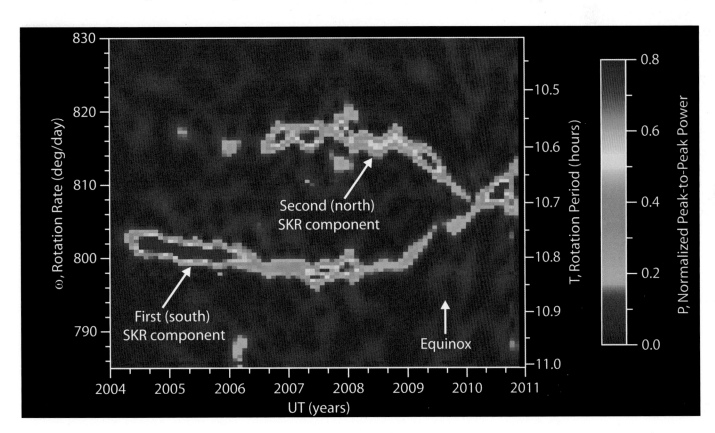

SOUTHERN LIGHTS

A visible-light image of Saturn combined with an ultraviolet image of its aurorae, both taken by the Hubble Space Telescope. Image: NASA/ESA/J Clarke (Boston University)/Z Levay (STScI).

momentarily collapse before the broken field lines quickly snap back, reconnecting with each other and releasing magnetic energy that accelerates any charged particles within them towards the poles of Saturn, where the field lines converge. At the poles the particles excite hydrogen molecules, causing them to glow red or purple in visible light (depending upon the energy of the particles) but also brightly in other wavelengths too: infrared, ultraviolet, even radio waves. In 2008 Cassini dove through an active auroral zone for the first time, albeit 247 million kilometres above Saturn's cloud tops where the light extravaganza was occurring. High above the auroral arc, or oval, of light, Cassini detected powerful radio emissions

CARBON SOOT PRODUCED IN LIGHTNING STORMS CAN DRIFT DOWN TO THE LOWER PLANETARY DECKS WHERE IT IS COMPRESSED INTO 'DIAMONDBERGS'.

originating from fast moving electrons spiralling around magnetic field lines in the auroral region.

Disequilibrium

A year later, Cassini discovered that Saturn's southern lights are not identical to the northern lights. August 2009 was the time of Saturn's spring equinox, where the tilt of the planet was aligned with the Sun on the ecliptic plane. The rings were edge-on to the Sun and both Saturn's northern and southern hemispheres received equal heating from the Sun and equal gusts of the solar wind. So, all things being equal, the aurora in the north should have been identical to the aurora in the south. Instead, Cassini saw that the auroral oval at Saturn's north pole is smaller and more intense than the auroral oval in the south. For this to be the case, Saturn's internal magnetic field must be slightly uneven, with stronger magnetism in the north than in the south. In turn, this suggests that the dynamo in the planet's core is not symmetrical either.

Intriguingly, there seem to be other factors that also impact upon Saturn's aurorae, factors that begin

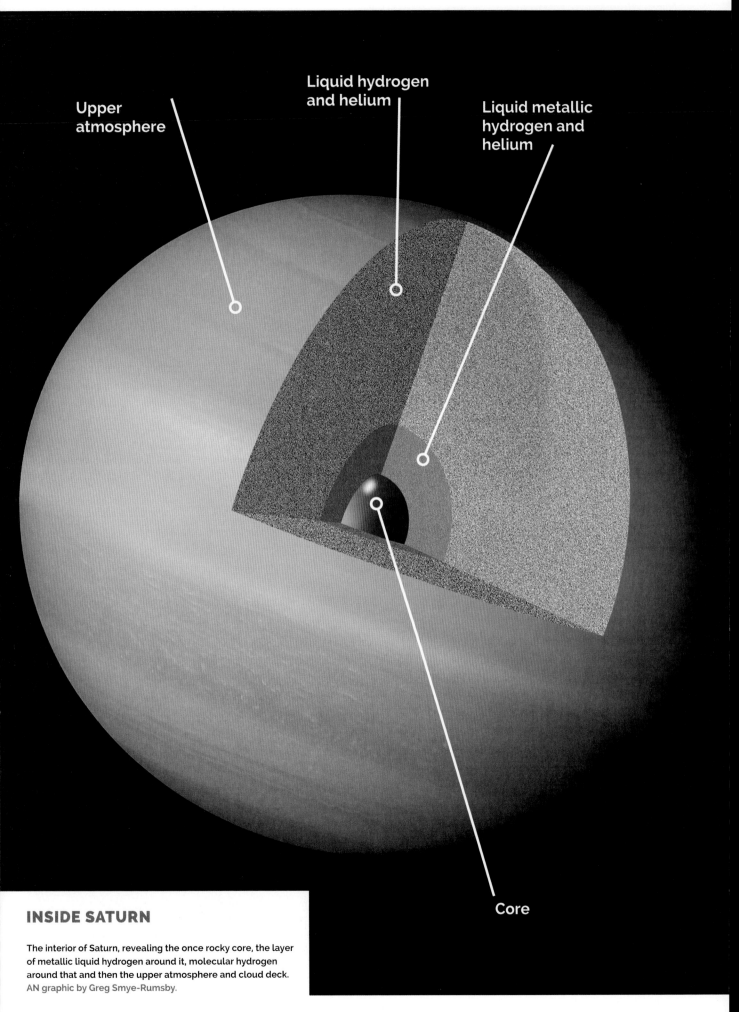

Upper atmosphere

Liquid hydrogen and helium

Liquid metallic hydrogen and helium

Core

INSIDE SATURN

The interior of Saturn, revealing the once rocky core, the layer of metallic liquid hydrogen around it, molecular hydrogen around that and then the upper atmosphere and cloud deck. AN graphic by Greg Smye-Rumsby.

TURNING DOWN THE HEAT

A false-colour infrared image of Saturn, captured with data from the Visual and Infrared Mapping Spectrometer on 1 November 2008. The image highlights Saturn's southern hemisphere, which has been emitting less and less heat (detected as thermal infrared emission, which appears red in this image) during Cassini's stay at Saturn. Saturn's rings appear blue, which is the colour used to indicate reflected light at short infrared wavelengths of two microns. Green indicates the reflection of slightly longer wavelengths at three microns. Image: NASA/JPL/ASI/University of Arizona.

WATER SPRAY

Saturn's moon Enceladus sports curtains of geysers in its south polar region, which spray vast quantities of water vapour into space around Saturn, contributing to the plasma environment there. Image: NASA/JPL–Caltech/Space Science Institute.

to draw our attention away from the ringed world itself and towards its enigmatic and varied moons. One bright ultraviolet spot in the auroral arc rotates in time with the orbit of the moon Mimas, while other bright spots and radio bursts seem to correlate with water vapour vented into space from fellow moon Enceladus. This vapour soaks the magnetosphere, becoming ionised and forming most of the plasma (a hot state of gas made from atoms that have lost their electrons) found in Saturn's magnetosphere. Yet despite this constant influx of material, the amount of plasma in Saturn's magnetosphere does not seem to be on the increase; it is being lost to interplanetary space, pushed out by magnetic currents that wash through the magnetosphere in time with the planet's seemingly unmeasurable rotation. Indeed, the surprising geological activity discovered by Cassini on Enceladus may explain many of the unusual things about the Saturnian system, some of which we will discover later in this book.

A SPRING IN SATURN'S STEP

October, 2007: a close-up of Saturn's northern hemisphere, where spring was fast returning. The atmosphere is gradually getting its creamy hues back, banishing the winter blues. Image: NASA/JPL–Caltech/Space Science Institute.

SPRING TAKES HOLD

This glorious portrait of Saturn, taken by Cassini in 2008, shows how the changing seasons has affected Saturn in the time since Cassini arrived there. Gone is the blue from its northern hemisphere, replaced by bands of hazy cloud that appear more mottled than those to the south, just a year prior to the equinox. If you compare the angle of the rings seen here to the image on pages 18–19, the change in the tilt of the planet with respect to the Sun appears clear. Image: NASA/JPL/ Space Science Institute.

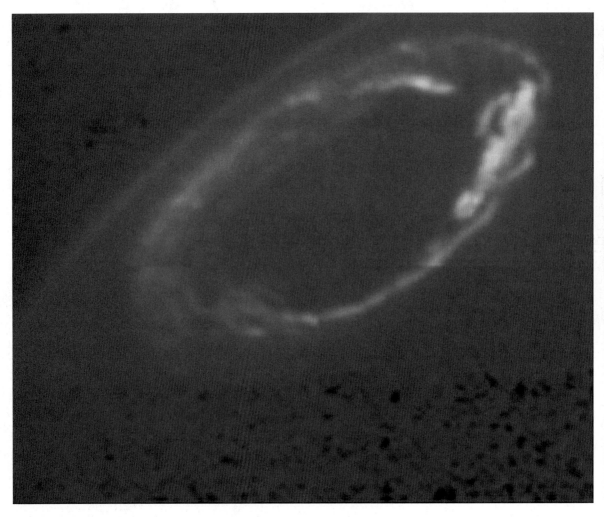

RING OF LIGHT

A composite image of one of Saturn's aurorae, composed of an infrared image from the CIRS instrument on Cassini, and ultraviolet data from the Hubble Space Telescope. Image: NASA/JPL–Caltech/University of Colorado/Central Arizona College/ESA/University of Leicester/University of Arizona/Lancaster University.

Magnetism is not the only thing that appears uneven on Saturn. We have alluded to the fact that Saturn is hotter than it should be, but it is also the case that the heat energy that it does emit is also lopsided, with more leaking into space from the planet's southern hemisphere than from its northern climes. Between 2005 and 2009, Cassini's Composite Infrared Spectrometer (CIRS) measured the energy loss from Saturn and found that, year-on-year, the planet gradually emitted less and less energy, but also that the southern hemisphere emitted a sixth of the energy released by the north. This pattern seemed to match the seasons; when Cassini arrived in 2004, Saturn's northern hemisphere was in winter and the southern hemisphere was basking in what passes for summer 1.4 billion kilometres from the Sun. Indeed, Saturn's northern hemisphere had turned an azure blue; as the north had grown cold, there grew a paucity of clouds in the atmosphere. The tilt of the planet, with the north angled away from the Sun, meant that sunlight entered the atmosphere at an oblique angle, meaning the light had to pass through a greater extent of the atmosphere. Because the clear atmosphere scatters blue light preferentially – just as on Earth – the

northern hemisphere appeared a frigid blue for a few years until Saturn's tilt became more balanced in the run-up to the 2009 equinox.

Things changed with the equinox. Liming Li, a planetary scientist at the University of Houston, Texas, has been leading astronomers in a multi-year study of Saturn's heat budget – how much heat the planet absorbs from sunlight and how much heat it emits into space. Li's group found that in the south the decrease in emitted energy continued as a result of both the increasing distance between the Sun and Saturn as the ringed planet moved slightly away along its elliptical orbit, and also the shift of the sub-solar latitude (the latitude directly underneath the Sun) northwards. In the north, however, specifically across a band of latitudes centred on 45 degrees north, the situation was turned on its head and between 2010 and 2011 nine percent more heat was emitted than before. And what was the cause of this huge increase in energy output? It was a colossal atmospheric storm, larger than anything ever seen before, that wrapped itself around the planet. Jupiter may roil and churn in a constant tumultuous fashion but, when unleashed, Saturn's storms rival anything the King of the Planets has to offer, as we will find out next.

WINTER IS COMING

Taken by Cassini on 29 July 2013, this view of Saturn shows the planet's southern polar region, growing blue as winter approaches and temperatures plunge to −172 degrees Celsius, while the north now enjoys summer, such as it is. Image: NASA/JPL/Space Science Institute.

The storm
to end all storms

Saturn's atmosphere is not as serene as it appears: raging winds, swirling vortices and massive storms tear through the clouds.

MEGA-STORM

By 25 February 2011, a mega-storm was in full flow in Saturn's atmosphere, its churning tail of clouds wrapped around the planet. Some of the clouds were able to drift southwards as they have circumnavigated the planet, until they ran into the head of the storm. Image: NASA/JPL–Caltech/Space Science Institute.

On 5 December 2010, a blemish 1,800 kilometres wide appeared in the northern hemisphere of Saturn's atmosphere, at a latitude of 33 degrees north. Peanut-shaped, it seemed incongruous amongst its creamy-hued surroundings and was dwarfed by the enormity of Saturn itself. Many similar disturbances have been seen on Saturn by Cassini over the past eight-and-a-half years; scientists thought nothing of it.

Then it grew.

Announcing its intentions through a cacophony of electrical disturbances as flashes of lightning flickered across the head of this enormous thunderstorm, it began expanding, first to a diameter of 5,000 kilometres, which is more than big enough to cover the entire United States of America from New York to Honolulu. Yet unlike Earth's storms, this was no spiral-shaped hurricane.

As the storm became caught on the gusts of jet streams that surged through the atmosphere, it spilled out, wrapping itself around the entirety of the planet's northern hemisphere and growing to over 300,000 kilometres in length. At its peak it covered a fifth of the hemisphere – around five billion square kilometres – a churning cavalcade of convective thunderstorms. Finally, after more than eight months of wind, thunder and lightning, the thunderstorm exhausted its power and fell silent in August 2011, leaving the swirling, agitated clouds to linger heavily in the atmosphere. It had been the longest-lived giant storm ever witnessed on the ringed planet, far outlasting the previous record holder, which was the great 150-day storm of 1903.

A multitude of questions cascaded through the minds of planetary scientists and atmospheric dynamicists. How did the storm start and why did it grow so large? What stopped the storm? And why do such storms only blow once every Saturnian year, which is 29 Earth-years long? Since records began the ringed planet has only experienced six storms of this magnitude: the first one to be observed occurred in 1876 and the most recent prior to the 2010–2011 storm appeared in 1990, lasting a mere 55 days. Crucially, the 2011 storm (some scientists have nicknamed it 'Ouroboros', for reasons that will shortly become clear) was the first time astronomers have

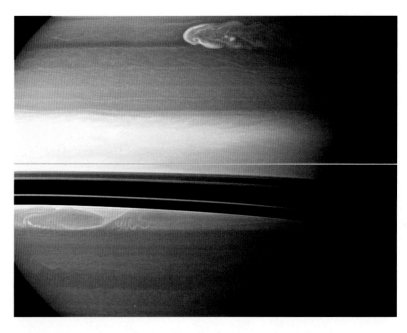

HIGHS AND LOWS OF THE MEGA-STORM

A different view of the mega-storm. These lurid colours are false, translated from near-infrared observations taken through filters that peer through differing degrees of absorption by methane in the clouds, with red and orange being the deepest clouds, white and blue representing the uppermost cloud deck and high altitude haze, and yellow and green being the clouds in between. Coding the cloud layers in these colours shows just what level the mega-storm was churning at inside Saturn's atmosphere. Image: NASA/JPL–Caltech/Space Science Institute.

been able to watch the evolution of one of these storms continuously and close up thanks to Cassini.

Cassini's Radio and Plasma Wave Science (RPWS) experiment was a key observer. It detected lightning from the storm at a rate ten times greater than that of any previous storm since Cassini entered orbit around Saturn. At its peak there were ten flashes of lightning every second and the radio bursts they emitted were often just a jumble.

Cassini's observations were assisted by an army of ground-based telescopes peering up from Earth towards the ringed planet. Some of the best results came from telescopes observing at thermal infrared wavelengths that showed the temperature of the storm clouds. They revealed how the storm clouds changed thanks to the convective transport of energy throughout the raging tempest, creating jet streams that wove through the storm instigating eddies and small vortices. As different atmospheric layers swirled and mixed together, molecules not normally seen in Saturn's cloud tops were dredged

AFTER MORE THAN EIGHT MONTHS OF WIND, THUNDER AND LIGHTNING, THE THUNDERSTORM EXHAUSTED ITS POWER AND FELL SILENT

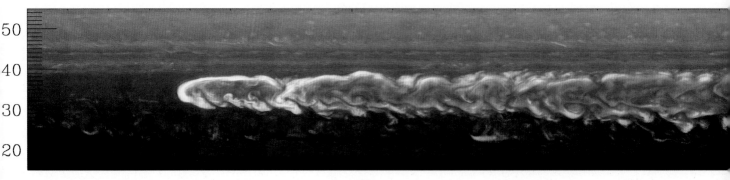

−100

Dec 5, 2010   Jan 2, 2011   Feb 25, 2011

Apr 22, 2011   May 18, 2011   Aug 12, 2011

up from below. These included acetylene, ammonia and phosphine and tracking the distribution and movement of these molecules via spectroscopic instruments provided a chemical tracer with which to follow the motions of the storm clouds.

Spring-time storm

On the face of it, the arrival of the storm seemed to have somehow been caused by the change in seasons. When Cassini arrived at Saturn the planet was tilted so that its southern hemisphere was basking in summer sunlight while its northern hemisphere shivered under the cloak of winter, so much so that the atmosphere to the north actually turned blue as haze, produced by ultraviolet light from the Sun reacting with molecules in Saturn's upper atmosphere, subsided in the pale winter light and more blue light was scattered. In August 2009 Saturn reached its equinox position, when the Sun shone directly over the planet's equator (see pages 66 to 73) and from then on the southern hemisphere has been gradually slinking

LIFE AND DEATH OF A STORM

Saturn's mega-storm, captured in its entirety from top left to bottom right. In the first panel the storm is barely visible as a small white spot on the terminator between day and night. Within a month it had blossomed and, over the following months the tail stretched out, wrapping around the planet's northern hemisphere until the head of the storm actually caught up with it and began swallowing it. This had a deleterious effect on the storm. The head had rotated out of view come May and by the time of the last image taken in August, the head of the storm had eradicated itself completely, leaving only turbulent clouds ringing the planet. Image: NASA/JPL–Caltech/Space Science Institute.

HEAD AND TAIL

A mosaic of images from Cassini showing the entirety of the storm laid out before us. The numbers on the bottom are degrees of longitude (centred on zero degrees), while running up the y-axis is latitude (centred on 35 degrees). In the middle, just above zero degrees longitude, is the spinning vortex, distinct from the head of the storm. When the head of the storm re-encountered the vortex in the tail, it was devoured. The contrast of this image has been enhanced to bring out the details in the storm, hence the unusual colours. Image: NASA/JPL–Caltech/Space Science Institute/Hampton University.

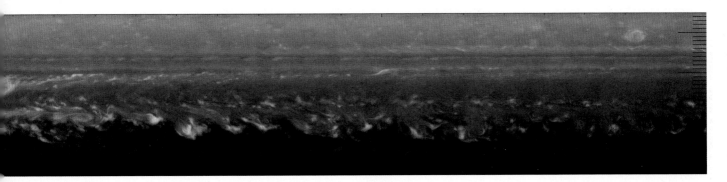

WHEN CASSINI ARRIVED AT SATURN IT SAW FREQUENT STORMS IN A REGION NICKNAMED 'STORM ALLEY'

towards winter, its atmosphere in the deepest south also turning an azure blue. Meanwhile, on the opposite side of the planet, northern spring is once again blossoming.

Andrew Ingersoll, who is a member of the Cassini imaging team from the California Institute of Technology and his student Cheng Li, suspect that the change of seasons so close to the eruption of the storm was more coincidence than consequence. Instead, they believe water is to blame.

Although there are no oceans on Saturn, there is plenty of water vapour in its atmosphere and, just like convective storms on Earth, water vapour helps drive storms on Saturn. As the mega-storms rage, they dump their mass of water into the bowels of the planet. This leaves the dry and hot hydrogen and helium mix in the clouds above lighter than the atmosphere below, a dichotomy that interferes with the natural process of convection whereby warm, wet air normally rises. It takes an entire Saturnian year for the upper clouds to grow cool enough to begin to sink and allow the warmer, wetter air to rise above them, kickstarting another great storm. Ingersoll likens it in some ways to a volcano, with pressure building up over nearly three

PATH OF STORMS

Another tempest rages along 'Storm Alley' (bottom right), followed by the pale sphere of the moon Tethys (the moon's shadow can be seen in the far north. Like other storms before it that have travelled down Storm Alley, this one was also radio loud, producing a noisy hiss from its frequent lightning. The Sun is shining from the south, casting the shadows of the rings on the northern hemisphere. Image: NASA/JPL/Space Science Institute.

decades before bursting out in energetic fashion. The whole process means that, in a way, the mega-storms have their own natural timer.

Incidentally, if this is correct, then it also explains why giant Jupiter, a planet sporting an atmosphere absolutely riven with storms, does not experience anything as explosive as Saturn's mega-storms. In 1996 NASA's Galileo spacecraft dropped a probe into Jupiter's atmosphere, yet it happened to fall through a region that was bone dry. Although scientists believe there is water vapour in Jupiter's clouds, Saturn's lower atmosphere probably contains far more.

So we think we now know why these mega-storms arise, but what allows them to persist so long remains frustratingly murky. Right from the beginning of the 2010–2011 storm, thermal energy began rising up from the lower atmosphere, convective currents rippling upwards into the stratosphere where they manifested themselves as two hotspots. Here they would normally be expected to run out of energy but instead of cooling and fading away they only grew stronger and hotter and, in April 2011, five months after the storm had appeared, they eventually coalesced into a single vortex of hot air some 80 degrees Celsius hotter than the surroundings, moving through the storm's tail behind the bright head of the storm. This vortex was analogous to Jupiter's churning cyclones such as the Great Red Spot or Red Spot Junior (Oval BA) and about the same size as the

SPOTTY STORMS

Storms cover the atmosphere in Saturn's northern hemisphere like a rash of spots in this image taken on 16 November 2008. The largest of the storms are several thousand kilometres across. Image: NASA/JPL/Space Science Institute.

THE CALM BEFORE THE STORM

Saturn appears relatively calm in this glorious image taken on 18 July 2009, just a month before equinox (note how the shadow of the rings appears so thin) and just over a year prior to the breakout of the largest Saturnian storm ever seen. Image: NASA/JPL/ Space Science Institute.

JET SET

Look closely to upper right hand side of this image looking down on Saturn and its northern hemisphere. The odd colours should give away the fact that this is a false-colour image, to represent infrared wavelengths of light that we cannot see with our eyes. Do you see something odd in the picture? There's a bright orange line streaking through the atmosphere – that's the sign of one of Saturn's jet streams blowing through the clouds. Half way along the jet stream seems to divert southwards and to the left of this change in direction a thicker, blurrier version of the jet stream can be seen. The jet stream exists at 42 degrees north and was there back in the days of the Voyager missions too. The orange colour (along with red) has been used to denote clouds that are deep in the atmosphere, showing how deep-rooted the jet streams really are. Image: NASA/JPL–Caltech/Space Science Institute.

latter. However, whereas Jupiter's monstrous cyclones are anchored in the lower atmosphere where conditions are more dynamic, Saturn's vortex was much higher up in what are normally calmer skies. Also, Jupiter's cyclonic storms have clear eyes, just like terrestrial hurricanes. On Saturn, the giant vortex was filled with storm clouds and lightning. And in the end, the presence of the vortex became the storm's downfall.

By the time the vortex formed the storm was out of control. It had grown so large that the storm-head was literally beginning to run into its own turbulent wake – just like the Ouroboros, the ancient symbol of a dragon eating its own tail. After wrapping itself around the planet, in June 2011 the head of the storm encountered the giant atmospheric vortex that the storm itself had spawned. For reasons that are still unclear, the vortex was able to suck the life out of the storm-head, causing it to fade away. On 28 August 2011 the last lightning bolt rippled through the stormy clouds. After 267 days, the storm to end all storms was over. Except, it wasn't quite.

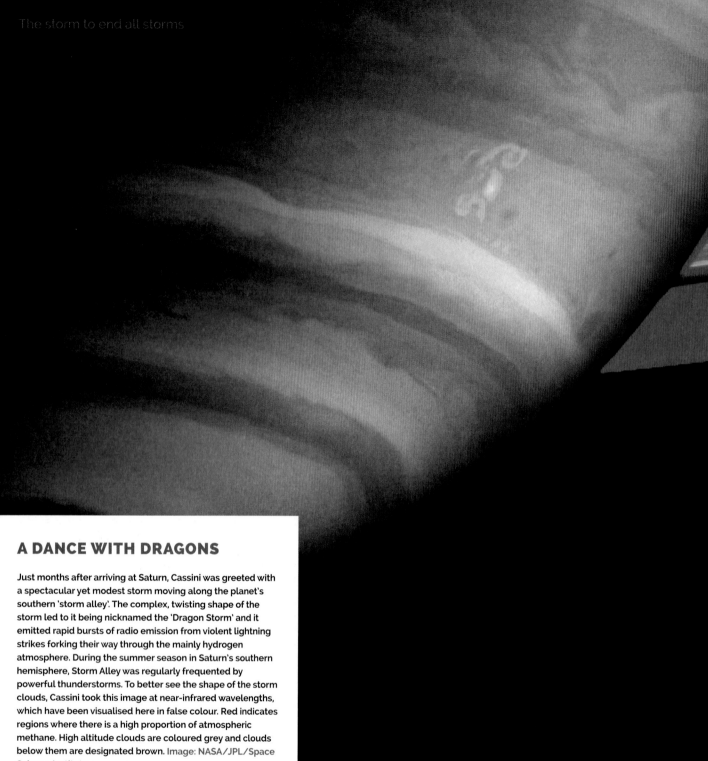

A DANCE WITH DRAGONS

Just months after arriving at Saturn, Cassini was greeted with a spectacular yet modest storm moving along the planet's southern 'storm alley'. The complex, twisting shape of the storm led to it being nicknamed the 'Dragon Storm' and it emitted rapid bursts of radio emission from violent lightning strikes forking their way through the mainly hydrogen atmosphere. During the summer season in Saturn's southern hemisphere, Storm Alley was regularly frequented by powerful thunderstorms. To better see the shape of the storm clouds, Cassini took this image at near-infrared wavelengths, which have been visualised here in false colour. Red indicates regions where there is a high proportion of atmospheric methane. High altitude clouds are coloured grey and clouds below them are designated brown. Image: NASA/JPL/Space Science Institute.

A storm that size is not going to simply vanish into thin air without leaving behind a legacy. Although the clouds visibly faded from view, in infrared light it was apparent that something was still stirring: the giant oval vortex, the storm-eater itself, continuing to swirl away malevolently and yet now completely invisible to the eye. When two ground-based telescopes, the European Southern Observatory's Very Large Telescope in Chile and NASA's Infrared Telescope Facility on Mauna Kea in Hawaii, inspected the aftermath on Saturn, the vortex was still clear to see. The infrared observations, led by Dr Leigh Fletcher of the University of Oxford, confounded all expectations – the vortex was something quite unique, according to Fletcher, who says that it was the first time such a phenomenon had been observed on any planet in

the Solar System. Given the usually calm and low-energy layer of the atmosphere where the vortex formed, it shouldn't have been able to exist in the first place, never mind have outlasted the storm from which it was born. It eventually dissipated by the end of 2013.

Mysteries and answers

The mega-storm of 2010–2011 has proven to be an eye-opener as to how little we truly understand what goes on beneath the cool creamy hues of the ringed planet's atmosphere. That scientists did not expect such a long-lived storm and accompanying vortex to propagate through Saturn's stratosphere simply indicates the gaps in our knowledge. By studying and coming to terms with the storm's behaviour it is going to help us fill in those gaps. It

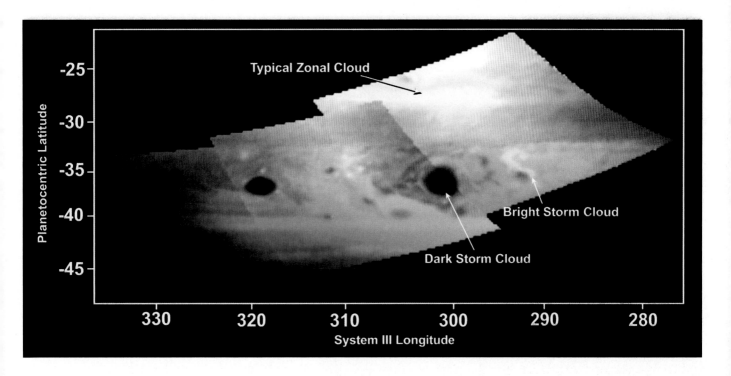

is also an opportunity for comparative planetology – the comparison of processes on one planet with those on another. We can compare the storm on Saturn with the storms on Jupiter or even storms on Earth, or use the planets in our Solar System as examples for figuring out what is happening in the atmospheres of distant extra-solar planets, where conditions can be even more extreme.

Saturn is not exactly quiescent when a mega-storm isn't raging. Though its atmosphere is not as turbulent on average as Jupiter's, smaller storms do break out on Saturn all the time. Prior to 2009's equinox, it was summertime in the planet's southern hemisphere. When Cassini arrived at Saturn in 2004 it began to see frequent storms in a region that scientists nicknamed 'Storm Alley' – a band 35 degrees south, which coincidentally – or perhaps not – is about the equivalent southern latitude to that at which the great storm of 2010–2011 broke out in the north. One storm after another blew a gale along this alley, but all were small and isolated, twisted knots of atmosphere sailing a calmer ocean of gas. Despite their diminutive stature they could be very long-lived, even longer than the 267 days of the 2011 mega-storm. Indeed, the longest-lived storm on Saturn was observed in 2009 in Storm Alley, a raging, record-breaking cyclone that endured for 334 days; however, it was 100 times smaller than the north's giant storm. A little larger are the occasional white ovals that appear on Saturn and are visible from Earth – comedian and amateur astronomer Will Hay most famously discovered a white spot on Saturn in 1933. These cyclonic storms are linked to Saturn's mega-storms and manifest themselves in the northern hemisphere as the seeds upon which the mega-storms grow.

The winds that blew the mega-storm around the planet are jet streams, just like those that aeroplanes ride across the Atlantic Ocean. On Earth the fastest of these swiftly moving currents of air have been clocked at 400 kilometres per hour. Without venturing into Saturn's atmosphere and riding the jet streams, how can we measure how fast they blow?

LIGHTNING STRIKES

A false-colour infrared image of a turbulent thunderstorm on Saturn. Bright clouds are rich in ammonia that has been dredged up to the cloud tops by rising convection currents. Lightning strikes convert methane in the atmosphere into dark carbon soot, left in the wake of the bright thunderstorms and visible as the dark spots. Image: NASA/ JPL/ASI/University of Arizona.

Tony Del Genio, an atmospheric scientist at NASA's Goddard Institute for Space Studies in New York, has spent his time investigating the relationship between the mega-storms and the jet streams. When water changes phase, from vapour into a droplet, it releases energy in the form of latent heat, which further heats the rising air struggling to break out from deep in the atmosphere. If there is a region of Saturnian air where water is condensing and rising, it creates a horizontal temperature difference with the blob of air next to it that is sinking and evaporating its water.

"Once those horizontal temperature differences are created on a planet that rotates rapidly enough, there will be low-pressure centres that are transporting momentum laterally," says Del Genio. This creates the winds of the jet streams. The storm literally blew itself around the planet.

Tracking the jet streams requires taking advantage of Saturn's (albeit uncertain) rotation. Cassini photographs a region of the atmosphere at different infrared wavelengths, penetrating to layers of various depths. On the planet's next rotation, Cassini takes more pictures. These data are then run through computer algorithms that look for regions of the atmosphere, such as clouds, which appear the same from one rotation to the next but which have perhaps moved relative to other atmospheric features. A simple calculation dividing the distance the cloud has travelled by the time interval between photographs provides the wind speed, which on occasions has been caught blowing at a staggering 1,800 kilometres per hour. The winds on Saturn make the gales of Earth's jet streams feel like a breeze.

It is clear that the more active Saturn's atmosphere is, the more we learn about it. In that sense, Cassini has been orbiting Saturn at a fortuitous time when massive storms have been tearing up the atmosphere. So while we may dread windy weather on Earth, we can't wait for the winds to rise again on the ringed planet.

THE WINDS ON SATURN MAKE THE GALES OF EARTH'S JET STREAMS FEEL LIKE A BREEZE

INTO THE VORTEX

Venus has one. Jupiter and Saturn both have them. Titan, the largest moon orbiting the ringed planet, has one. Even Earth has one. We're talking about the giant polar vortices in their atmospheres, but what is generating these twisting, swirling maelstroms?

"They might have a common cause, but I don't think we know enough about the vortices on the other planets to really tell," says Tony Del Genio of NASA's Goddard Institute for Space Studies. Take Titan's south polar vortex, the most recent of the vortices to be discovered, in 2012. Its elongated shape featured an interior mottled by turbulent clouds surrounded by a hood of wispy, spiral strokes painted in softer hues. According to Del Genio, its structure is reminiscent of open cellular convection similar to that seen over Earth's oceans, but at a much higher altitude. He speculates that the vortex forms as a response to seasonal cooling as the seasons change and winter approaches the southern hemisphere – a similar vortex was spotted by the Cassini spacecraft over Titan's north pole in 2004, indicating that the direction of Titan's atmospheric circulation has switched around since then.

However, Saturn's puzzling north polar vortex is somewhat different. Rather than the swirling peanut shape of Titan's vortex, Saturn sports a bewildering hexagonal vortex, with six clear and fairly straight sides. Cassini observed it in 2009 as spring fell on Saturn's northern hemisphere, but it was first observed back in 1980 and 1981 during the Voyager 1 and 2 fly-bys. The hexagon is huge, located at 77 degrees north latitude and, at 30,0000 kilometres across with each side of the hexagon measuring 13,800 kilometres, it is wide enough to fit the Earth in twice, with room to spare for the Moon too.

The hexagon appears to be bordered by a 400 kilometre per hour jet stream, which cuts off the inside of the hexagon from the outside atmosphere. Observations by Cassini indicate that within the hexagon there are fewer large haze particles than there are suspended in the clouds just outside the wall of fast-moving air on the edge of the hexagon. Along this edge are driven massive hurricanes, which rotate in the opposite direction to the hexagon. The largest are approaching 3,500 kilometres in size, twice as large as any hurricane ever recorded on our planet. The gas giant planets like Saturn seemingly like to do things big.

While the hexagon is remarkable, it is understandable to scientists who study the complex nature of atmospheres. Straight-sided shapes naturally occur when wind speeds sharply decrease with latitude, which leads to turbulent flow between the sections of the atmosphere rotating at different speeds. This turbulence breeds a number of atmospheric vortices that interact with each other before settling around the border of what has become shaped like a hexagon. For all this to happen, the atmospheric characteristics have to be very precise. That's why we do not see hexagons on other planets in the Solar System.

Intriguingly, because the jet stream hexagon is an atmospheric wave deeply rooted in Saturn's interior, it does not seem to be affected by seasonal changes and rotates every ten hours, 39 minutes and 23 seconds. It has been mooted that this could this be the true rotation period of Saturn, but this hypothesis remains unconfirmed.

And what is at the south pole, I hear you ask? Just another atmospheric vortex, recirculating gas around the atmosphere. No hexagons, jet streams or hurricanes. On any other world the southern vortex would be fascinating, but on Saturn, in the shadow of the northern hexagon, it barely gets a mention!

DOWN THE WHIRLPOOL

A close look at the vortex at the centre of Saturn's hexagon. The eye of the storm is 2,000 kilometres across, sucking Saturnian air into it.
Image: NASA/JPL–Caltech/Space Science Institute.

SWIRLS IN THE SOUTH

At the opposite end of the planet is the southern vortex, a straight-forward whirlpool surrounded by a wall of high cloud and swirling thunderstorms that form a tenuous ring in the otherwise clear air of the vortex. Normally in a hurricane on Earth convection of warm air occurs in the cloudy wall of the eye of the storm, but in Saturn's southern vortex it is occurring in patches in the eye too, hence the smaller storms. However, despite this convection, the air is mostly downwelling, being sucked into the interior of the planet where it will be recirculated. Image: NASA/JPL/Space Science Institute.

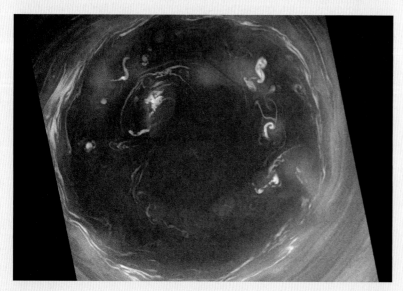

POLAR FORTRESS

Looking down on Saturn's hexagon, with its whirling hurricane dead centre, we can see the yellow-green jet stream that creates the hexagonal shape, like a giant wall bordering some ancient fortress. A second, paler coloured storm is patrolling around the hexagon's periphery. Although it is not apparent from the picture, the jet stream blows at a higher altitude than the central storm, which is at the well of the atmospheric vortex. The images here are presented in false colour, with red indicating deep clouds and green higher-altitude clouds. Image: NASA/ JPL–Caltech/Space Science Institute.

THE HEXAGON IS
HUGE, WITH EACH SIDE
MEASURING 13,800
KILOMETRES, AND IT IS
WIDE ENOUGH TO FIT
THE EARTH IN TWICE,
WITH ROOM TO SPARE
FOR THE MOON TOO

SEEING THROUGH THE HEXAGON

The six-sided hexagon at Saturn's north pole, seen here in infrared light as captured by the VIMS instrument on board Cassini. Saturn's north pole was hidden from the Sun when this image was taken, but infrared light produced by Saturn's own interior heat was detectable. Hence in infrared light Cassini is able to see below the clouds to a depth of 75 kilometres, where the clouds finally become opaque even to infrared light. These clouds appear bright in the image, which has been contrast reversed. The image clearly shows the writhing perimeter of the hexagon and the knotted clumps of the hurricane vortices that ride around it. Image: NASA/JPL/University of Arizona.

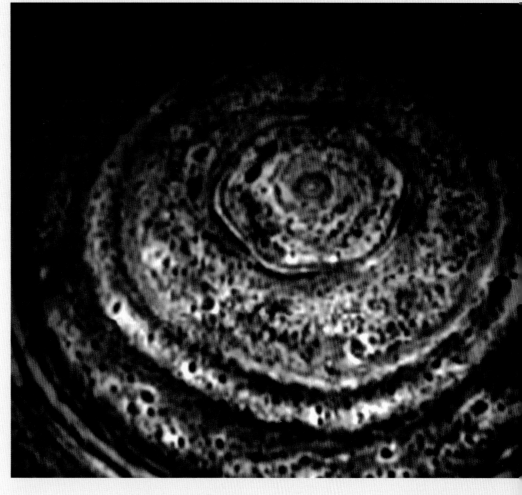

The age of the ringmaster

Saturn's rings are not just the planet's crowning glory, but the jewel of
the Solar System. Their origins are lost in the mists of time but,
thanks to Cassini and some clever detective work, their
secrets are gradually being pried away.

SATURN IN VINYL

A north polar view of Saturn, looking down on the backlit rings that make them look like a giant vinyl record. Saturn itself has been removed from the image, having been overexposed to bring the fainter rings into the picture, but its presence is still strongly felt with its shadow plunging part of the rings into darkness. Note the thin, wiry F-ring around the edge of the A-ring. This image was assembled from 27 separate image taken on 21 January 2007 and stitched together. Image: NASA/JPL/Space Science Institute.

Saturn's crown of gloriously dazzling and intricate rings is one of the jewels of the Solar System, contributing significantly to the planet being the most beguiling world to orbit the Sun. Saturn may not be the only world with rings, but in comparison the anaemic bands around Jupiter, Uranus and Neptune pale into insignificance. The astonishing intricacy is nothing less than exquisite artwork, unrivalled among the other planets. Only Saturn's are so massive, bright and colourful, to the point of being iconic.

For centuries the rings have prompted questions about their nature. How old are they? How did they form? Why are they so bright? What are they made of? Prior to Cassini's arrival, the rings were considered to be relatively young, maybe formed from a giant comet that passed too close to Saturn around 100 million years ago and was shredded. Such a relatively recent formation (well, 'recent' when compared to the 4.6-billion year age of the Solar System) would explain why the rings are so bright – there has not been enough time for the infall of dirty meteoritic dust to pollute and darken them. There's a problem with this though: if the rings really are transient then what is the chance that, over four-and-a-half billion years of history, the rings' existence should coincide with the existence of the human race?

Thanks to Cassini, that perspective has now been irrevocably changed. Could the rings really be ancient while somehow remaining forever young? New insights drawn from Cassini's careful observations are suggesting that could very well be the case.

Ringleaders

It would do to know a little bit about the rings first. There are seven principal rings named alphabetically in order of their discovery but not in distance order from Saturn. Many of these rings are composed of hundreds of narrow ringlets, looking like the grooves on a vinyl record. The closer we look at Saturn's rings, the more intricacy we find.

First up is the D-ring, just 8,000 kilometres above Saturn's cloud tops and discovered by Voyager 1. Then comes the dark C-ring, followed by the wide and bright B- and A-rings. Beyond them are the thin F- and G-rings before we arrive at the diffuse E-ring, which is a billowing torus of water-vapour belched out by the moon Enceladus. These are the main rings, but not the only rings: several more faint outer rings are associated with debris sputtered from the surfaces of nearby moons by tiny meteorites, the gravity of the moons then constraining these rings in tights orbits.

The estimated total mass of all the rings is 3×10^{19} (thirty million trillion) kilograms, which is equivalent to the mass of Saturn's

397 kilometre-wide moon Mimas. The rings stretch 270,000 kilometres from one end to the other, yet their thickness is only an estimated ten metres. The particles in the rings range from as small as a centimetre to giant boulders of ice several metres across and they can clump together to form small moonlets embedded in the rings.

Clean water

The composition of the rings would, at first glance, appear to point to their origin in the break up of an icy comet, rather than a partially rocky moon that fragmented under Saturn's gravitational tides.

"The particles are quite bright with albedos of roughly 50 percent [meaning that they reflect 50 percent of all sunlight that falls on them] and we can see nice clean spectral features of water-ice, so we have a pretty good idea that the rings are almost all water-ice," says Jeff Cuzzi, a Cassini scientist from NASA's Ames Research Center. "Also, we have ground-based microwave observations at centimetre wavelength that show that the rings don't emit very much microwave energy. This is easily understood in terms of their size, but what it does require is that they must be more than 90 percent water-ice."

> RING PARTICLES RANGE FROM AS SMALL AS A CENTIMETRE TO GIANT BOULDERS OF ICE SEVERAL METRES ACROSS

Cuzzi favours a young age for the rings. One of his reasons is that they rings seem to be unexplainably bright – were the rings old, they would surely have been dirtied by dark meteoritic debris over billions of years, just as the rings around the other giant planets have.

"There is a constant infall of meteoritic debris," says Cuzzi. "It's pretty dark, being around a third carbon, a third rock and a third ice, and it pollutes the ring material pretty quickly, darkening it up."

Admittedly the rings (in particular the C-ring) do have a reddish tint, but this is from dark organics in the ice such as tholins, fine-grained hematite and polycyclic aromatic hydrocarbons, and not necessarily from meteoritic debris.

Another reason why the rings must be young, Cuzzi says, is the existence of tiny moonlets that 'shepherd' the rings, their gravitational pulls and pushes confining the rings to their orbits. The moonlets presence only makes sense if the rings are young, according to Cuzzi. They are beginning to spin away from Saturn, taking angular momentum from the rings through torques and spiral density waves that ripple through the rings.

"What this means is that the little moons that we see today can't have been in their current locations for much more than a couple of hundred million years," says Cuzzi. For example, Atlas – the shepherd moon on the outer edge of the A-ring – would have taken less than 100 million years to migrate to its current position, 80,000 kilometres from Saturn's cloud tops. The important point

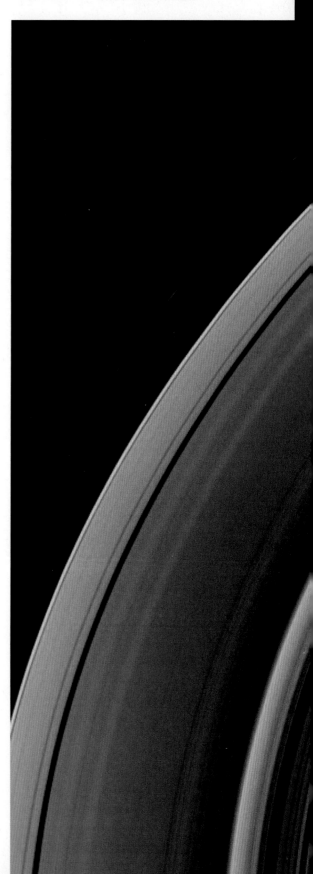

GRACEFUL CURVES

Looking at the un-illuminated, backlit side of the rings without all the glare of reflected sunlight can provide a subtle view, as we see here. Look carefully around the edge of the A-ring and you will spot the tenuously thin F-ring, shadowed by two small moonlets that appear as pinpricks of light: Janus (top) and Pandora. The alternating bright parts of the F-ring are bright clumps in the ring that moved during the exposure, which was captured on 7 February 2008. Image: NASA/JPL/Space Science Institute.

Colombo Gap

Maxwell Gap

D Ring

C Ring

B Ring

74,500km

92,000km

SERENE SCENE

Saturn's rings meet its cream-hued atmosphere in this portrait
taken on 28 February 2009. Image: NASA/JPL/Space Science
Institute. Image: NASA/JPL/University of Colorado.

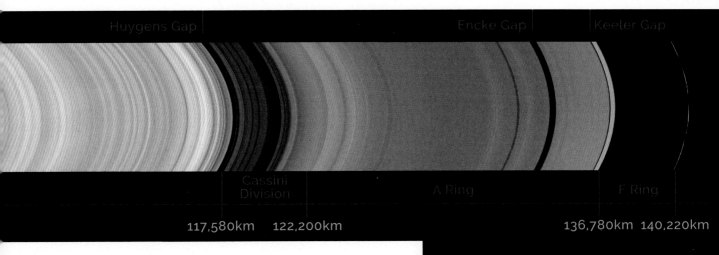

Huygens Gap — Encke Gap — Keeler Gap

Cassini Division — A Ring — F Ring

117,580km   122,200km   136,780km   140,220km

is that to conserve the angular momentum of the ring system, the rings should have begun to fall towards the planet. If the rings really are old, the moonlets should have spun away and the rings mostly fallen into Saturn's atmosphere by now, argues Cuzzi. Clearly they haven't, so that must mean the weight of evidence stacks up on the side of young rings rather than old, right? Well, actually, perhaps not.

Ring waves

Larry Esposito is a man who has history with Saturn's rings. Based at the University of Colorado in Boulder, USA, in 1979 he dug into data from the Pioneer 11 space probe to discover Saturn's wayward F-ring. Today he is the Principal Investigator of the Ultraviolet Imaging Spectrograph (UVIS) on board Cassini and is still studying the planet's ring system. He has discovered what he believes indicates that the rings can be as old as Saturn itself, while remaining fresh-faced. To make this discovery, Esposito and his team working with UVIS had some assistance from far away: the light of distant stars.

From Earth, Saturn is rarely seen to occult – that is, move in front of – a star. On the other hand, stellar occultations are a far more frequent event for Cassini as Saturn covers a much larger area of sky when seen up close by the spacecraft. Of most interest is when the rings themselves actually occult a bright star – the way the starlight flickers through the rings and is scattered by the ring particles can inform us about the specific size of the material that makes up the rings, for example. However, UVIS' observations of the stellar occultations discovered something quite interesting about the way Saturn's moons wield influence over the size of the ring particles, their evolution and ultimately the continued youthful appearance of the rings.

The gravity of certain moons around Saturn, including Mimas, Janus, Epimetheus and even Titan, can create density waves within the rings – regions where the ring particles can pile up before relaxing again in the troughs of the wave. In particular there are density waves in Saturn's B-ring instigated by a 2:1 gravitational resonance with the tiny moon Janus, which is only 190 kilometres across (in other words, for every two orbits the particles in the B-ring make, Janus makes exactly one, meaning that ring particles come into close contact with Janus' gravity at certain points in their orbit).

During the occultations UVIS found that at the crest of these waves there is a drop in the size of the particles where the optical depth – the degree of transparency in the rings – reaches its peak. Correspondingly, in the trough of the wave the particles are found to be at their largest. Together these are the biggest and smallest grains seen anywhere in the B-ring. It appears that the density waves, caused by orbital resonances between the moons and the rings, stir up the particles so that in the troughs they stick together to build into larger particles, then at the crest of the wave they collide and break up once again. Each wave goes past a given point in the rings every 14 hours, during which the aggregates form and then fragment, a constant churning cycle that keeps turning over the water-ice and maintaining the rings' fresh, youthful appearance by diluting any dark meteoritic dust. It is a remarkably gentle process too, with the collisions between the ring particles taking place at mere walking pace.

"The process can persist for billions of years in stirred-up regions, where collisions take place at speeds of metres per second," says Esposito. "Therefore, crystals of ice could survive over the age of the Solar System at these velocities."

Not all the larger particles can be broken up this way – some are more solidly held together by their own gravity. These are harder to disrupt, but the extra mass increases the collision speeds up to ten metres

THE CONSTANT REPLENISHMENT HELPS KEEP THE RINGS LOOKING YOUNG AND HEALTHY, EVEN THOUGH THEY MAY BE MUCH OLDER

ICY EDGES

Cassini's UVIS instrument captured this ultraviolet view of Saturn's rings. Measurements in ultraviolet have shown that over 90 percent of the material in the rings is made from water-ice. This particular image was taken right at the beginning, during Cassini's orbital insertion manoeuvre that took the spacecraft through the plane of the ring system. The red coloured rings indicate the dirtier material of the Cassini Division and the Encke Gap. Image: NASA/JPL/University of Colorado.

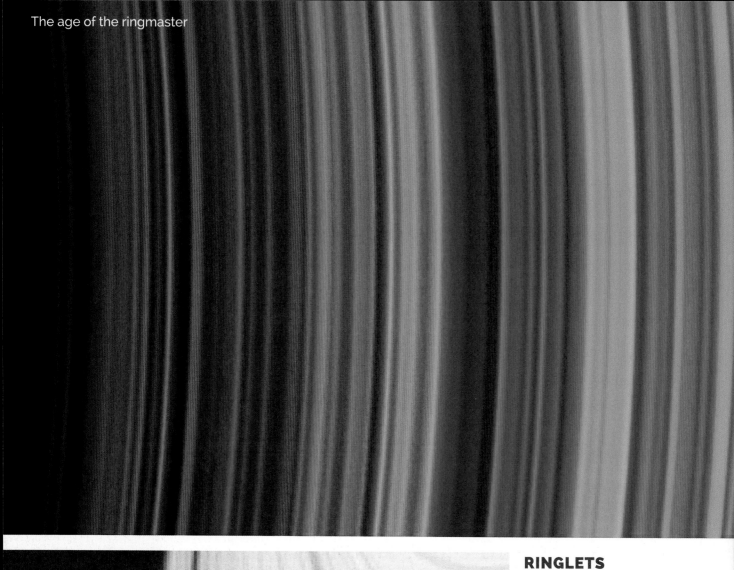

RINGLETS

Myriad ringlets can be seen in this close up of the C- and B-rings. The redder the rings in this false-colour ultraviolet image, the dirtier they are. the more turquoise rings are mostly water-ice. Image: NASA/JPL/University of Colorado.

BIRTH OF A MOON

A bright arc of material is seen on the edge of the A-ring on 15 April 2013. Is this evidence of material in the rings being disrupted by the presence of an unseen moonlet that has just formed from the rings themselves? Image: NASA/JPL–Caltech/Space Science Institute.

per second, fast enough to kick grains of ring material out of the rings altogether and into haloes above and below the ring plane, as observed by UVIS in 2004 around the density waves, centred 100 kilometres from the resonance, with the brightest part of the halo 450 kilometres from the ring plane. Another instrument, the Visual and Infrared Mapping Spectrometer (VIMS), saw the largest grains where the haloes are centred, with smaller grains at greater distances.

The constant churning of clumps of ring material can also create gaps, or wakes, in the rings that are described as 'propellers' and exist in a region in the middle of the A-ring that has subsequently been nicknamed the 'propeller belts'. Here the clumps clear out spaces in

the rings immediately before and behind them, with the largest clumps reaching a kilometre in size and being capable of kicking particles half a kilometre above or below the plane of the rings. Sometimes these clumps are torn apart, or alternatively they can grow into small moonlets themselves. Indeed, Cassini Imaging Team member Professor Carl Murray of Queen Mary, University of London believes he has seen this very moment of moon creation happen.

Giving birth

The birth-day for this particular moonlet was 15 April 2013, when it – or rather, the disturbances in the rings that its gravity stirred up – was spotted by Cassini's

RAINBOW BRIGHT

With the Sun directly behind Cassini on 12 June 2007, bright sunlight surges onto the rings, creating a halo of light scattered by the icy ring particles. The rainbow effect is actually caused by the motion of the spacecraft relative to the halo as it took images separately in red, green and blue filters. Image: NASA/JPL/ Space Science Institute.

narrow-angle camera as the moonlet began to depart the rings that had spawned it. Normally the edge of the A-ring is razor sharp, but on this day Cassini observed several protuberances from the edge of the ring and an arc of bright ring material, 1,200 kilometres in length and a fifth brighter than the surrounding ring particles, being swept along by what was likely a brand new but unseen moon no larger than a kilometre across. Cassini was 1.2 million kilometres from Saturn when it spotted the disturbances and at that distance the moonlet would have been too small to be seen. Cassini will get another chance to spot the object, which Murray nicknamed 'Peggy', when the spacecraft swoops closer to the edge of the A-ring in late 2016 to find out whether a fully formed moon really has departed the rings to join its siblings in orbit around Saturn, or whether Peggy was really only a loosely held together clump of icy ring material that has since fallen apart.

"The theory holds that Saturn long ago had a much more massive ring system capable of giving birth to larger moons," says Murray. "As the moons formed near the edge, they depleted the rings and evolved, so the ones that formed earliest are the largest and farthest out."

The continual creation of new moonlets answers one half of Jeff Cuzzi's concerns about the relationship between the shepherd moons and the age of the rings.

"Cassini data show that both aggregation and destruction processes are ongoing in Saturn's rings," says

DELVING INTO THE OCCULT

A key method of surveying Saturn's rings is to watch how the block – or occult – the light of a bright background star or, in this case, how they block a radio signal from Cassini to Earth. Cassini beamed back three simultaneous radio signals at wavelengths of 0.94, 3.6 and 13 centimetres and, when scientists on Earth received them, they could infer how the rings had blocked and distorted the signals. The degree of interference from the rings told scientists which rings contained a denser distribution of material, information that is then replicated here by presenting the rings in false colour. The white band in the B-ring indicates where material is densest; purple signifies a deficiency of particles smaller than five centimetres, green is where there are particles present smaller than five centimetres and blue indicates rings that contain a large number of particles smaller than one centimetre. Image: NASA/JPL.

AN OBJECT, PERHAPS A LARGE COMET OR A SMALL MOON, MAY HAVE COME TOO CLOSE TO SATURN AND BEEN TORN APART BY THE GIANT PLANET'S GRAVITY TO FORM THE RINGS

BACKSCATTER

Above: from the correct viewing angle, the spoke particles scatter light and appear bright. The spokes have been seen more frequently since Saturn's 2009 equinox – this image was taken on 6 September 2009, less than a month after the equinox. Image: NASA/JPL/Space Science Institute.

Spokes on a wheel

One of the rings' biggest mysteries are the elusive 'spokes' first seen by Voyager 1 as dirty-looking streaks that extend outwards and rotate with the planet in a manner described as being like 'spokes on a wheel' by NASA scientist Richard Terrile, who discovered them in Voyager's imagery. Curiously, Voyager 1 saw them as dark while approaching the planet, but light as the spacecraft moved away from them. The inference was that the spokes are comprised of tiny charged particles of dust, each one no larger than a millionth of a metre, that are elevated above the B-ring by electrostatic or magnetic forces and which, from the correct viewing angle, can appear to scatter light and become bright.

What causes them remains a puzzle. One popular hypothesis is that micrometeoroids are constantly striking the rings, sputtering out clouds of charged particles that are then elevated above the B-rings by electromagnetic forces. An alternative is that they are linked to lightning storms on Saturn, which could produce clouds of electrons that then find themselves moving towards the rings along magnetic field lines. This would perhaps explain why the spokes are often seen mirroring longitudes on Saturn that produce Saturn Kilometric Radiation during thunderstorms, and also why there is some evidence that they are seasonal: Cassini did not find the spokes until 5 September 2005 and the spokes have been seen more frequently since Saturn's equinox in 2009.

Either way, their link to Saturn's magnetic field seems a strong one. They rotate in time with the planet's magnetic field, although differential rotation of the widespread orbits the particles take causes them to spread out. They have been seen to grow 6,000 kilometres in mere minutes and persist for hours at a time. They are beautiful but ephemeral and continue to vex scientists and push Cassini's ability to detect them to the limit.

WHEN SATURN SPOKE

Spokes shimmering across Saturn's B-ring, as seen on 26 November 2008. Image: NASA/JPL/Space Science Institute.

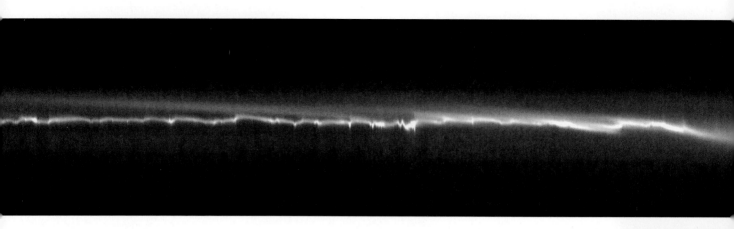

FREAKY F-RING

Saturn's F-ring is one of the most fascinating of all the planet's rings. It's not the biggest and it's not the brightest, but its behaviour is the most bizarre, as is evident in the wacky details in this image. The picture has been artificially straightened, but this does not account for its tortured appearance. The ring is shepherded by a tiny moonlet named Prometheus (its companion moonlet, Pandora, is believed to have a negligible affect on the ring) that tugs on the ring particles, while there are also believed to be myriad smaller objects sat within the ring itself, that distort it, unwinding it like a length of string. However, the wispy horizontal streaks in the image are, alas, little more than imaging defects. Image: NASA/JPL/Space Science Institute.

Esposito. "These small moons can survive for 10 million to 100 million years before they are destroyed by an impact. The fragments form a ring and are subsequently ground to dust, while new moons are formed at the edge of the rings that replace the former moons." If the moonlets have limited lifespans then they do not have enough time to generate the spiral density waves that can cause the rings to fall into Saturn. There's another upside to this constant replenishment – like anti-ageing creams, the process helps keep the rings looking a young and healthy 100 million years old, even though they may mostly be much older in truth.

Peeling a moon

So Saturn is seemingly capable of creating moons, but in the distant past the ringed planet may have been adept at destroying them too, providing a possible origin for the rings. It is clear that there is a lot of activity in the rings. They may not even remain exactly as we see them in the future and, following that logic, they were therefore not necessarily the same in the past. There has been much speculation as to how they formed, with two main theories coming to the fore. One is that the rings are just leftover debris from the formation of Saturn and its moons, a hypothesis bolstered by the fact that all the giant planets have rings, although why Saturn's should be so different is not explained. An alternative theory is that an object, perhaps a large comet or a small moon, came too close to Saturn and was torn apart by the giant planet's gravity to form the rings. This theory dates all the way back to the nineteenth century and the French astronomer Édouard Roche, when he developed the idea of the Roche limit, a point in orbit around a planet beyond which the gravitational tidal forces are so strong

they can pull even a moon apart. He even had a name for the unfortunate moon that had been destroyed: Veritas (the Roman goddess of truth). Now a new model developed by Robin Canup of the South-West Research Institute in Colorado dramatically expands on Roche's idea by suggesting that there was not just one Veritas, but many.

Saturn's moon Titan is odd, not in the sense of its intrinsic characteristics (although with a hydrocarbon-rich atmosphere, lakes and rivers of liquid methane and ethane, all manner of organic chemistry and a possible underground water ocean, it is certainly unique) but by the fact that it is the only large moon to orbit Saturn; with a diameter of 5,152 kilometres it is 2,000 kilometres larger than Rhea, the ringed planet's second largest moon. Compare this to Jupiter, which has four moons in Titan's class. Why does Saturn not have more large moons?

Canup thinks they fell into Saturn itself billions of years ago, tumbling one after another on decaying orbits caused by their interaction with the disc of primordial material from which they formed and that Titan is the only survivor from that time (for the record, Canup has developed a similar theory for Jupiter too). Her computer simulations show that the last moon to fall – let us call it Veritas for the sake of historical continuity – was peeled like an onion. First, the moon began to flex under the mighty tidal forces at play, causing its ice to soften and melt, allowing all the rock contained within the moon to sink to the core. As Veritas crossed the current orbit of Saturn's B-ring, the gravitational forces stripped away the outer layers of water-ice, leaving behind only the rocky core that fell to its doom, becoming a part of Saturn. The ice layers spread out into a bloated belt around Saturn, containing far more mass than the rings do today (Titan's mass is 1.35×10^{23} kilograms, compared to the current mass of the rings provided earlier in this article). The icy particles in this belt began to collide with one another, the energy of the collisions causing the belt to spread out further. Some of the particles followed Veritas into Saturn, while in the other direction some were swept up by the moons, or even coagulated and accreted into small moons themselves. The densities of many of Saturn's moons appear to support this origin theory, as they are unusually rich in water-ice.

Whether such a theory can be conclusively proven is uncertain – perhaps one day we will detect the actual formation of planetary rings around an exoplanet. If

A FEW KINKS TO IRON OUT

A closer, more detailed view of the F-ring in the aftermath of Prometheus passing by. The core of the ring is the brightest part, while streamers of fainter material ripped from the core are seen on either side. Although Prometheus had left the scene of the crime by the time this image was taken on 23 October 2008, the kinks in the ring that its gravity caused remain. Image: NASA/JPL/Space Science Institute.

THE DAY THE EARTH SMILED

The world was able to celebrate the Cassini mission with this epic vista of a backlit Saturn, the planet caught in silhouette as Cassini looked back towards the direction of the Sun and the inner Solar System. The Sun is being eclipsed by Saturn, but visible at bottom right is a little blue spot: Earth. A campaign was launched to encourage people to look back up at Saturn and Cassini while the spacecraft was capturing the 141 wide-angle camera images that have gone into creating this astounding mosaic.

The image clearly displays all of Saturn's major ring bands, from the D- and C-rings closest to the planet, the major B- and A-rings, the black gulfs of the Cassini Division and the Encke Gap, the bright line of the F-ring, and the elusive and diffuse G- and E-rings, with Enceladus slap bang inside the latter. Image: NASA/JPL–Caltech/Space Science Institute.

Mars

Pallene's ri

Venus

Janus

Janus' ring

Prometheus

Epimetheus

Clumps

Look closely and you can see the plume of water vapour erupting from Enceladus' geysers that is feeding the E-ring.

Tethys

Mimas

Pandora

Earth and Moon

Our pale blue dot, seen from the orbit of Saturn. Look closely and you can se a tiny dot – just a pixel – next to our planet. That is the Moon.

Canup's model is correct for both Saturn and Jupiter, then rings around gas giants may be fairly common. On the other hand, if the rings did form when an unfortunate and unusually large comet passed too close to Saturn, then the glorious rings may be a rare occurrence in planetary systems, and Saturn's rings could be quite young, depending upon when the comet's doomed encounter took place.

The consensus has switched, from young rings during the early days of Cassini's mission, to the more detailed evidence that points to old but constantly replenished rings. There's still time for a twist in the tale, however. Shortly before the end of its mission in 2017, Cassini will drive through the rings, between the inner C-ring and the top of Saturn's atmosphere, placing it in prime position to measure the exact mass of the rings, which until now has been uncertain. If the rings are less massive than expected, that might point to a comet being their origin, but if they are more massive, it may mean the rings are the ancient remains of a large moon and are almost as old as the planet itself.

"We will just nail that whole question of the ring mass for sure, and that's really the way to tell the age," says Cuzzi.

Regardless of how massive and how old the rings are, there is one thing that we do know to be true: that every time we gaze at Saturn, we should feel fortunate to have such a spectacular sight on our cosmic doorstep.

NIGHT FALLS

A vertigo-inducing view of the terminator between day and night on Saturn, looking down on the rings as they slip into the shadow of the planet. Yet nighttime on Saturn is never truly dark – scattered light from the rings falls back onto the planet, casting an eerie twilight. This image was taken on 20 March 2009. Image: NASA/JPL/Space Science Institute.

CRESCENT MOON

Nowhere else in the Solar System can you see scenes such as this one. We see an oblique view of the rings, Saturn's shadow cutting across and almost parallel to them, with two moons, Mimas (closest to camera) and Epimetheus (in the background) 'photo-bombing' Cassini's picture. Note the phases of the moons and, if you look closely, you can make out the outline of a crater on Mimas close to the terminator. Image: NASA/JPL/Space Science Institute.

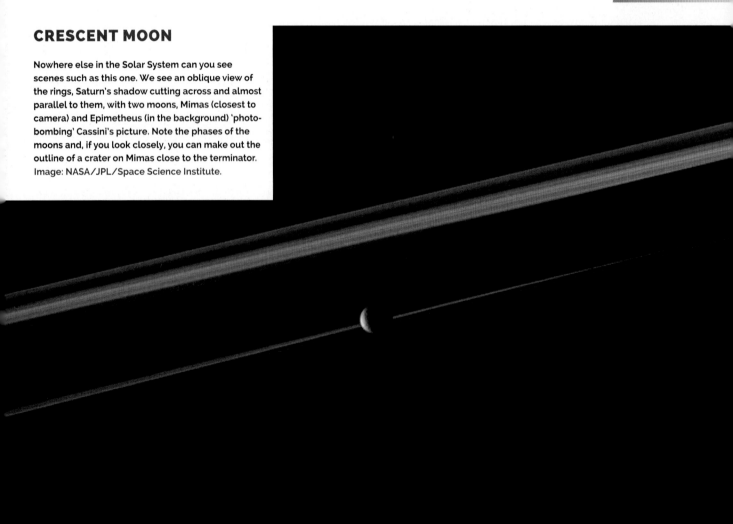

The rings of Saturn

D: 66,900–74,5210 kilometres from the centre of Saturn, 8,668 kilometres above the planet's cloud tops. Saturn's innermost ring, made up of three ringlets, is tenuous and faint, to the point of being transparent. Cassini has detected it moving 200 kilometres closer to Saturn.

C: 74,658–92,000km. The C-ring (sometimes called the Crepe Ring) is made of darker material than the bright A- and B-rings. It is about five metres thick.

B: 92,000–117580km. The heavyweight of Saturn's ring system, the B-ring contains the most mass, 2.8×10^{19} kilograms, and is the largest and brightest of the rings. It is made up of many ringlets that all contribute varying hues and brightnesses, and is up to 15 metres thick.

Cassini Division: 117,580–122,170km. Between the B and A-rings is what at first appears to be a large gap named the Cassini Division. However, this 4,600 kilometre band is not a gap at all, but a region of dark ring material, similar in composition to the C-ring.

A: 122,170–136,775km. Up to 30 metres thick, the A-ring alone contains an estimated 6.2×10^{18} kilograms of material, equivalent to the mass of Saturn's moon Hyperion.

Encke Gap: 133,589km. More of a true gap than the dusty Cassini Division, the Encke Gap resides within the A-ring and contains several distinct ringlets.

F: 140,180km. Lying around 3,000 kilometres from the A-ring, the F-ring is a bizarre, tangled, thin ring that is shepherded by two small moons, Prometheus and Pandora.

G: 166,000–175,000km. A thin, diffuse ring too faint to be seen on the accompanying image. Its brightest section is an arc of material at its inner edge.

E: (Not on image) 180,000–480,000km. A wide (2,000 kilometres) and diffuse belt of water vapour, fed by the geysers on Saturn's moon Enceladus. It is too faint to be seen in this image.

Image: NASA/JPL–Caltech/Space Science Institute.

D   C   B   A   F   G   E

Encke Gap

Cassini Division

Shadowlands

When Saturn reached equinox in 2009 and its rings were aligned edge-on to the Sun, the shadows that were subsequently cast contained information necessary to unravel some of the many mysteries about the rings' hidden structures.

A TEAR IN THE RINGS

Mimas' shadow cuts a dark wound into the colourful spectacle of Saturn's rings in this image dated 8 April 2009. Image: NASA/JPL/Space Science Institute.

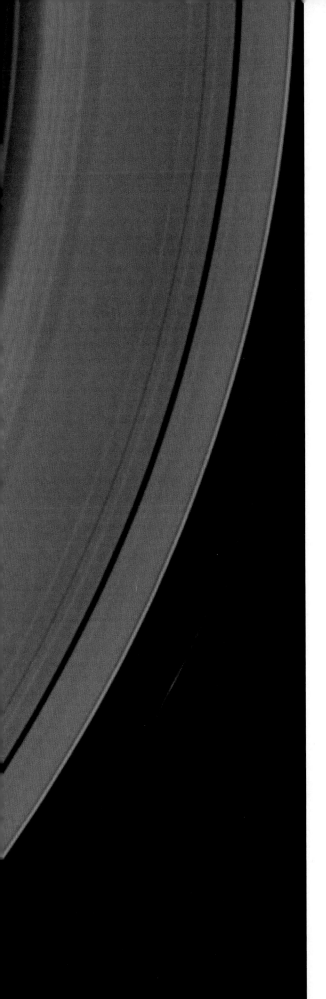

The shadows slipped away, slowly, gradually dropping southwards as the Sun moved northwards. For five years after Cassini arrived at Saturn, the angle of the Sun shining through the glorious rings had been from below, casting their finely defined shadows against the cold winter skies of the north. As the seasons sedately progressed, spring began to blossom in the north as the angle of the Sun began to change, climbing higher and higher towards the equator. Then, come 11 August 2009, the Sun found itself directly above Saturn's equator, illuminating the rings edge-on. The shadows of those rings on Saturn vanished and both north and south enjoyed equal light.

It was a unique time. The equinox, just like on Earth, signified a change of season throughout the Saturnian neighbourhood. After that, the Sun moved into the northern hemisphere and shadows and winter descended on the south.

The equinox is often described as a ring-plane crossing. With Saturn tilted by 26.7 degrees, the angle of the rings to the Sun and the plane of the Solar System changes as the planet traverses its 29.7-year orbit and our relative viewpoint shifts. Twice a Saturnian year – or approximately every 15 years on Earth – we and the Sun appear to pass through the plane of Saturn's rings during the equinox, causing the rings to 'disappear' as we see them edge-on. With the Sun directly above Saturn's equator, the rings no longer cast a shadow: only their approximately ten-metre thick edge is illuminated, plus any clumps of ring material or moonlets that may have been raised up above them. Cassini watched these structures cast shadows that lengthened as 2009's equinox approached, revealing a three-dimensional ring system in a way that has not really been possible before or since.

Indeed, 2009 was the first time scientists have been able to watch this event up close, thanks to the ringside seat afforded to Cassini. The views included the shadows of Saturn's many moons falling across the rings and onto the golden-hued globe of the ringed planet. As a comparison, we are used to regularly seeing the moons of Jupiter casting their shadows on the giant planet's globe and any decent amateur telescope will show you these shadows transiting across Jupiter. This is because Jupiter barely lists at all – its rotational axis and the plane of its moons' orbits are angled towards the Sun by a mere three degrees, which is not enough to take them out of alignment with the Sun. Saturn's large tilt, which results in the orbital plane of the moons also being tilted, means that we only see their shadows around the time of equinox.

The first moon seen to cast a shadow was the 113 kilometre-wide Epimetheus on 8 January 2009, followed a month later by 30 kilometre-wide Pan. The likes of

"WE THOUGHT THE PLANE OF THE RINGS WAS NO TALLER THAN TWO STORIES OF A MODERN-DAY BUILDING, BUT INSTEAD WE'VE COME ACROSS WALLS MORE THAN TWO MILES HIGH."

FALLING SHADOWS

Just a year away from equinox, on 22 August 2008, Cassini captured this profile of Saturn with the shadow of its ring system now much narrower and closer to the equator as the Sun-angle diminishes. Image: NASA/JPL/Space Science Institute.

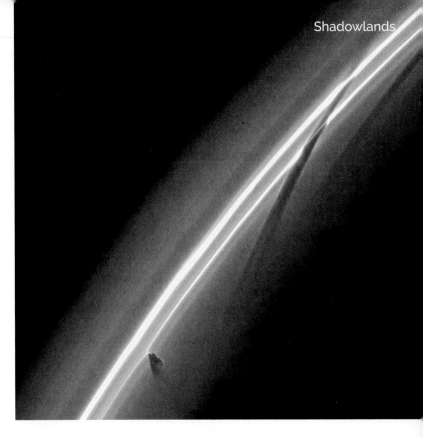

Tethys, Titan and Mimas were also caught throwing shadows onto the rings, the shadows growing like dark splinters cutting into the bright, icy ring particles. While the shadows could not tell us anything new about the moons that we did not already know about, they did reveal to us small moons that we did not know about, hidden deep within gaps in the rings. As they orbit Saturn, the gravity of these unseen moons can disturb the ring particles, creating spiralling density waves or, in the case of the tiny moon Daphnis in the A-ring's Keeler Gap, vertical waves towering one-and-a-half kilometres high. These waves are enormous when you consider the thickness of the rings, but they only become noticeable at equinox when they start to cast a shadow.

Ring mountains

Diminutive Daphnis was a real star of the show. At just eight kilometres wide it is tiny, although by no means is it among the smallest moonlets of Saturn – Aegaeon, for example, which lurks within Saturn's G-ring, is 250 metres across. Daphnis wavers about the 42-kilometre wide Keeler Gap in an eccentric, inclined orbit. It is the inclined part of the orbit that is key here; the up and down motion of the moon imparts an up and down wave-like motion on the ring material every time Daphnis moves close to the ring, causing the propagation of giant waves four kilometres high along the edges of the gap. At equinox these towering waves cast their shadows 500 kilometres across the A-ring, revealing their presence.

Carolyn Porco, the Cassini Imaging team leader from the Space Science Institute in Boulder, Colorado, summed up the findings when she said, "We thought the plane of the rings was no taller than two stories of a modern-day building, but instead we've come across walls more than two miles high."

Something happened in 1984

One of the biggest shocks to come out of Cassini's observations of the equinox was the discovery of vast, undulating waves seen extending 17,000 kilometres across Saturn's C-ring and right to the edge of the B-ring. Cassini had observed them in 2006 and at the time they were thought to be confined to just the innermost D-ring, with an amplitude of one kilometre. The shadows that the corrugating waves, or ripples, cast became more apparent in the low-angled sunlight of the equinox, revealing their full, stunning extent.

"It looks like something happened in the early 1980s to get this pattern going, but we are still trying to figure out what could have disturbed such a large part of the rings," says Matthew Hedman of Cornell University in New York. In 2006 Hedman argued that the ripples in the D-ring had been caused by a small comet or asteroid impacting the ring during early 1984, less than three years after Voyager 2 had flown past. This caused the ring material to become slightly inclined with respect to Saturn's gravitational field. Further evidence that Saturn's rings are constantly bombarded by 'space junk' came during Cassini's observations of the rings during the equinox, when it spotted bright streaks 5,000 kilometres long in the rings. These streaks were debris clouds from where objects a metre or two in size had smashed into the rings and disintegrated, scattering icy ring particles into space.

SHADOW OF A SHEPHERD

The gravity of the shepherd moon Prometheus is able to torture Saturn's F-ring, twisting and tearing aggregates of matter within the ring this way and that, pulling streamers out above the plane of the rings. This picture was taken on 14 January 2009 and both the distorted ring (top and middle) and Prometheus itself (bottom left) cast shadows. Image: NASA/JPL/Space Science Institute.

GREEK ROMANCE MEETS ROMAN BEGINNINGS

The shadow of 179-kilometre wide moon Janus crosses Saturn's A-ring (although Janus itself is not visible in the image), dwarfing the shadows cast by eight-kilometre wide moonlet Daphnis and the mountains of ring matter that it elevates on the edge of the thin Keeler Gap near the top left of the image. The wider gap closer to the shadow of Janus is the Encke Gap. This image was snapped on 11 July 2009.

CASTING A LONG SHADOW

Spokes above Saturn's B-ring appear bright in contrast to the barely illuminated rings and the long splinter of shadow belonging to Mimas, which is out of frame in this image taken on 9 September 2009. Image: NASA/JPL/Space Science Institute.

A SHADOW OF TITANIC PROPORTIONS

The dark splodge sat on Saturn's cloud-tops is the giant shadow of Titan, following the curvature of the planet as seen on 7 November 2009. Only at equinox do Saturn's moons leave their shadows on the face of the planet. Image: NASA/JPL/Space Science Institute.

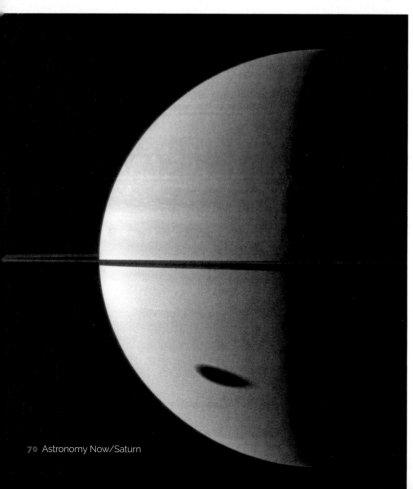

However, with the revelation that the corrugated ripples extend into the C-ring as well, the impact theory came under fire because it struggled to explain the huge scale of these ripples. The ripples in the D-ring had first been detected in 1995 by the Hubble Space Telescope, when it observed Saturn's rings occulting the star GSC5249-01240. As the star's light flitted in and out between the rings, Hubble measured the wavelength of the corrugation to be 60 kilometres, twice the current wavelength. Because Saturn is oblate rather than spherical, its shape affects the orbits of the rings, causing the longitude of their periapse (each ring's closest point to Saturn) to precess and the longitude where the rings cross the equator (the node) to move backwards by a few degrees per day. This is called differential nodal regression.

This precession means that the longitude of periapse increases with time, while the regression means that the longitude of the ascending node decreases with time. As the rings regress at different speeds, the point at which they cross the equator moves in and out of phase with each other, both above and below the rings because of their inclination, creating a vertical distortion with peaks and troughs. These are what we see as the corrugated ripples. As the nodes move backwards with respect to longitude on the planet, they cause the corrugated pattern to spiral tighter and tighter with each revolution, thus explaining why the wavelength was larger in 1995 than it is today. By working backwards and 'unwinding' this spiral to see how many times it has wrapped around, we find it was created in 1984. Despite the problems with the theory, the impact model is still the leading candidate, particularly as Hedman has discovered that Jupiter's dark main ring also features a corrugated spiral pattern dating back from the Comet Shoemaker–Levy 9 impacts in 1994. If the twin Voyager spacecraft, which visited Saturn in 1980 and 1981 respectively, had only got there a few years later they might have seen something very interesting.

Miniature moons

Besides the Keeler Gap there are another dozen or so gaps interspersed in Saturn's magnificent rings. One of the most famous is the Encke Gap, which is home to the small moon Pan, which was discovered by the Voyager probes and which is believed to control the behaviour of the numerous ringlets found within the gap. During the equinox, Cassini witnessed clumps in the kinked, partial ringlets within the Encke Gap casting shadows over 350 kilometres long, right across the gap and onto the A-ring. Meanwhile, similar features were also observed in the Colombo Gap in the C-ring, which is controlled by a gravitational resonance with the giant moon Titan.

Meanwhile, many more tiny moonlets were turning up, answering questions that had been asked prior to the Cassini mission about the range of objects that can be found within the rings. In the A-ring a moonlet 400 metres across cast shadows 350 kilometres long and created a 'propeller' feature 130 kilometres in size, one of the largest propellers ever seen. Another moonlet bobbing up and down in a gap in the B-ring was estimated to be even smaller, just 200-metres across, making it one of the smallest moonlets ever discovered. Intriguingly, it did not feature a propeller, possibly because of the higher density

SERENE SATURN

Saturn's second largest moon Rhea glides along the ring plane, the ring's shadows barely edging out beneath them. On Saturn's limb, below the rings, is a small dark spot that is the shadow of the moon Tethys. Saturn appears serene, pictured here on 4 November 2009, but just over a year later the largest storm even seen on another planet would appear to wreak havoc. Image: NASA/JPL/Space Science Institute.

SPIN THE PROPELLER

A large 'propeller' moves through Saturn's A-ring just outside of the Encke Gap, as seen on 13 August 2009. The propeller is just a few kilometres long and is created by a tiny moonlet a few hundred kilometres across, which is still large enough to cast a shadow at equinox. Image: NASA/JPL/Space Science Institute.

of the B-ring material, which more easily fill gaps left by the moonlet than the particles in the A-ring.

Whether or not all these tiny bodies are permanent features or just temporary agglomerations is uncertain, but Cassini's shadow observations at equinox has made it clear that the objects embedded within the rings can span a wide range of sizes, with even the smallest moonlets capable of kicking up a fuss amongst the ring particles. None of these observations would have been possible without the timing of the equinox.

"The equinox was a moving spectacle to behold, and one that has left us with far greater insight into the workings of Saturn's rings than any of us could have imagined," says Carolyn Porco. "We always knew it would be good. Instead, it's been extraordinary."

DARK RINGS

Less than a month after the equinox, on 4 September 2009, the rings are still close to edge-on with the Sun, but their slim shadow has now dropped south of the equator. The dot just below the rings is the moon Mimas. Because the Sun is still at a shallow angle to the rings in this image, the rings appear dark. Image: NASA/JPL/Space Science Institute.

A SHEPHERD'S FLOCK

A MOON AND ITS RING

Saturn's tiny moon Anthe and the arc of ring material that it drags around with it. In this image Anthe (the bright spot) is moving towards the bottom right, with most of the arc in front of it, but over time Anthe moves back and forth throughout the arc. Anthe is tiny – just two kilometres across – and the ring particles are believed to have come off Anthe as micrometeoroids have battered its surface, spewing dust out into space. This picture was taken on 3 July 2008. Image: NASA/JPL/Space Science Institute.

TWO MOONLETS WITH ONE SHOT

The twin tiny moons Anthe (top left) and Methone (bottom right) along with the arcs of ring material that they carry around with them. Image: NASA/JPL/Space Science Institute.

MISCHIEVOUS MIMAS

The diminutive moon Mimas seen above the plane of the rings on 31 January 2011. Note the flat edge on the right limb of Mimas – this is the wall of the giant crater Herschel. As the innermost of Saturn's larger moons, Mimas wields significant influence over the rings and the shepherd moons, carving gaps and trapping moonlets into lockstep via gravitational resonances. Image: NASA/JPL/Space Science Institute.

SPACE EGG

Ovoid-shaped moon Methone, captured in a rare close up by Cassini. At just three kilometres in diameter, Methone is not large or massive enough to have grown into a spherical shape and its elongated nature may be a clue as to how it formed. Image: NASA/JPL–Caltech/Space Science Institute.

Many of the equinox observations involved tiny moonlets, but given that they are so small, less than a kilometre across in many cases, what is their importance in the grander scheme of things? Some of the moonlets are sometimes described as shepherd moons, for they keep the ring material in check, but if anything it turns out that many of these moonlets are merely sheepdogs belonging to a much larger shepherd. At 397 kilometres across, Mimas is by no means Saturn's biggest moon, but it is the closest of the larger moons to Saturn and its rings. Its gravity reaches out, clutching many of the small moonlets and forcing them into resonant orbits, i.e. orbital periods that are an exact fraction of Mimas' and thus they feel an extra pull from Mimas' gravity. For example, Anthe and Methone are two small moons located between Mimas and Enceladus. Each is trailed by their own partial 'ring' of material and both are in resonant orbits with Mimas. It is Mimas' gravitational tugs that prevent the arc material from spreading all the way around Saturn to form a fully-fledged ring. Exactly how the moonlets' relationship with Mimas arose is a bit of a puzzle, but there are two possible solutions.

"One idea that connects all the small moons is that there was some event, some object, that broke up in the inner part of the Saturnian system," says Carl Murray, a Cassini Imaging Team member from Queen Mary, University of London. Fragments of this disintegrated larger moon would have scattered far and wide, with many pieces falling into Saturn itself. The moonlets that we see today would just be the leftovers from that event, chunks of debris that got lucky and found themselves in resonant orbits with Mimas, locking them there.

"Another possibility is that, because of the torques they exert on the rings, the tiny moons are moving out very slowly," adds Murray. In this case, as the moonlets wind outwards, the first major moon they will encounter will be Mimas, which will prevent any further movement by trapping them in resonant orbits. "Either way, it appears that Mimas has a role in maintaining some of the smaller moons and the arcs of ring material."

In charge of managing all of Cassini's science, Linda Spilker of NASA's Jet Propulsion Laboratory describes her work on the greatest ever planetary exploration mission.

Interview
Linda Spilker, Cassini Project Scientist

What does your role as Cassini's Project Scientist involve?

I oversee all of the science that we can do with Cassini and make sure we have the right scientific balance within the budget and schedule that we have. With the Cassini mission we pretty much have five areas that we focus on: the planet itself of course, the rings, the large moon Titan, the remainder of the icy satellites, and then the magnetosphere, so you can imagine you have all of these conflicting requests, and I work with the science teams to come up with the best balance.

How far in advance do you plan Cassini's tour around Saturn's neighbourhood?

We plan the tour many years ahead, and again it is to get the right balance of science, so we'll spend part of our time in the equatorial plane, we'll spend part of our time at higher inclinations, we'll look for good fly-by opportunities of Enceladus and so on. We basically use Titan as our tour engine; we get not only incredible views of Titan but its gravity also helps shape our orbit.

We've planned the mission in three phases. For the first four years [2004–2008], called the 'Prime Mission', we had the tour completely planned out and were working on it very early on. Then once we knew we had

MISSION MANAGER

Cassini Project Scientist Linda Spilker with a replica of the spacecraft.

approval for funding for the next two years [2008–2010], which we called the 'Equinox Mission', we also had a tour decided upon early for that period of time, in particular making sure that we could get into those unique orbits where we could see rings edge-on to the Sun. Then, as we got NASA funding and approval to go forward, we planned out the entire seven years of what we now call the 'Solstice Mission', which will end when Cassini ends its mission near the Saturn solstice in 2017.

When planning these phases, we had lots of meetings to take all of the requirements from the various science groups and instrument teams on what kind of science they want to accomplish, and then our tour designers came up with a whole suite of different tours. We looked at them and tried to mix and match, taking parts of various tours and stitching them together, and of course we had to do all of this within our fuel budget. So we are in the middle of a plan for seven years but we can still make small tweaks: sometimes we can go a little closer or further away from an icy satellite, or maybe tweak an orbit a little bit to get a nice stellar occultation by Dione for example, which we're intrigued by because Dione is potentially another world that might be active like Enceladus. So we can make small changes and tweaks within the framework of when we're going to be at high inclination, when we're going to be in the equatorial plane and so on.

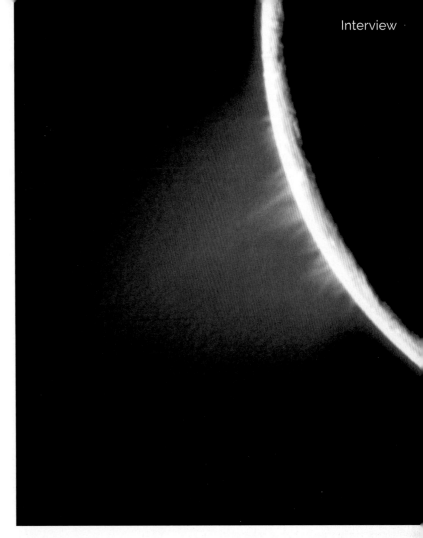

You have been involved with Cassini since the 1980s. Has it surpassed your expectations?

I actually started at the Jet Propulsion Laboratory in 1977, shortly before the launches of Voyager 1 and Voyager 2 and they were just tremendous missions to work on. What really got Cassini started is when we flew by Saturn in 1980 and 1981 with Voyager 1 and Voyager 2, and we looked at Titan and saw a world that was the size of Mercury but was completely covered with haze, so that we couldn't see through to the surface. So a group of scientists both on the European side and on the NASA side started working even then, in the mid-1980s, towards a mission that ultimately became Cassini, with the idea of a Saturn orbiter and what became the Huygens probe to explore Titan. I worked on Voyager all the way through to the Neptune fly-by in 1989, but starting in 1988 I also began to support [Cassini's] science definition team and became part of putting together the science objectives in each of those five areas I mentioned – the planet, the rings, the magnetosphere, Titan and the icy satellites – and [defining these objectives] is so important for how we designed the spacecraft, the instruments that we selected, that sort of thing. It was a really wonderful transition because I'd been there for the Voyager fly-bys of Saturn and then to be able to think about the next mission to go back there was just an incredible opportunity.

Has Cassini surpassed my expectations? That's a really good question and I would have to say yes, Cassini has exceeded what were my expectations at the time. I think a good example would be the geysers coming out of the south pole of Enceladus, that was just so amazing and remarkable. Landing safely on the surface of Titan and then using RADAR and other instruments that we purposefully carried to look through the haze to see how Earth-like Titan's surface appeared, I think that was just incredible. We weren't expecting that we would find river channels and lakes and sand dunes and so many things that are so familiar and the key was that methane was playing the role on Titan that water plays here on Earth. It can form clouds, it can rain, it can fill lakes. Those two things in particular [Enceladus and Titan] far exceeded anything that I could have imagined.

The Imaging Science Subsystem takes a lot of the glory, but what things are the other instruments doing that deserve to be in the public limelight?

We can make a lot of other remarkable discoveries and increase our understanding by looking at different wavelengths or by looking with other instruments besides the cameras. For instance, a good example is the RADAR instrument, that's the instrument that really can see through the haze and give us maps of the surface of Titan. [Another example is that] it wasn't the cameras that first really detected the presence of geysers at Enceladus, it was the magnetometer team. They came back to us after the early fly-bys of Enceladus and said, "there's something really odd here, Saturn's magnetic field lines aren't going down to the surface as they would on an airless body, [it's forming

EMANATIONS

The geysers of Enceladus, spraying water vapour into space, were a huge surprise to the Cassini team. This image was captured on the second closer fly-by of the moon on **27 November 2005.** Image: NASA/JPL/Space Science Institute.

MYSTERY WORLD

Probing beneath the hazy atmosphere of Titan provided the impetus to develop the Cassini mission. Image: NASA/JPL/Space Science Institute.

a] the tail that looks a little bit like a comet, there's something strange going on at the south pole." For our next fly-by of Enceladus they wanted Cassini to go a lot closer and take a more detailed measurement and it was during that fly-by that we noticed the south pole was hotter than it should be, we had an occultation of a star that happened to cross through the area below the south pole and led to us actually detected jets coming out [and obscuring the star]. Only later the imaging team said yes, we did have some pictures but we weren't sure what they meant, but now that we know what's going on they are probably some early pictures that we had of them as well.

There have been lots of other stars of the show. A good example has been, in a way that we didn't imagine, how we sampled the geysers coming out of Enceladus' south pole. There we used our Ion and Neutral Mass Spectrometer and our Cosmic Dust Analyser. The first instrument, the mass spectrometer, sampled the gas and the dust analyser sampled the icy grains and that's how we found out for the first time that not only was

there water vapour and water-ice particles but there's a whole host of other complex molecules and perhaps an environment in Enceladus' ocean that might support life.

Cassini will remain in orbit until 2017 so that it can witness the northern summer solstice. What can we expect from this?

When we look at solstice we'll see the northern hemispheres of both Saturn and Titan at one extreme, at summer. At Titan we'll get good views of the north pole and we're interested to see whether the winds pick up, will we see evidence of waves on the lakes and will we see more clouds form because the predictions tell us that there should be more clouds and methane rain falling on Titan. With the rings we'll get the highest angle ever, so the rings will be heated to their highest amount and we'll just get really good views of the rings themselves. Then of course there is the magnetosphere, that magnetic bubble that Saturn is in – how will it change with the changing solar

COOL BLUE

The cool blue of Saturn's northern hemisphere in winter, streaked by the shadows of the rings and joined by the moon Mimas, as seen on 7 November 2004. Image: NASA/JPL/Space Science Institute.

illumination? Will there be changes in the solar wind pressure and how will that affect the magnetic field that Saturn is in? Then there are the icy satellites and what's really cool is that, as we approach solstice, we're getting a change to take a good look at the north poles of these moons. For instance, an Enceladus fly-by in October 2015 will give us a chance to look in detail at its north pole and look for evidence of whether the north pole was ever active or whether there are ancient 'tiger stripes' [fractures in the surface from which the geysers erupt] or any example of something that might indicate possible emission, because when we first arrived it was northern winter, so the north poles of all of the moons were in darkness.

"WE USE TITAN AS OUR TOUR ENGINE; WE GET NOT ONLY INCREDIBLE VIEWS BUT ITS GRAVITY ALSO HELPS SHAPE OUR ORBIT."

WE MUST RETURN

Saturn has far too many mysteries left to not go back once Cassini's mission is at an end. If nothing else, we will want to see more spectacular pictures such as this, which Cassini captured on 15 April 2008. Image: NASA/JPL/ Space Science Institute

A GRAND VIEW

This is the view of Saturn taken from the orbit of Iapetus, one of the outer moons, on 10 September 2007. Because Iapetus is slightly inclined to the plane of the rings, Saturn appears to have a tilt when seen from its viewpoint. Image: NASA/ JPL/Space Science Institute.

How are you feeling about the impending end of the mission?

There are many exciting things about the end of the mission. During our last 22 orbits we will actually dive into the narrow gap between the innermost ring and the top of Saturn's atmosphere, and by getting in that close to Saturn we'll get really exquisite measurements of Saturn's magnetic field and its gravity field, we'll measure the mass of Saturn's rings more accurately and get a chance to sample a place where no spacecraft has ever flown before. Part of what we're going to try and do is directly sample the atmosphere as we get to those very close final orbits and also early on to directly sample the ring particles and measure their composition directly, again with the Cosmic Dust Analyser.

So there's exciting new science, although it will be really hard and sad at the end because it will be like saying goodbye to a really good friend. I've been with Cassini since she was just an idea and I was there to see the development of the spacecraft, its launch and then to be there for Saturn orbit insertion and see her take her first steps in the Saturn system. Along the way we have also grown the Cassini family and I think that will be the hardest part – when the mission ends the Cassini family, the Cassini team, will go their separate ways and end an era that has seen so many friendships.

Looking to the future, has Cassini left a lot for future missions to discover and explain?

Yes, Cassini has left some very interesting questions. In NASA's New Frontiers line there is a proposal for a new mission that would go back to Saturn with a probe to basically go into the atmosphere and sample below the depths that we can sample with Cassini, very similar to the Galileo probe to Jupiter [which plunged into Jupiter's atmosphere in 1996]. Of course, since we didn't know anything about the geysers on Enceladus before launch, Cassini didn't really carry any instruments that we could use to answer the

question of whether its ocean is habitable. If it is, could there possibly be life? So we'd like a mission to go back with the right instruments to fly through the plumes of Enceladus multiple times and make those measurements and start to answer that question. If there is life, is it life that's very different from the life that we're used to thinking about on Earth? Or does life have something in common? Any life that evolved in the ocean of Enceladus wouldn't have been in contact with anything that could have made its way to Earth or Mars or something like that. Then for Titan it would be interesting to sample the methane seas; there's an early proposal for a Titan boat to make measurements in a methane sea. There's an intriguing question: could you have some kind of unusual life that could use methane instead of water? And we just want to understand more about the very interesting environment that we found on Titan. So there are lots of reasons to go back and lots of things that remain to be explored.

If there was one take-home message from your experiences with Cassini that could be applied to future planetary missions, what would it be?

I would probably say, be prepared for surprises. That certainly was the case for Titan, and then the geysers coming from Enceladus. Be open to having your whole paradigm shifted by something that you might discover.

THERE ARE MANY EXCITING THINGS ABOUT THE END OF THE MISSION, ALTHOUGH IT WILL BE HARD SAYING GOODBYE TO A REALLY GOOD FRIEND

SUMMER ON SATURN

As the solstice beckons in 2017, summer has shifted to the northern hemisphere while the south lurks in winter and shadow, as seen in this image taken on 6 May 2012 that also shows Titan in front of the rings. Image: NASA/JPL–Caltech/ Space Science Institute.

SMALL but not forgotten

The big moons take the glory, but the small moons have been some of the biggest surprises to scientists studying Saturn.

Saturn's retinue of smaller moons are often overlooked in favour of the big hitters like Titan, Rhea and Enceladus. They are small and icy, not much more than porous rubble piles made of the detritus left over from the creation of the larger moons and the rings. Saturn has 62 moons in total, but 49 of them are smaller than 50 kilometres wide. While these small moons are nothing out of the ordinary in themselves – they are cratered and irregularly shaped – their orbits and interactions with other moons are extraordinary and quite unlike anything else seen in the Solar System.

Cassini has not visited all of them, but here are a few of the more notable small moons that Cassini has caught up with.

Atlas

Like many of these small moons, Atlas was discovered by scientists inspecting images beamed back by Voyager 1 in 1980. Atlas is named after one of the Greek titans because, as one of the closest moons to Saturn, it holds the rings on its 'shoulders'. It has a bizarre shape too, looking a bit like a flying saucer with a spherical bulge surrounded by an equatorial ridge, which is probably made of ring particles swept up by the moon.

Atlas skirts the outer edge of Saturn's A-ring, but it is not a shepherd moon: the edge of the A-ring is kept sharp by gravitational resonances from the small moons Janus and Epimetheus, which are a little further out. Atlas does make up for it though by having its own ring arc.

Atlas at a glance

Dimensions:	41 × 35 × 19km
Mass:	6.6 × 10^{15}kg
Density:	0.46g/cm^3
Orbital radius from Saturn:	137,670km
Orbital period:	14 hours and 22 minutes
Discovered:	1980

FLYING SAUCERS

Images showing Atlas (the two on the left) and fellow small moon Pan and their distinctive 'flying saucer' shapes. The ridges running around their equators are believed to come from dusty material that has been gathered up by the moons. The ridge represents 27 percent of Atlas' volume and 10 percent of Pan's, so they account for quite a lot of material. Images: NASA/JPL/Space Science Institute.

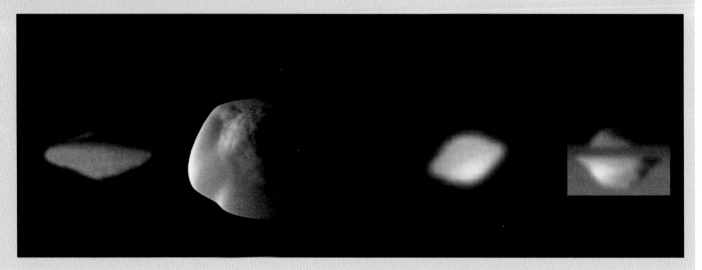

Prometheus and Pandora

SOFTENED MOON

Right: Cassini's best view of Pandora as it skirts the outside edge of Saturn's F-ring. Fractures that run through the moon may have an effect on the dust overlying the surface, causing it to almost fill in the craters and make them appear softened. **Image: NASA/ JPL/Space Science Institute.**

The behaviour of Saturn's F-ring, with its braids and twists, is closely linked to its shepherd moon, Prometheus, which orbits on the inside of the F-ring. Pandora, an eighty-kilometre-wide moon on the outside of the F-ring, was once though to also be a shepherd, but Cassini observations have shown that Pandora has no gravitational effect on the ring. Nevertheless, Prometheus and Pandora are only separated by the F-ring and come within 1,400 kilometres of each other every six years. Both are spotted with craters no larger than 30 kilometres, which have a softened appearance because of dust filling them in.

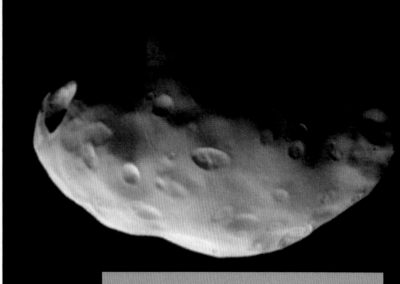

Pandora at a glance

Dimensions:	104 × 81 × 64km
Mass:	1.4×10^{17}
Density:	$0.49g/cm^3$
Orbital radius from Saturn:	141.720km
Orbital period:	15 hours and 6 minutes
Discovered:	1980

OUT OF THE SHADOWS

Left: On 27 January 2010 Cassini performed a rare fly-by of Prometheus and snapped this shot as the elongated moon began to move out of the shadows. **Image: NASA/JPL/Space Science Institute.**

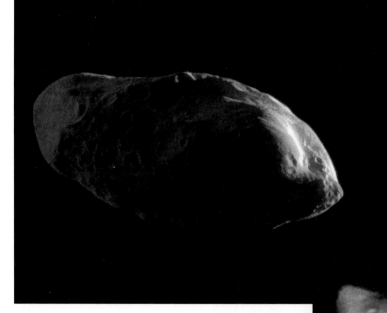

PROMETHEUS THE POTATO

Right: Fully illuminated, Prometheus' odd, baked potato-like shape is clear to see. **Image: NASA/JPL/Space Science Institute.**

Prometheus at a glance

Dimensions:	137 × 79 × 59km
Mass:	1.6×10^{17}kg
Density:	$0.48g/cm^3$
Orbital radius from Saturn:	139.380km
Orbital period:	14 hours and 36 minutes
Discovered:	1980

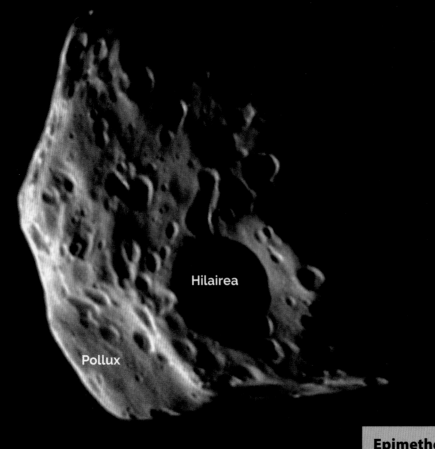

Hilairea

Pollux

EERIE EPIMETHEUS

Epimetheus emerges from the shadows, showing a craggy face of craters. This is a false-colour view that highlights differences in the way the surface material reflects light. At bottom left is a reddish crater with the softened walls called Pollux. The crater in shadow is called Hilairea. Image: NASA/JPL/Space Science Institute.

Epimetheus at a glance

Dimensions:	130 × 114 × 106km
Mass:	5.3×10^{17}kg
Density:	0.64g/cm³
Orbital radius from Saturn:	151,410km
Orbital period:	16 hours and 40 minutes
Discovered:	1966

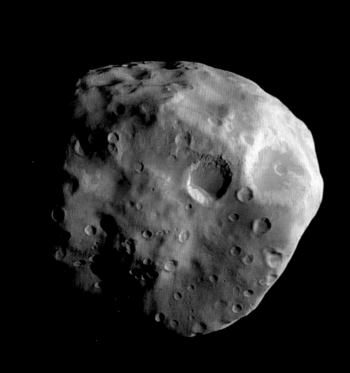

TERRIFIC TERRAIN

Epimetheus presents two types of terrain: one that is smooth and darker and another that is brighter and slightly yellow. The brighter terrain is fractured and might be some kind of icy 'bedrock'. Image: NASA/JPL/Space Science Institute.

Epimetheus and Janus

If you think Pandora and Prometheus like to race each other around Saturn, then you will find Epimetheus and Janus to be really fast and furious.

These two moons are bizarre: they are co-orbital, which means they essentially share the same orbit, with one slightly closer to Saturn and one slightly further away. In fact, for 12 years after their discovery in December 1966, nobody realised they were actually two objects in the same orbit.

There is no danger of the two colliding, despite their shared orbit. The closest they can come to each other is 15,000 kilometres, although the difference between their orbital radii can be as small as 50 kilometres. Every 24 hours, the inner moon of the two creeps another quarter of a degree around Saturn and eventually it catches up with the outer moon. Each time they pass, the gravity felt between the two saps the momentum of the outer moon and speeds up the inner moon. This causes the outer moon's orbit to degrade and the inner moon's to widen, leading to the two switching orbits every four years and continuing this cycle ad infinitum.

How could two moons end up doing this orbital tango? It is likely they are formed from the disruption of a single, larger moon not long after Saturn formed. Perhaps the larger body was struck by something else, or more likely gravitational tides from either Saturn or one of the larger moons wrenched them apart.

Epimetheus and Janus also orbit within a faint dust ring, likely produced from tiny bits of dust sputtered from their surfaces by many micrometeoroid impacts.

JANUS IN PROFILE

Taken from a distance of 33,000 kilometres on 30 June 2008, Cassini captured this startling view of Janus in shadow, with only its southern limb illuminated. Image: NASA/JPL/Space Science Institute.

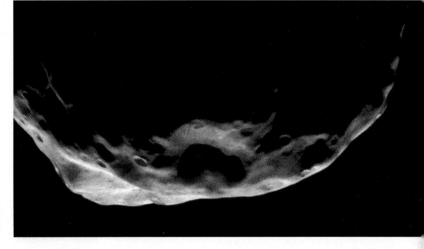

Janus at a glance

Dimensions:	203 × 185 × 153km
Mass:	1.9×10^{18}kg
Density:	0.63g/cm³
Orbital radius from Saturn:	151,460km
Orbital period:	16 hours and 40 minutes
Discovered:	1966

THERE'S A HOLE IN THE MOON

A deep, shadowed crater dominates this view of Janus. Image: NASA/JPL/Space Science Institute.

FANTASTIC JANUS

Cassini caught Janus gliding in front of the face of Saturn on 25 September 2006. Image: NASA/JPL/Space Science Institute.

Telesto and Calypso

Two more co-orbital moons, Telesto and Calypso were spotted in ground-based observations just prior to Voyager 1's arrival in 1980. However, unlike Epimetheus and Janus, they are not just co-orbital with each other, but also share an orbit with the large moon Tethys. When we say they share an orbit, what we really mean is they are trapped in Tethys' Lagrangian points. These are stable gravitational points where objects can be suspended as the gravitational attraction between two bodies precisely balances. There are five stable Lagrangian points around an object, with Telesto and Calypso found at the leading L4 point and trailing L5 point respectively. It is a similar situation to Jupiter, which has asteroids, named the Trojans, grouped in the Jovian L4 and L5 positions. As such, Telesto and Calypso are sometimes called 'Tethys trojans'.

TINY TELESTO

Telesto is a surprisingly smooth moon with very few craters. On a larger moon we might put this down to some form of resurfacing, but on tiny Telesto another, unknown, process may be at work. Image: NASA/JPL/Space Science Institute.

Telesto at a glance

Dimensions:	33 × 24 × 20km
Mass:	Uncertain
Density:	Uncertain
Orbital radius from Saturn:	294,619km
Orbital period:	1 day, 21 hours and 20 minutes
Discovered:	1980

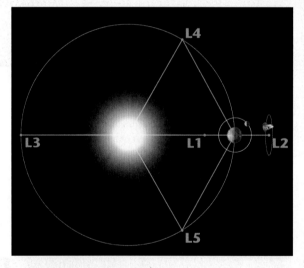

LOCKED IN ORBIT

A diagram showing the Lagrangian points between Earth and the Sun. The image shows a spacecraft at L2. In this case, substitute Earth for Tethys and the Sun for Saturn, and you will find Telesto at the L4 point and Calypso at L5. Image: NASA/WMAP Science Team.

CALYPSO!

Telesto's fellow trojan, Calypso, also sports a smooth visage in this image, taken on 13 February 2010 from a distance of 21,000 kilometres. Image: NASA/JPL/Space Science Institute.

Calypso at a glance

Dimensions:	30 × 23 × 14km
Mass:	Uncertain
Density:	Uncertain
Orbital radius from Saturn:	294,619km
Orbital period:	1 day, 21 hours and 20 minutes
Discovered:	1980

Helena and Polydeuces

These are another pair of trojan moons, this time caught in the Lagrangian points of Dione. Like Telesto and Calypso, Helene and Polydeuces were discovered by ground-based observations in 1980. Helene has been imaged in detail by Cassini, but Polydeuces, which is tiny, has been seen only as a small, egg-shaped smudge from distance.

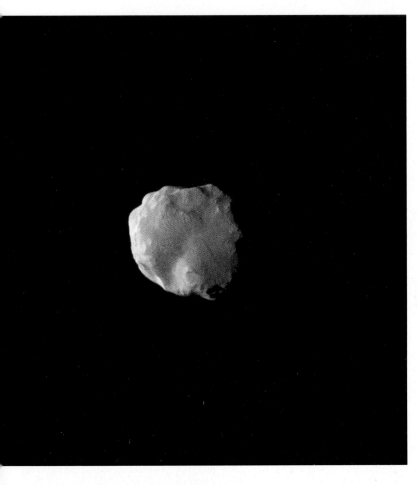

ALL ALONE IN THE NIGHT

A view of Helene, showing grooves, gullies and craters against the starkness of black space. Image: NASA/JPL/Space Science Institute.

A SENSE OF SCALE

Just how diminutive small moons like Helene are is really brought home in images such as this, taken on 3 March 2010, where the atmosphere of giant Saturn is the backdrop. Image: NASA/JPL/Space Science Institute.

HELLO HELENE

Cassini had this close encounter with Helene on 18 June 2011. Image: NASA/JPL/Space Science Institute.

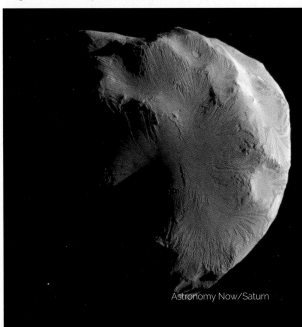

Astronomy Now/Saturn

Helene at a glance

Dimensions:	43 × 38 × 26km
Mass:	Uncertain
Density:	Uncertain
Orbital radius from Saturn:	377,396km
Orbital period:	2 days, 17 hours and 45 minutes
Discovered:	1980

Polydeuces at a glance

Dimensions:	3 × 2.5 × 2km
Mass:	5 × 10^{13}kg
Density:	0.5g/cm^3
Orbital radius from Saturn:	377,396km
Orbital period:	2 days, 17 hours and 45 minutes
Discovered:	2004

Mimas

Once thought to be rather boring, Mimas has proven to be a moon of wonderful surprises.

Mimas at a glance

Diameter:	425 × 393 × 381km
Mass:	3.75 × 10^{19}kg
Density:	1.15g/cm^3
Orbital radius from Saturn:	185.539km
Orbital period:	22 hours and 36 minutes
Discovered:	1789

LOOKING HERSCHEL IN THE EYE

Mimas' giant crater Herschel bears down on Cassini's cameras in this portrait of the moon, captured during the close fly-by of 13 February 2010. Mimas has a marble-esque appearance thanks to myriad craters that have bright walls but dark floors of dust left behind by ice sublimating in sunlight. The floor of Herschel also appears quite smooth, filled with frozen lava. Image: NASA/JPL/ Space Science Institute.

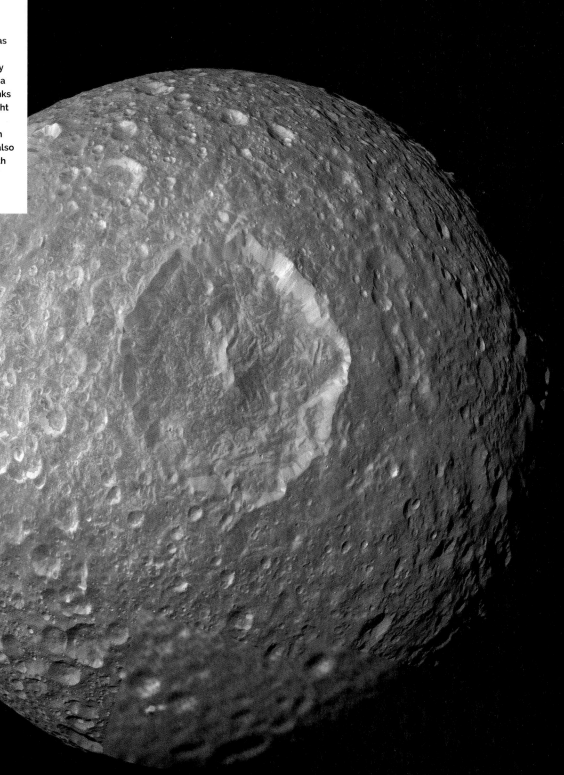

Mimas nearly never made it through adolescence. Over four billion years ago it was hit so violently – whether by an asteroid or a comet or even a fellow small moon of Saturn we cannot say – that Mimas was almost completely smashed apart. Instead, the cosmic crash left the enormous crater (well, enormous relative to the size of Mimas) that we call Herschel, after William Herschel who discovered Mimas. It is 130 kilometres across – fully a third of the diameter of Mimas – and sports deep crater walls and a rugged central peak. The size of the crater is such that, had the impactor been any larger, Mimas would have been obliterated.

As it is, Mimas survived and has actually become an important moon with regards to the evolution of the rings. As the innermost of Saturn's larger moons, it wields influence over some of the rings and inner shepherd moons. Its gravity helps keep the Cassini Division clear, as ring particles there orbit twice for every one orbit that Mimas makes. Each time their orbits coincide, Mimas tugs on the ring particles, pulling them clear of the Division. Another resonance is with Pandora, which orbits three times for every two orbits Mimas makes, while the boundary between the C- and B-rings is created by a 3:1 resonance with Mimas. Had fate not fallen on the side of Mimas all those billions of years ago, the rings might look a little different today.

Arcade games

Mimas' giant scar has left it looking eerily similar to the Death Star from *Star Wars*, although this analogy has become so frequently used that it is beginning to get a little worn now. So Mimas is in need of some rebranding.

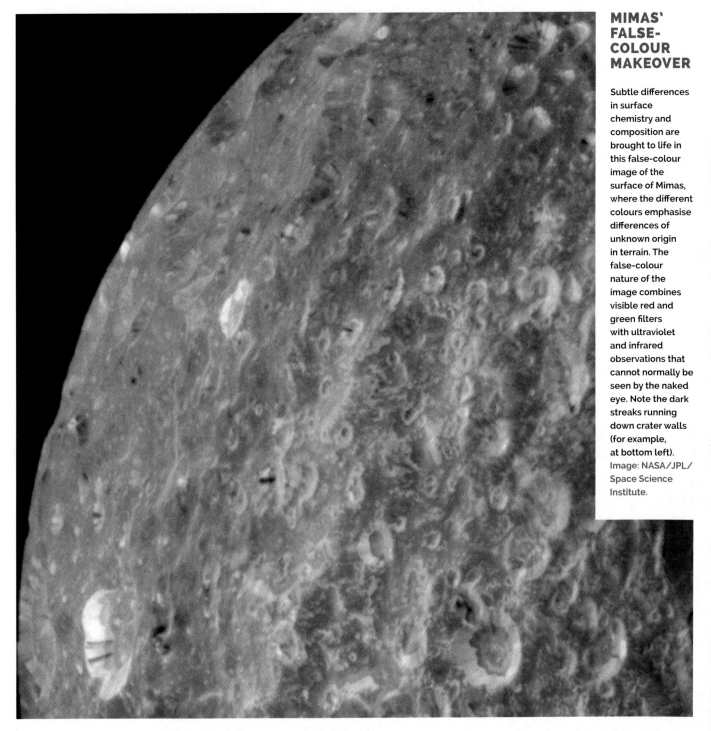

MIMAS' FALSE-COLOUR MAKEOVER

Subtle differences in surface chemistry and composition are brought to life in this false-colour image of the surface of Mimas, where the different colours emphasise differences of unknown origin in terrain. The false-colour nature of the image combines visible red and green filters with ultraviolet and infrared observations that cannot normally be seen by the naked eye. Note the dark streaks running down crater walls (for example, at bottom left). Image: NASA/JPL/Space Science Institute.

HANGING MARBLE

Mimas hangs in space in front of Saturn, its hemispheres split by night and day. As the innermost of Saturn's larger satellites, Mimas is able to control some of the activity in the rings with its gravity. Image: NASA/JPL/Space Science Institute.

THE PAC-MEN OF SATURN

Mimas and Tethys and their wedge-shaped temperature variations, which are believed to be caused by high-energy electrons hitting their surfaces and altering the heat conductivity of the ice there. Image NASA/JPL–Caltech/GSFC/SwRI.

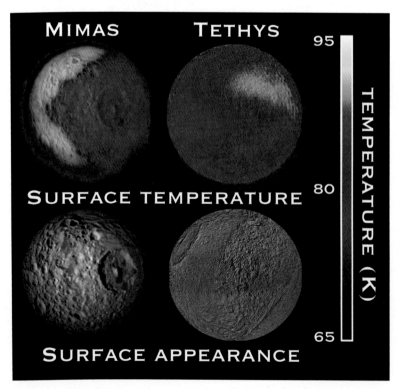

Rather than an instrument of planetary destruction, how about looking upon Mimas as one of the first computer game heroes? When Cassini studied the thermal emission emanating from Mimas' surface using its Composite Infrared Spectrometer, scientists were amazed to see that the hottest point was not just after high noon on the equator, but on the morning limb. Furthermore, the emission created a wedge-shape feature that looks just like the open mouth of Pac-Man! To add to the authenticity, there is even a warm 'pac-dot' centred on Herschel Crater, poised for Pac-Man to eat and whose steep five-kilometre-deep walls can trap a modest amount of heat. Computer-game silliness aside, the pattern is a puzzle to scientists. Mimas' surface temperature is normally around –196 degrees Celsius, but the Pac-Man shaped region is fifteen degrees warmer.

One possibility is that Mimas has differing types of ice on its surface. Dense, smooth ice reflects heat from the Sun away into space, while powdery ice, a bit like snow on the ground, can absorb more heat and warm the surface, re-radiating that heat into space as infrared light. This sounds plausible, except for Pac-Man's sharp boundaries – how could nature create such a precise shape? Two years later, in 2012, a second 'Pac-Man' was found on Tethys. Whatever was causing the anomalous features had to act the same on both moons, meaning that whatever it is, it was external to both Mimas and Tethys. The focus therefore fell onto the storm of high-energy electrons that is trapped within Saturn's powerful magnetosphere, through which both Mimas and Tethys sail. The electrons bombard their leading hemispheres, steadily hammering powdery ice into hard, packed ice. The leading hemispheres then appear cooler than the trailing hemispheres and the wedge-shape is just a natural result of this head-on bombardment.

The Pac-Man is not the only hidden pattern on Mimas. Herschel Crater has also 'earned its stripes', sporting bands of light and dark in its walls. They were spotted by Cassini on 13 February 2010 during the spacecraft's closest fly-by of Mimas. The dark streaks trail downwards towards the floor of the crater, which is filled by more dark markings and rimmed by another notably dark stripe. Scientists suspect that it is a case of brighter ice evaporating in sunlight, leaving behind a dark, dusty layer of silicate and carbon-rich materials, perhaps deposited by tiny meteorites. Gravity inevitably sets to work on these dark materials, pulling them down slopes to where they accumulate at the bottom of the crater.

Deeper underground

Mimas has mysteries that lurk underground as well as above ground. Mimas is small, around 400 kilometres in diameter, so it should have lost most of the core heat that it was born with. It should just be solid ice and rock, all the way through.

HEAT EMISSION FROM THE SURFACE OF MIMAS CREATES A WEDGE-SHAPE FEATURE THAT LOOKS JUST LIKE THE OPEN MOUTH OF PAC-MAN!

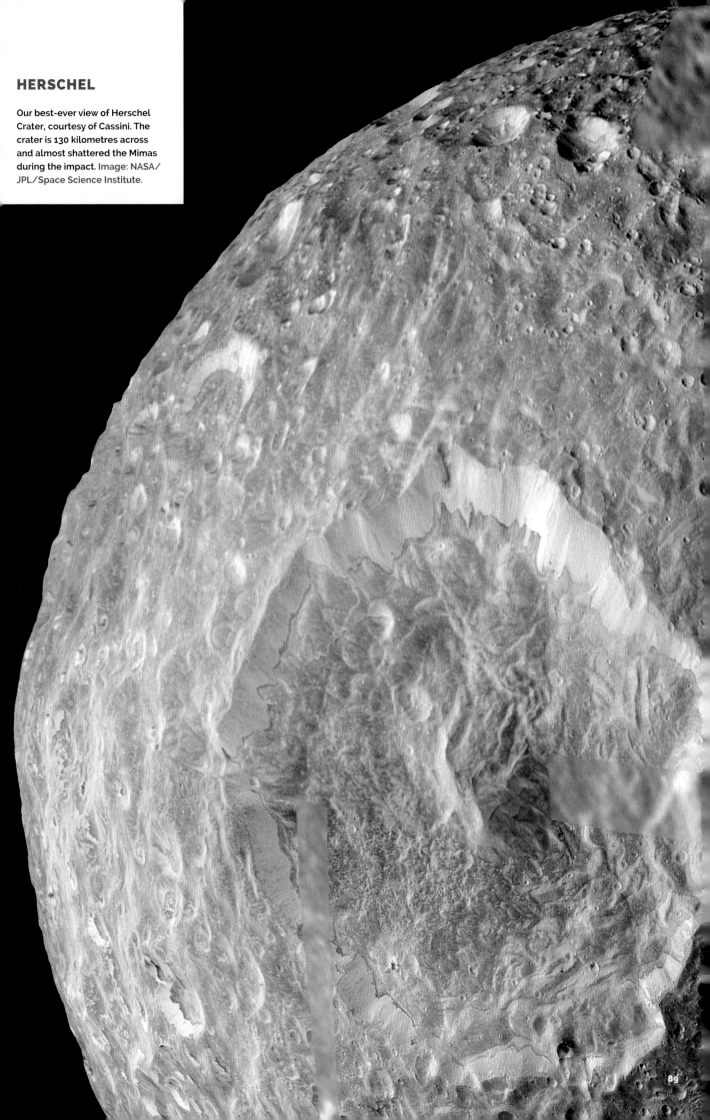

HERSCHEL

Our best-ever view of Herschel Crater, courtesy of Cassini. The crater is 130 kilometres across and almost shattered the Mimas during the impact. Image: NASA/JPL/Space Science Institute.

DEATH STAR

A famous view of Mimas and its crater Herschel that gives the impression of the Empire's Death Star in *Star Wars*. Image: NASA/JPL–Caltech/Space Science Institute.

Over time, scientists observing Mimas with Cassini began to notice that it behaved oddly. Like a ball with a weight inside it, Mimas seems to wobble from side-to-side during its orbits of Saturn. This is evident from a phenomenon known as libration, wherein Cassini is able to see a little of the far side of Mimas that is brought into view because of the wobble. This would happen if Mimas' interior is unevenly shaped, perhaps like a rugby ball, which would unbalance the distribution of mass inside Mimas and instigate the wobble. The cores of planets and larger moons should relax into spheres not too long after they formed; if Mimas really has somehow retained this rugby-ball core, perhaps caused by the fast rotation of the moon after either its formation or the impact that created

Herschel, then it would be a geological record of Mimas' early days, frozen in time.

There's an even more exciting prospect, however. A school of thought that suggests that Mimas' wobble is incurred by its core sloshing around in a global ocean of water. It is hard to believe though; for one thing, Mimas does not retain the heat necessary to keep water liquid. Furthermore, there is no geological sign on the surface of an ocean below, such as on Jupiter's moon Europa, for example, which exhibits chaotic terrain and large fractures where water may have welled up from below. Mimas, in contrast, is just bleak and cratered. If there is a Mimantean ocean, then it resides between 24 and 31 kilometres below the surface.

STARK RELIEF

The truth about the nature of Mimas and its giant crater is finally emerging from the shadows thanks to Cassini. Image: NASA/JPL/Space Science Institute.

HAD FATE NOT FALLEN ON THE SIDE OF MIMAS ALL THOSE BILLIONS OF YEARS AGO, THE RINGS MIGHT LOOK A LITTLE DIFFERENT TODAY

INTO SPACE

Looking out into space beyond the cratered texture of Mimas' surface. Mimas has borne the brunt of many 'space invaders' that have impacted on its grey, icy surface. So many craters pockmarking Mimas tells us that its surface is extremely ancient, as opposed to a body with few craters such as Enceladus, which frequently resurfaces itself thanks to 'spray' from its geysers. Image: NASA/JPL–Caltech/Space Science Institute.

Enceladus

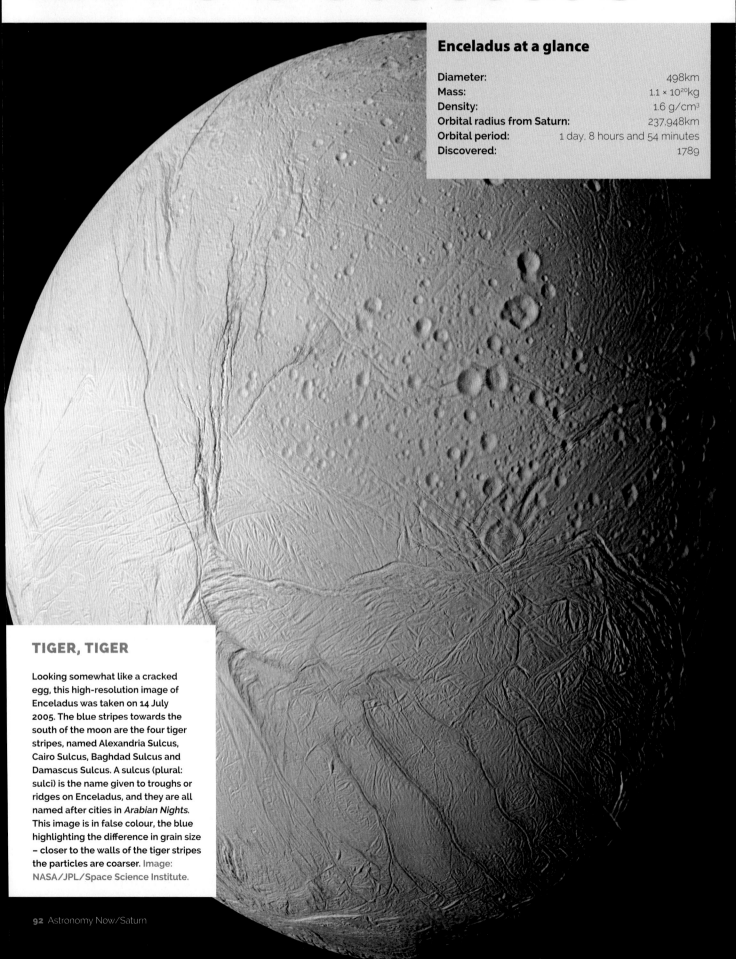

Enceladus at a glance

Diameter:	498km
Mass:	1.1×10^{20}kg
Density:	1.6 g/cm³
Orbital radius from Saturn:	237,948km
Orbital period:	1 day, 8 hours and 54 minutes
Discovered:	1789

TIGER, TIGER

Looking somewhat like a cracked egg, this high-resolution image of Enceladus was taken on 14 July 2005. The blue stripes towards the south of the moon are the four tiger stripes, named Alexandria Sulcus, Cairo Sulcus, Baghdad Sulcus and Damascus Sulcus. A sulcus (plural: sulci) is the name given to troughs or ridges on Enceladus, and they are all named after cities in *Arabian Nights*. This image is in false colour, the blue highlighting the difference in grain size – closer to the walls of the tiger stripes the particles are coarser. Image: NASA/JPL/Space Science Institute.

When Cassini arrived at Saturn, nobody ever thought that little Enceladus would be one of the most active moons known.

Move over, Europa; step aside Mars; when it comes to seeking possible habitats for life elsewhere in the Solar System, there's a new player in town. Enceladus (pronounced En-sell-A-dus), a snow-white moon of Saturn, has sprung from nowhere to become one of the leading contenders in the search for alien life. When Cassini arrived at Saturn in 2004, nobody had any indication that Enceladus might be out

FOUNTAIN VIEW

At the top is a backlit view of Enceladus taken on 27 November 2005, with sunlight shining through the curtains of water vapour spewing out from the tiger stripes in the surface. At the bottom is an enhanced false-colour view of the exact same scene, showing the full extent of the plume. When see like this, it is not hard to imagine how it could deflect Saturn's magnetic field. Images: NASA/JPL/Space Science Institute.

of the ordinary. Then a chance discovery by Cassini's magnetometer team changed everything.

Enceladus is not a magnetic moon. It does not produce its own magnetic field and there seemed to be no reason why it would interact with Saturn's magnetosphere any differently than the other airless, icy moons. So when Cassini made its first fly-by of Enceladus in February 2005, the magnetometer team-leader, Professor Michele Dougherty of Imperial College London, did not expect to see anything in the magnetometer data – in fact, so unlikely was it to find anything that she did not even look at the data until a few days after the fly-by. When she finally did, there was a surprise waiting for her.

"We found there were perturbations in the magnetic field that were the type of perturbations that you would expect to see if Enceladus were acting as an obstacle to the flow of plasma," she says. Saturn, its magnetic field lines and the plasma trapped within them all co-rotate at more or less the same speed and the field lines should pass through Enceladus while the plasma should go around it. "But that's not what we saw," Dougherty tells *Astronomy Now*.

Enceladus was acting as though it had either a magnetic field of its own or a sizeable atmosphere that was deflecting Saturn's magnetic field lines, preventing them from reaching the moon's surface. It was so out of the blue that Dougherty thought it might be a technical fault, but on the second fly-by the following month, when Cassini buzzed Enceladus at an altitude of just 500 kilometres, the onboard magnetometer instrument again recorded the magnetic field lines draping around Enceladus, but this time the effect seemed to be focused on the moon's south pole. Dougherty became convinced that they were seeing evidence of some kind of atmosphere, but that did not make sense. Enceladus is small, just 498 kilometres across and, as such, it lacks the gravity to hold onto an atmosphere dense enough to block Saturn's magnetic field. The only explanation was that something was continually outgassing from Enceladus to constantly replenish the atmosphere, yet on such a small moon that seemed too bizarre. To attempt to get to the bottom of these peculiar observations, on Cassini's next visit to Enceladus in July 2005 it flew 173 kilometres above the moon's south pole and this time the spacecraft's entire arsenal of scientific instruments were on the lookout for anything odd. They found it.

"The only way we could model the observations that we saw was to have a neutral jet of water vapour spraying up from the south pole and becoming ionised [electrically charged] so that the field lines would essentially drape around the plume," Dougherty says (the electric field generated by the ionised particles in the plumes interacts with the magnetic field and deflects it). "The really great thing about the fly-by was that all the other instruments saw the atmosphere too – well, it's not really an atmosphere, but more of a plume. I think that shows the strength of the Cassini spacecraft in that there are all these different instruments onboard and you're able to put all the data together and get an overall picture about what's going on."

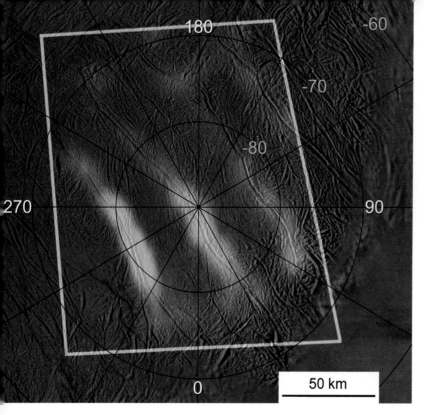

Tiger stripes

Discovering the plumes of water vapour was only the beginning. The next significant task was to understand why there were plumes in the first place and where they were emanating from. Scientists immediately drew analogies with Jupiter's moon Io, which experiences volcanic activity over practically every square kilometre of its surface thanks to the way its interior is kneaded by the gravitational tidal forces from Jupiter next door. The same process occurs on Enceladus, except that instead of red hot molten lava spewing out, this icy moon throws up water vapour instead. High-resolution imagery of Enceladus' south pole revealed a series of linear fractures running across the surface. Nicknamed 'tiger stripes', Cassini measured the temperatures within these cracks to be far higher than at the surface of Enceladus, approaching zero degrees Celsius at depths of just 300 metres. Add in a little ammonia to act as an anti-freeze and water could clearly be kept liquid at these temperatures, which presumably grow even warmer the deeper one goes into Enceladus' interior.

TAKING THE TEMPERATURE

A heat map across the four main tiger stripes at Enceladus' south pole. The brightest tiger stripe, on the left-hand side, is Damascus Sulcus, with temperatures reaching –90 degrees Celsius. While this temperature is not even nearly warm enough for liquid water, we must remember that the surface is exposed to space and that the stripes' jump in temperature suggests that a much warmer source lies just a few hundred metres below, from which heat is escaping. In this image, at least three of the tiger stripes are fully active, with the fourth on the right just partially active when this image was taken on 14 July 2005. Image: NASA/JL/GSFC/Space Science Institute.

INSIDE A TIGER STRIPE

A diagrammatic view of how the plumes erupt. Water laden with minerals and dust grains is fed upwards through fractures leading to reservoirs, which in turn are fed by a large underground sea (not depicted in this illustration). The water in the fractures is highly pressurised, turning it into vapour that then bursts outwards when the tiger stripes open. Icy fallout then settles on the ground either side of the tiger stripe. Image: NASA/JPL–Caltech/Space Science Institute/Ron Miller.

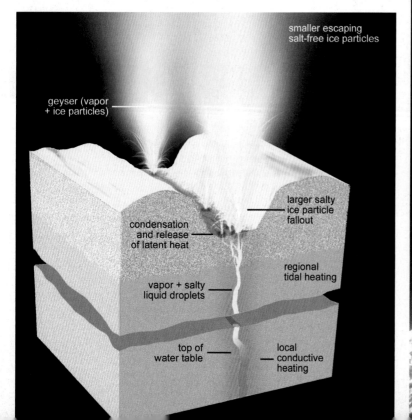

"The tiger stripes are much warmer than they have any right to be, which implies there are warm temperatures pretty close to the surface," says Andrew Ingersoll of the California Institute of Technology."

From the beginning the eruptions have been described as plumes or geysers, but recent analysis of images taken by Cassini show that they erupt as faint curtains all along the length of the tiger stripes, with the bright plumes that we see simply being where this curtain is folding back on itself along the jagged path of the tiger stripes. Their spray can reach 1,500 kilometres into space, although in truth 90 percent of the icy particles that are ejected from the tiger stripes cannot escape Enceladus' gravity and end up snowing back onto the surface, leaving a fine powder 100 metres deep and composed of particles just a millionth of a metre across, which would be perfect for skiing on! All this snow keeps the surface of the moon looking constantly fresh and smooth, filling in craters and ridges and ultimately causing Enceladus to become the most reflective body in the known Solar System.

THE TIGER STRIPES ARE MUCH WARMER THAN THEY HAVE ANY RIGHT TO BE, WHICH IMPLIES THERE ARE WARM TEMPERATURES PRETTY CLOSE TO THE SURFACE

The ten percent that does escape into space forms Saturn's diffuse E-ring, which is centred on Enceladus. The E-ring itself is found within a broader torus of water vapour that can only be seen in infrared light and which was discovered by the European Space Agency's Herschel Space Telescope. The water vapour contained within this torus gradually falls onto Saturn in a kind of rain; through this mechanism, Enceladus becomes the only moon in the Solar System to be capable of chemically altering the atmosphere of its parent planet. Furthermore, as we have seen, the icy particles become ionised, or electrically charged, when they interact with

LAND OF THE PLUMES

Jets of water vapour are seen bursting up from the tiger stripes in this image taken on 2 February 2010. From left to right the tiger stripes are Alexandria Sulcus, Cairo Sulcus, Baghdad Sulcus and Damascus Sulcus. Image: NASA/JPL/ Space Science Institute.

the high-energy plasma in Saturn's magnetosphere. This effectively generates an electric current between Enceladus and Saturn, much like the Io Plasma Torus – an electric field looping between Io and Jupiter – is fuelled by sulphur ions from Io's volcanoes. The link between moon and planet can approach energies as high as 80,000 electronvolts and this electric loop generates an aurora above the ringed planet. Meanwhile, icy particles direct from the E-ring fall onto the leading hemispheres of some of Saturn's other moons, including Rhea and Tethys, giving them a fresh coat.

Underground ocean

Returning to Enceladus, the big mystery for Cassini to solve was, where is all this water vapour coming from? The temperature measurements of the tigers stripes implied that liquid water could be supported beneath the surface and this has obvious consequences for the potential for life within Enceladus.

The hope amongst scientists was that Enceladus habours an ocean, or at least a sizeable underground lake, but some scientists suggested another explanation, by looking at how water vapour could be generated by the frozen walls of the tiger stripes rubbing together as Saturn's gravity flexes Enceladus. The friction of this action would melt the ice in the walls and turn it directly into water vapour.

This theory did not last long once Cassini began a number of daredevil flights through the plumes, beginning in 2008. Although obviously none of its onboard instruments had been designed to specifically study the plumes, mission scientists were able to employ the Cosmic Dust Analyser (CDA) and the Ion and Neutral Mass Spectrometer in ways that had not been intended, in order to 'taste' Enceladus' geysers. The first such passage through the plumes was on 13 March 2008, speeding through them at 15 kilometres per second. Although there was the risk of large particles in the plumes striking Cassini and doing the spacecraft some misfortune, Cassini emerged unscathed. Later flights through the plumes took place at an altitude of just 25 kilometres. The CDA discovered salts mixed in with the icy particles and water vapour, as well as carbon dioxide, methane, acetylene and propane. Furthest away from Enceladus the grains are relatively small and low in salt, as you would expect as the lightest particles would be able to travel the largest distances, but much closer to the moon the grains that the CDA tasted were larger and rich in sodium and potassium – exactly what would be expected from an ocean

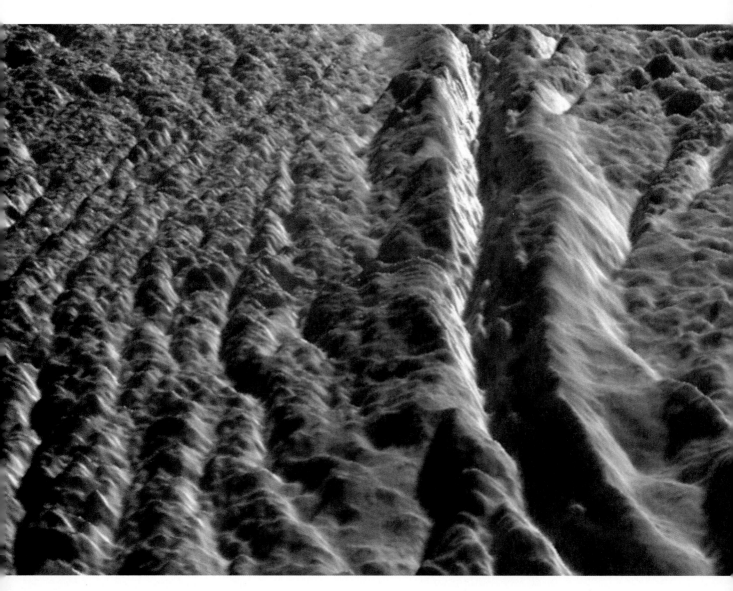

whose water is crashing against rock on the sea floor. Boundaries between liquids and solids such as this are havens for life in Earth's oceans. Cassini's CDA also detected sodium, plus carbonates such as soda, in the E-ring. All these discoveries pointed towards, but could not conclusively prove, the existence of an underground ocean, perhaps running 50 to 80 kilometres deep, located at the south pole.

Rock on the ocean floor, particularly ultramafic rocks high in magnesium and iron that have been raised up from the moon's upper mantle, chemically interact with water, generating other minerals including serpentine, hence the process being known as serpentisation. It results in the water becoming alkaline, which makes it friendlier to life. In addition, serpentisation also produces molecular hydrogen. This can be an important source of chemical energy for primitive life in deep-sea biospheres, which is exactly what we find around so-called 'black smokers' at the bottom of Earth's oceans.

"The discovery of serpentisation makes Enceladus an even more promising candidate for a separate genesis of life," says Christopher Glein of the Carnegie Institution of Washington. "It provides a link between geological and biological processes."

THE PRESENCE OF METHANE, AN ALKALINE PH AND HYDROTHERMAL ACTIVITY IN THE SEA IS GREAT NEWS FOR THE POSSIBILITY OF LIFE

Serpentisation is an example of hydrothermal activity, evidence for which Cassini has detected based on the amount of nano-sized grains of silica found in the plumes. Hydrothermal activity in general occurs when seawater gets into rock on the sea floor, reacts with it and emerges from the rock as a hot solution of all kinds of minerals, including silica. This is how the tiny dust grains that erupt into space in the plumes form: this hot solution of water and minerals rises to the top of the ocean, where it comes into contact with cooler water, allowing the dissolved minerals to condense into grains. The water containing the grains continues to rise through fractures in the frozen ceiling of ice above the sea, where it is stored in pressured reservoirs a few hundred metres below the tiger stripes – these reservoirs are the warm spots that Andrew Ingersoll alluded to. When Saturn's gravity periodically pulls the tiger stripes open, the mixture of water and dust grains bursts out, spewing from the fractures at rates of between 200 and 250 kilograms every second.

DIVING INTO DAMASCUS

Left: A simulated image showing an angled, elevated view close to Damascus Sulcus. Although simulated, the image uses real data to show the rippled terrain close to the tiger stripes. Image: NASA/JPL/Space Science Institute/Universities Space Research Association/Lunar and Planetary Institute.

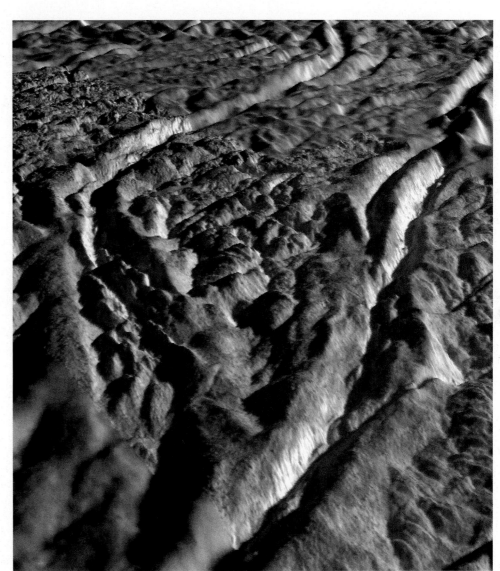

BAGHDAD SULCUS

Right: Another simulated view looking along Baghdad Sulcus, showing the tiger stripe split into two branches, with each trench up to two kilometres across. The walls of the trenches are up to 100 metres high. Image: NASA/JPL/Space Science Institute/Universities Space Research Association/Lunar and Planetary Institute.

Alien life?

Methane has also been tasted in the plumes and scientists think there are two possible sources of this gas, both involving phenomena known as clathrates, which are crystalline lattices of ice that can trap molecules including methane. In one case, hydrothermal activity could release methane from the rocky sea floor, but the pressure deep down there would quickly crush the methane into icy clathrates. However, if the release of methane from the rock is greater than the rate at which the clathrates can form, then the ocean will become loaded with methane, which then rises upwards and is blown out along the curtain of plumes emanating from the tiger stripes.

BEYOND ENCELADUS

Cassini's narrow-angle camera gazes beyond Enceladus, to the sunlight side of the rings of Saturn beyond, seen at an angle of just a degree above the ring-plane. Image: NASA/JPL/Space Science Institute.

The second source of methane could be the ceiling of ice above the sea. This ice is primordial, having formed at the same time that Enceladus itself did and has been locked inside the moon ever since. If this ice begins to melt and merge into the ocean, it could release methane, which again could form clathrates or super-saturate the ocean.

Scientists were already pretty convinced that Enceladus harbours a hidden ocean when Cassini produced the clinching evidence in the form of gravity data. Every time Cassini flies past a moon, be it Enceladus or one of the other moons, the moon's gravity slightly alters the spacecraft's trajectory. During three fly-bys of Enceladus between April 2010 and May 2012,

scientists monitored the changes in Cassini's trajectory by how its radio carrier signal was Doppler shifted. This allowed them to accurately measure not only Enceladus' overall gravitational field, but to also detect a 'negative mass anomaly' at the moon's south pole. In other words, they found a region underneath the south pole that was less dense – and hence produces less gravity –than its surroundings. The only explanation is the existence of a large sea inside a cavity fifty kilometres below the surface.

The presence of methane, an alkaline pH and hydrothermal activity in this sea is all great news for the possibility of life existing inside Enceladus. We should be careful to point out that just because the environment inside Enceladus may be hospitable to some forms of life, that does not necessarily mean that there is life. The potential for life, however, ranks Enceladus amongst the likes of Mars, Europa and Titan as the best places in the Solar System where astrobiologists could look for simple, microbial life. In many ways Enceladus is the most promising location because, unlike on Europa where future missions will have to drill or melt their way through a few dozen kilometres of ice to reach the ocean, there is a clear way to access Enceladus' underground ocean through the tiger stripes. It may be that there is not even any need to enter the ocean – the ocean comes to us, squirted out as plumes through fractures. Although Cassini's instruments were not built to detect biological matter within the plumes, a future mission to Enceladus will be capable of making these measurements.

"If there is some really interesting chemistry then it would be cause to get excited," says Ingersoll. "If there were actual life, then a lot of that might be coming out for us to measure."

If that is true, then that is when things will get really interesting!

CLOSE ENOUGH

On 5 October 2008 Cassini flew within a mere 25 kilometres of Enceladus' surface before speeding away and taking this picture as it looked back. The tiger stripes and south pole are seen to be just emerging from the morning terminator at the lower right. At the top (north) of the picture is a deep, dark chasm named Labtayt Sulcus, which is a kilometre deep. Image: NASA/JPL/Space Science Institute.

SQUEEZE AND RELEASE

Enceladus' geysers are driven by the changing gravity of Saturn as the moon orbits it on an elliptical (slightly oval rather than perfectly round) trajectory, at times being closer to Saturn than at other points in its orbit. When it is closest to Saturn, the tiger stripes are slammed shut. However, when Enceladus reaches the point in its orbit where it is a little bit further away, Saturn's gravitational tidal forces act to open up the tiger stripes, causing the plumes to burst open in full flow, as can be seen in the distant image on the left, compared to the image on the right when Enceladus is at its closest and quietest.

THERE ARE CRATERS TOO

Enceladus' terrain is not all about the tiger stripes. There are craters aplenty too, although not nearly as many as is seen on the other moons of Saturn. The craters, over geological timescales, are rapidly filled in by icy particles falling fro the sky out of the plumes. The constant fine snowfall acts to soften the edges of the craters, while in between them run narrow, parallel grooves that are relics of Enceladus' ancient tectonic legacy. Image: NASA/JPL/Space Science Institute.

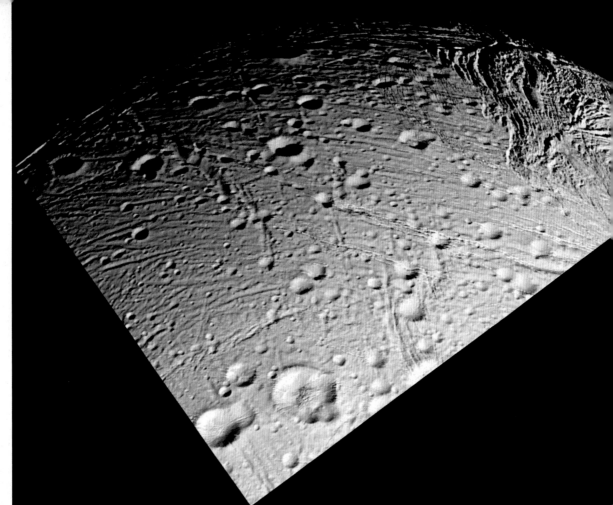

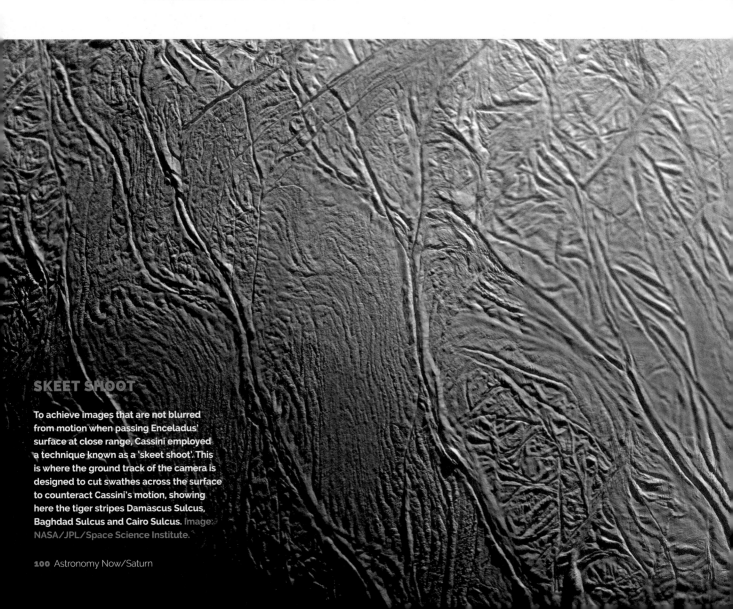

SKEET SHOOT

To achieve images that are not blurred from motion when passing Enceladus' surface at close range, Cassini employed a technique known as a 'skeet shoot'. This is where the ground track of the camera is designed to cut swathes across the surface to counteract Cassini's motion, showing here the tiger stripes Damascus Sulcus, Baghdad Sulcus and Cairo Sulcus. Image: NASA/JPL/Space Science Institute.

A LAND WITHOUT STRIPES

The tiger stripes are conspicuously missing from Enceladus' north polar region, pictured here. The image is looking southwards, with the north pole in shadow when this image was taken on 12 March 2008. The two overlapping craters near the middle are called Ali Baba (top) and Aladdin (bottom). Were there once tiger stripes at the north pole too, which have since become inactive and filled in with fresh fallout from the plumes emanating from the other pole? Cassini will be looking for evidence of them during its final two fly-bys. Image: NASA/JPL/Space Science Institute.

SNOWBALL IN SPACE

Enceladus looks calm and serene in this image, taken from a distance of 170,000 kilometres. There is no hint of the plume curtains, or of the ocean that lies beneath. Image: NASA/JPL–Caltech/Space Science Institute.

A RAIL OF CURTAINS

For ten years, scientists thought that the eruptions from
Enceladus' tiger stripes were in discrete plumes, but it has
since been realised that the entire length of the tiger stripes are
erupting all at the same time, producing a curtain of water vapour.
This false-colour image highlights the presence of the curtains.
Image: NASA/JPL–Caltech/Space Science Institute/PSI.

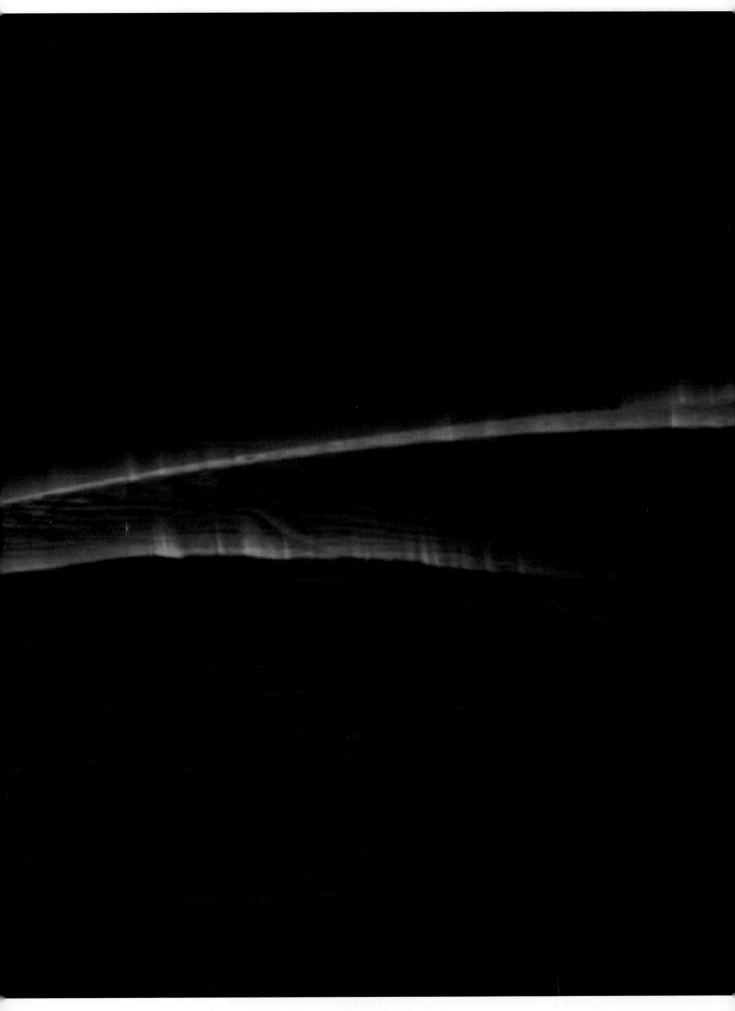

Tethys

The third major moon out from Saturn
is Tethys, a medium-sized world of ice and craters.

Tethys at a glance

Diameter:	1,066km
Mass:	6.2 × 10²⁰kg
Density:	0.98g/cm³
Orbital radius from Saturn:	294,619km
Orbital period:	1 day, 21 hours and 18 minutes
Discovered:	1684

A HINT OF DARKNESS

The dark tint to Tethys' trailing
hemisphere is clear to see in this
enhanced colour image taken on 11
April 2015. Because Tethys is always
tidally locked – meaning its rotation
on its axis matches its rotation around
Saturn, so that it always shows the
same face to the ringed planet
– the trailing hemisphere always
faces opposite Tethys' direction of
motion, allowing the dark material
to accumulate. Image: NASA/JPL–
Caltech/Space Science Institute.

There is a wonderful variety to Saturn's many moons. Even when at first glance they may look similar, when we look deeper each moon has its own unique character, with blemishes and faults and standout characteristics. Take Tethys (pronounced Teth-iss). It is cold, cratered and barren. Yet it wears a crater so large it could engulf Mimas and has a giant chasm that encircles three-quarters of the moon. For some unexplained reason it is the least dense of all the major Saturnian moons, made from water-ice nearly all the way through, while on its surface subtle colour variations hint at complex processes. So Tethys may be cold, cratered and barren, but it certainly is not dull.

The Odyssey

Discovered in 1684 by Giovanni Domenico Cassini at the same time that he found Dione (Cassini could also claim Rhea and Iapetus as his discoveries, plus the eponymous Cassini Division in the rings), most of the major discoveries about Tethys came three centuries later with the fly-bys of the Voyager probes and then the arrival of the Cassini spacecraft. The aforementioned gigantic crater is named Odysseus, after the Greek hero perhaps better known to us as Ulysses. At 445 kilometres across, it is wider than Mimas, which as we have already seen in a previous section also sports a giant crater called Herschel, which is a third of Mimas' diameter. There are clear differences between the appearance of Odysseus and that of Herschel. The walls and floor of Odysseus seem to curve with the shape of Tethys, whereas Herschel has punched a chunk straight out of Mimas and its walls appear straight when viewed edge-on from a distance. When Odysseus was born, Tethys was still quite young and warm from its formation, so much so that beneath the surface water may have been liquid, or at least slush, rather than hard ice when the impact that created Odysseus struck. Tethys' insides were therefore more malleable and the crater was able to 'relax' into the softer ground.

All that water-ice makes Tethys the least dense of Saturn's large moons. There is rock in there somewhere,

THE ODYSSEY

The eye of Tethys – the giant crater Odysseus – stares back at Cassini in this image taken on Christmas Eve 2005. The crater's terraced rim towers five kilometres above its surroundings. Inside the crater floor is relatively devoid of smaller craters, indicating it is younger than the surface beyond Odysseus, while in the middle of the inner ring of mountains inside the crater is a central pit that is up to four kilometres deep. Central pits inside craters such as this may form when ice beneath the impact is melted and drains away through fractures cracked open by the force of the collision. This leave an empty space into which the crater sags. Image: NASA/JPL/Space Science Institute.

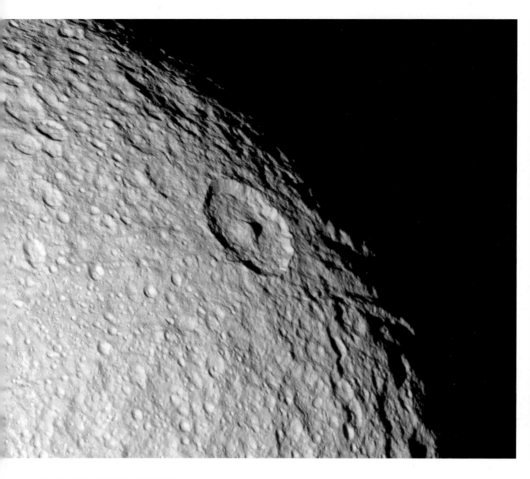

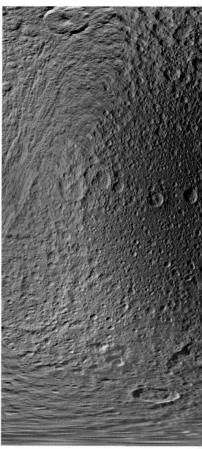

SON OF ODYSSEUS

The 90 kilometre-wide crater Telemachus (fittingly named alongside Odysseus; in Ancient Greek legend Telemachus was Odysseus/Ulysses' son) on the terminator between night and day. Above Telemachus is the ruins of another large crater that must be much older, judging by its state of erosion. Image: NASA/JPL/Space Science Institute.

A MAP OF THE WORLD

An enhanced colour Mercator projection of Tethys, highlighting the darker trailing hemisphere and the mighty Odysseus. The equatorial band on the right-hand side of the image is the mouth of the Pac-Man. The resolution of the map is 250 metres per pixel. Image: NASA/JPL–Caltech/Space Science Institute/Lunar and Planetary Institute.

ICY LANDSLIDES

Tethys' landscape almost looks like it has melted. It hasn't – we must remember this is not hard, immovable rock that what we see on a lunar landscape. What we are seeing is the ice relaxing, blunting the edges of craters and fractures in the ground so that they look soft. The double crater at bottom right has experienced landslides on its walls, further reducing their sharpness. Image: NASA/JPL/Space Science Institute.

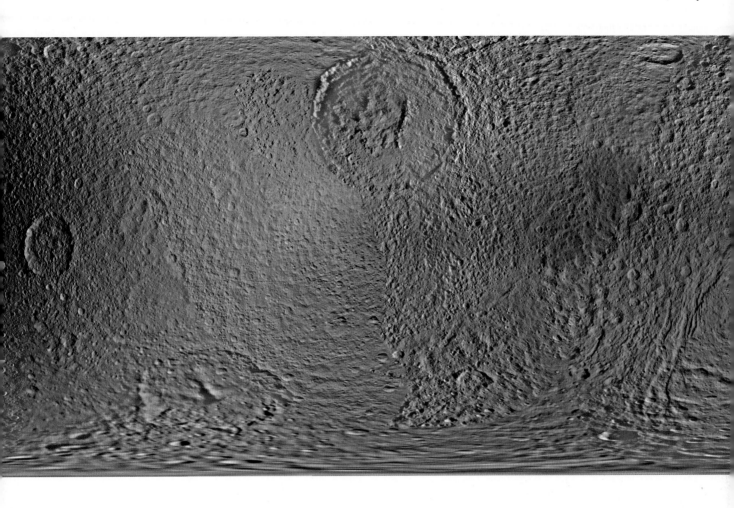

and if it has all sunk deep into Tethys and settled into the core, then that core of rock is no larger than 300 kilometres across – the rest of Tethys is made entirely from ice. Nobody knows why, but one popular theory that could explain a lot of intriguing features about the Saturnian system is that many of the icy moons, including Tethys, are made of the cast-offs of one or more Titan-sized moons that were destroyed; ripped apart by Saturn's gravitational tides and swallowed by the planet. The theory stems from comparing Saturn to Jupiter, its closest relative in the Solar System. Jupiter has four giant moons akin to Titan, namely Io, Europa, Ganymede and Callisto. Why does Jupiter have a quartet of giant moons and Saturn merely one? The solution, developed by Robin Canup of the Southwest Research Institute in Boulder, Colorado, is that once upon a time Saturn did have more large moons like Titan. However, just as interactions with the planet-forming disc around young stars can sap angular momentum from planets, causing them to migrate inwards, the same happened to Saturn's moons. One by one they fell into Saturn (see page 60 for more details about this hypothesis) until there were just two left. Titan was far enough out from Saturn to not spiral in before the disc of gas, water-vapour and dust from which moons formed dissipated. The other moon, however, was swallowed like its lost siblings. When it reached a point known as the Roche limit, Saturn's gravitational forces were able to overcome the stability of

the moon and begin stripping icy layers from it. The moon was destroyed, but these icy layers became the rings – or at least some of them – and also formed or contributed to many of the icy moons, including Tethys. Alas, this may be a theory difficult to prove, at least without observing this process in action around some distant exoplanet. For now it must remain a tantalising hypothesis.

Torn Tethys

The other gigantic geological feature on Tethys is the huge Ithaca Chasma, which is 2,000 kilometres long (half the length of the immense Valles Marineris on Mars), 300 kilometres wide and three kilometres deep. This huge fracture that splits Tethys' sides was likely opened up when the slushy interior of the moon began to freeze solid billions of years ago. As we know, when water freezes it expands. On Tethys there is a lot of water to expand, more than enough to crack the moon's shell and result in this huge chasm, along with a number of other, smaller, faults scattered around Tethys.

There are more subtle features on the surface too. With all that ice reflecting sunlight, Tethys is the second brightest moon orbiting Saturn (Enceladus is the brightest). Its leading hemisphere is actually 10 to 15 percent brighter than its trailing hemisphere, creating a kind of watered-down version of Iapetus' two-toned hemispheres, which we will learn more about in a later chapter. Tethys' leading hemisphere is being blasted by icy particles from Saturn's thick E-ring, which Tethys orbits just outside of. Meanwhile the trailing hemisphere is being turned darker by two processes. One process involves ions bombarding Tethys and chemically altering the surface particles. The second process sees a light drizzle of dark dust – the same stuff that

ITHACA CHASMA IS A GIGANTIC GEOLOGICAL FEATURE 2,000 KILOMETRES LONG, 300 KILOMETRES WIDE AND THREE KILOMETRES DEEP

LOOKING SOUTHWARDS

The 245-kilometre wide crater Melanthius, found in Tethys'
southern hemisphere in this image taken on 23 July 2006.
Image: NASA/JPL/Space Science Institute.

covers half of Iapetus and fills in the deep craters of Hyperion – raining onto Tethys. This dark material is believed to originate from the outermost moon Phoebe (see pages 174 to 177) and may be composed of minerals such as hematite and 'nanophase' iron (nanophase alludes to the size of the grains being under 100 nanometres, or ten millionths of a metre).

Winning streaks

Beyond this hemispherical dichotomy, there is also the Pac-Man thermal emission, which we have mentioned in the chapter about Mimas. Unlike Mimas, however, Tethys' Pac-Man is vaguely visible to optical cameras too, having been first noted by Voyager 1. More mysterious are faint red streaks that arc across Tethys' cratered plains and were not discovered until 2015. The streaks are not visible to the naked eye, but are seen in enhanced images combining a number of filters. Found in Tethys' northern hemisphere, they became noticeable when the Saturnian system entered northern summer, with the polar regions becoming much better illuminated by the Sun than at any previous stage of Cassini's mission.

THE SECOND DEATH STAR

Mimas is not the only moon of Saturn to resemble the Death Star: the crater Odysseus helps Tethys also stake a claim to that title. Odysseus is an example of a double-ring crater, with the inner ring of mountains spanning 140-kilometres across. The two sets of rings are created from rippled shock waves running through the ice after the impact. Image: NASA/JPL/Space Science Institute.

OF ALL THE LARGE MOONS AROUND SATURN, TETHYS CONTAINS THE HIGHEST PROPORTION OF WATER-ICE

"The red arcs are just a complete surprise," Linda Spilker, Cassini's Project Scientist at the Jet Propulsion Laboratory, told *Astronomy Now*. "We saw hints of them back in 2005 but didn't really pay too much attention at the time."

What the streaks are composed of and where they came from is unknown, but scientists do know that they are fairly young, for they cover every other type of surface feature on the moon including recent deposits from Saturn's E-ring.

"It's so intriguing because it almost looks like material that has been spray painted onto the top surface," says Spilker. "The streaks are not aligned with any fractures or cracks, they just go across whatever they like as a light coating. One side of Tethys is coated with these E-ring particles, and yet the red material is even on top of that, so I wonder how old it might be."

There are numerous possibilities. Perhaps something has exposed ice that contain impurities, much like the dirty red markings of Jupiter's icy moon Europa. Another alternative is the material could have outgassed, implying Tethys could be active, or maybe there is another source of dusty material in the Saturnian system that is depositing material onto Tethys but which has not yet been identified. Well, Cassini has to leave something for the next mission to Saturn to follow-up on!

SCARRED LAND

Chasms and cliffs run along a surface pockmarked with craters. Here we see the tail end of the giant Ithaca Chasma, which is a bit like the Tethys equivalent of the Grand Canyon. Image: NASA/JPL/Space Science Institute.

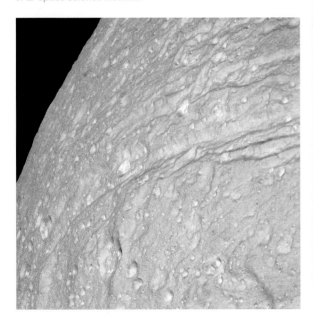

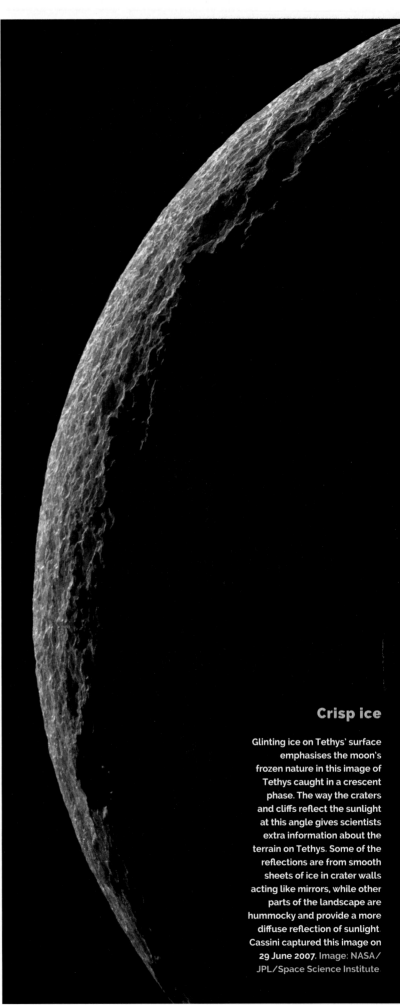

Crisp ice

Glinting ice on Tethys' surface emphasises the moon's frozen nature in this image of Tethys caught in a crescent phase. The way the craters and cliffs reflect the sunlight at this angle gives scientists extra information about the terrain on Tethys. Some of the reflections are from smooth sheets of ice in crater walls acting like mirrors, while other parts of the landscape are hummocky and provide a more diffuse reflection of sunlight. Cassini captured this image on 29 June 2007. Image: NASA/JPL/Space Science Institute

Tethys

SHADOW OF THE PAC-MAN

A faint band of darker material runs around Tethys' equator, forming
the mouth of the 'Pac-Man' seen more prominently in infrared light
looking at the moon's heat signature. Note the scar running along the
bottom right hand side of the moon – that's part of Ithaca Chasma.
Image: NASA/JPL/Space Science Institute.

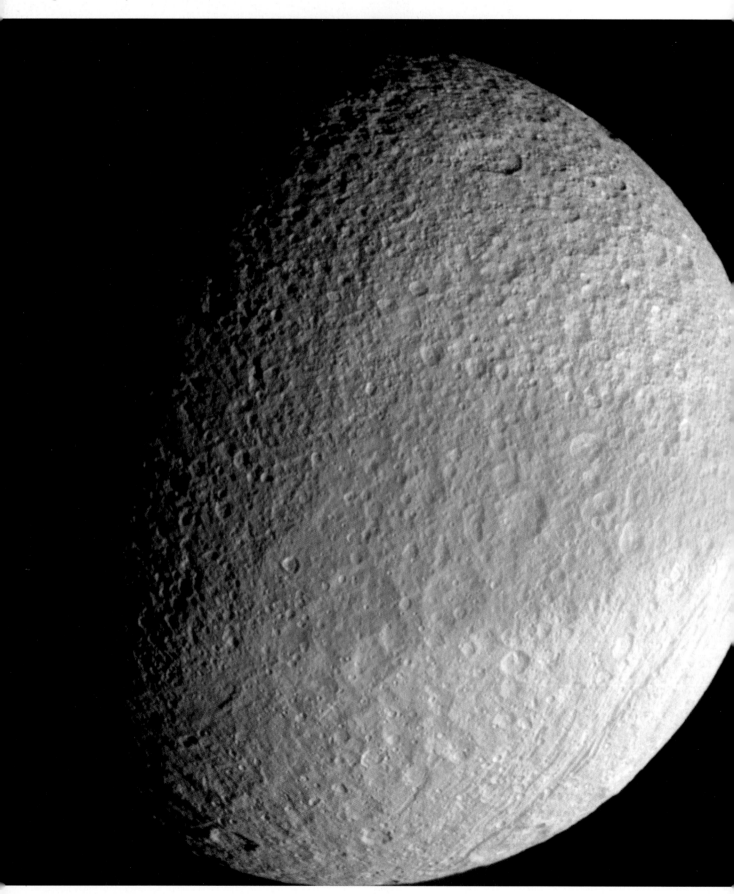

GRAND CANYON

The full glory of Tethys' giant canyon, Ithaca Chasma, dominates this view, imaged by Cassini on 10 May 2008. The giant canyon is 2,000 kilometres long. Image: NASA/JPL/Space Science Institute.

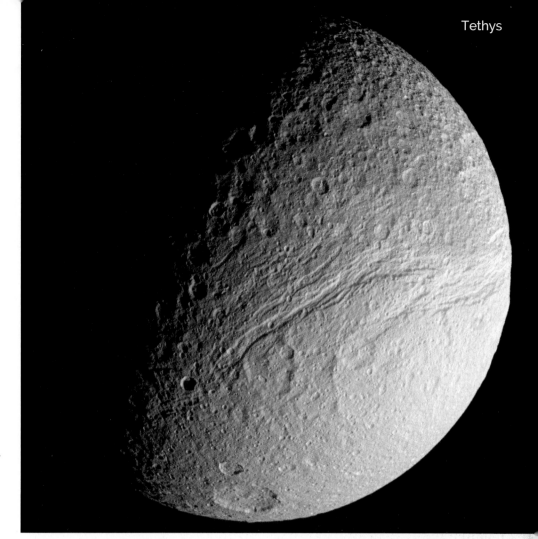

RED-FACED

Mysterious red streaks arc across the surface of Tethys, as seen in this enhanced-colour image taken on 11 April 2015. The streaks are a few kilometres wide and hundreds of kilometres long. their origin is currently a mystery. Image: NASA/JPL–Caltech/Space Science Institute.

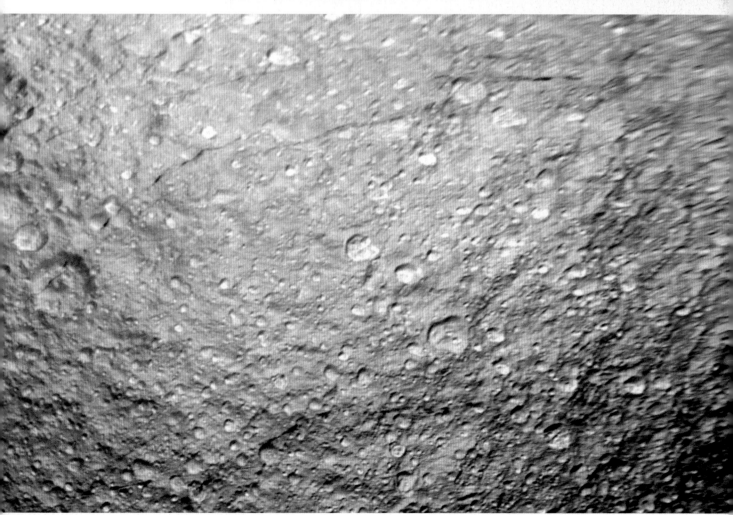

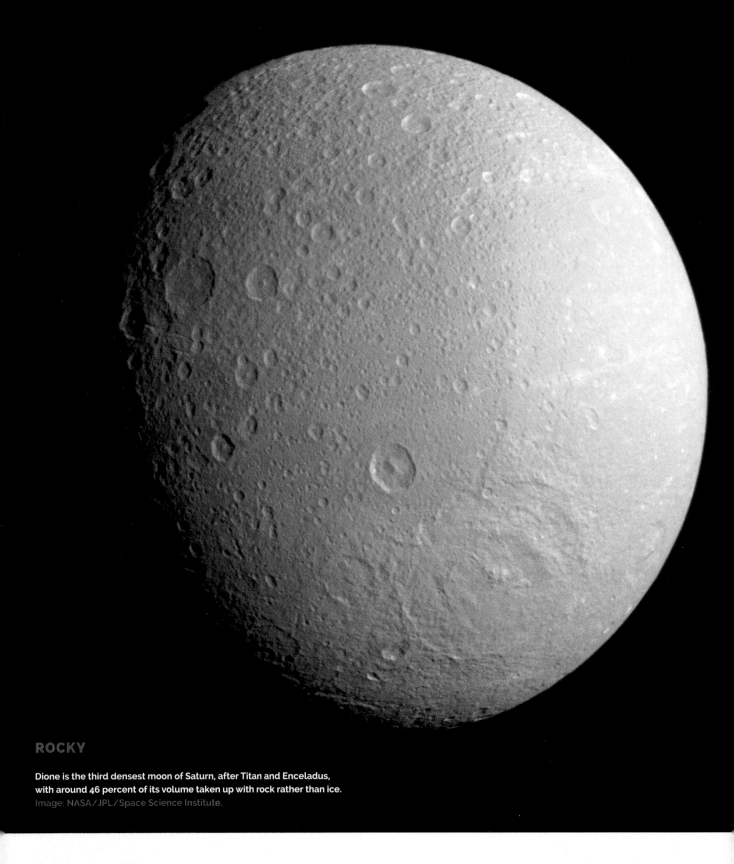

ROCKY

Dione is the third densest moon of Saturn, after Titan and Enceladus, with around 46 percent of its volume taken up with rock rather than ice.
Image: NASA/JPL/Space Science Institute.

Dione

If Enceladus is the moon that is, then Dione is the moon that was, with its glory days now far in the past.

Dione at a glance

Diameter:	1,129km
Mass:	1.1 x 10²¹kg
Density:	1.5 g/cm³
Orbital radius from Saturn:	377,396km
Orbital period:	2 days, 18 hours and 48 minutes
Discovered:	1684

Dione (pronounced Dye-OH-nee) is a moon of half-measures. While Enceladus is riotously spewing out water vapour from its tigers stripes, Dione is sputtering along. While Enceladus' ocean could be a potential hive of alien life, Dione's has likely mostly frozen solid. In many ways Dione is a fossil – a moon that was once active and thriving, but today has largely shut down.

And in a twist of fate, Dione has a large hand to play in keeping Enceladus active. The two moons have settled into a 2:1 resonance, meaning that for every two orbits Enceladus makes of Saturn, Dione makes one, so that periodically they lie close to each other. This resonance helps keep Enceladus in its non-circular orbit, which results in changing gravitational forces opening and closing its tiger stripes and driving the water vapour plumes.

So why has Dione struggled to keep up with its more illustrious fellow moon? Perhaps the tidal forces that Enceladus feels are stronger than those experienced by Dione, or maybe Enceladus contains more radioactive rock releasing heat to warm the ocean. Whatever the case, Dione seems to have had a far more interesting past than its present.

On its trailing hemisphere is a huge mountainous ridge, 800 kilometres long and with peaks ranging one to two kilometres in height. The surface beneath the mountains dips underneath their weight by half a kilometre. This would only happen if the surface beneath the mountains, called Janiculum Dorsa, had been warm and malleable, which would have been the case had there been a sub-surface ocean when the

DIONE COULD BE A FOSSIL OF THE WONDROUS ACTIVITY CASSINI HAS DISCOVERED SPRAYING FROM SATURN'S GEYSER MOON ENCELADUS

LAST TRIP BUT ONE

A close-up of Dione's cratered surface, captured by Cassini on 16 June 2015 – the mission's penultimate visit to the moon. The rings of Saturn can be seen, edge-on, in the background. Image: NASA/JPL/ Space Science Institute.

mountains formed billions of years ago. Furthermore, also found in the trailing hemisphere is network of huge fractures, braided canyons and giant cliffs with bright walls. When the Voyager spacecraft both flew past Saturn and imaged Dione, their cameras could not resolve these canyons, known as Eurotas Chasmata, as anything other than bright wispy terrain and scientists thought they might be fresh material that had welled up from underground. Cassini's high-resolution eyes showed this was not the case, but perhaps these canyons could have been active, like Enceladus' tiger stripes, billions of years ago.

Scratch that. Scientists have discovered that there is some form of activity on Dione right now. The nature of it, though, is a complete mystery.

As Saturn rotates in its ten-hour-whatever period, its magnetosphere and all the plasma (negatively charged particles of gas) within it rotates along with Saturn. Like anything else that is spinning fast enough, the cloud of plasma in the magnetosphere flattens into a disc shape and streamers of electrons start to spin off it, to be ejected into interplanetary space. Using Cassini's

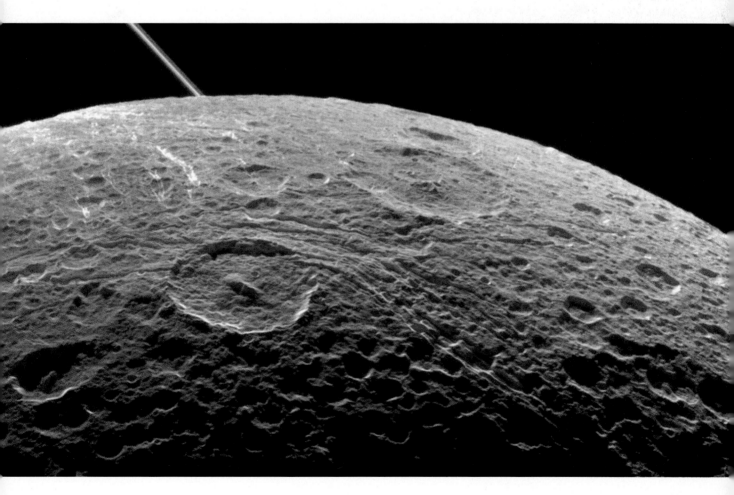

plasma spectrometer, scientists have tracked some of these electron streamers back to both Dione and Tethys. The implication is that some form of geological activity on these moons is spewing material out into space, which then becomes ionised before joining the general cloud of plasma. Whatever this activity is, it must be fairly low level because from looking at Dione (and Tethys) it is not immediately obvious.

"A picture is emerging that suggests Dione could be a fossil of the wondrous activity Cassini discovered spraying from Saturn's geyser moon Enceladus, or perhaps a weaker copycat Enceladus," says Bonnie Buratti of NASA's Jet Propulsion Laboratory, who leads Cassini scientists who study Saturn's icy moons. "There may turn out to be many more active worlds with water out there than we previously thought."

There's more. Molecular oxygen, in trace quantities, has been discovered forming a tenuous atmosphere, or 'exosphere' around Dione, just like on its larger sibling Rhea. When we say tenuous, we mean extremely sparse: Cassini's plasma spectrometer

SUNLIGHT, SUN-BRIGHT

Dione's dayside is overexposed in this image to bring out details from the moon's night-side. The large Eurotas Chasmata splits the moon. Image: NASA/JPL/Space Science Institute.

measured one molecule for every eleven cubic centimetres. As on Rhea, the oxygen is likely liberated from water-ice on the surface by sunlight or energetic particles trapped in the magnetosphere of Saturn.

"We now know that Dione, in addition to Saturn's rings and the moon Rhea, is a source of oxygen molecules," says Robert Tokar, a Cassini team member from the Los Alamos National Laboratory, in New Mexico, USA. "This shows that molecular oxygen is actually common in the Saturnian system and reinforces that it can come from a process that doesn't involve life."

Cassini made its last fly-by of Dione on 17 August 2015, which means that answers to exactly what is happening on Dione, and what happened there in the past, may have to wait until our next adventure at Saturn. Nevertheless, we know enough to be able to change our view of Dione from that of a boring, dead ice world to one that, at least once upon a time, was much more interesting and we are perhaps seeing the last vestiges of that today.

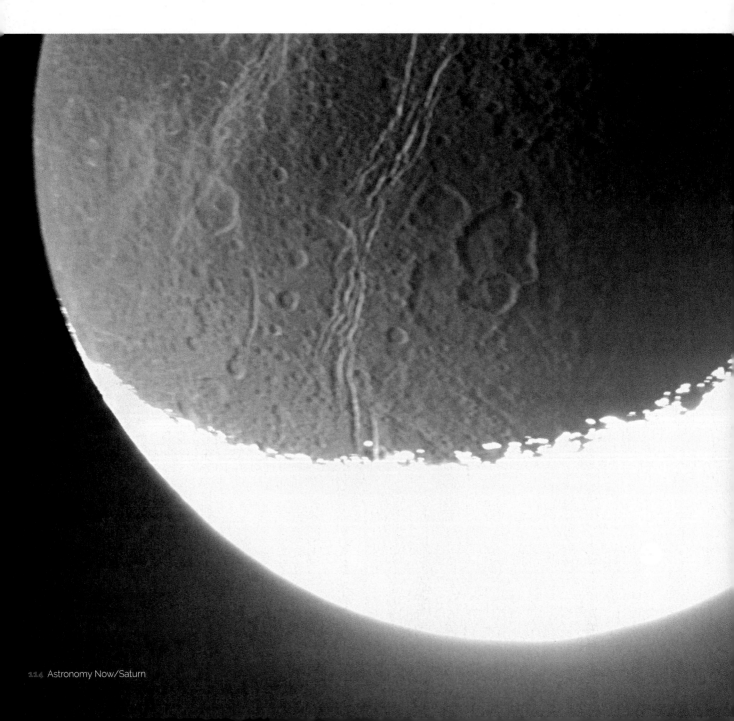

CHASMATA

The shiny canyons of Dione's Eurotas Chasmata may have formed a long
time ago when Dione's orbit was more elliptical, allowing gravitational tides
to rip the moon's surface open. This image was captured on 11 April 2015.
Image: NASA/JPL–Caltech/Space Science Institute.

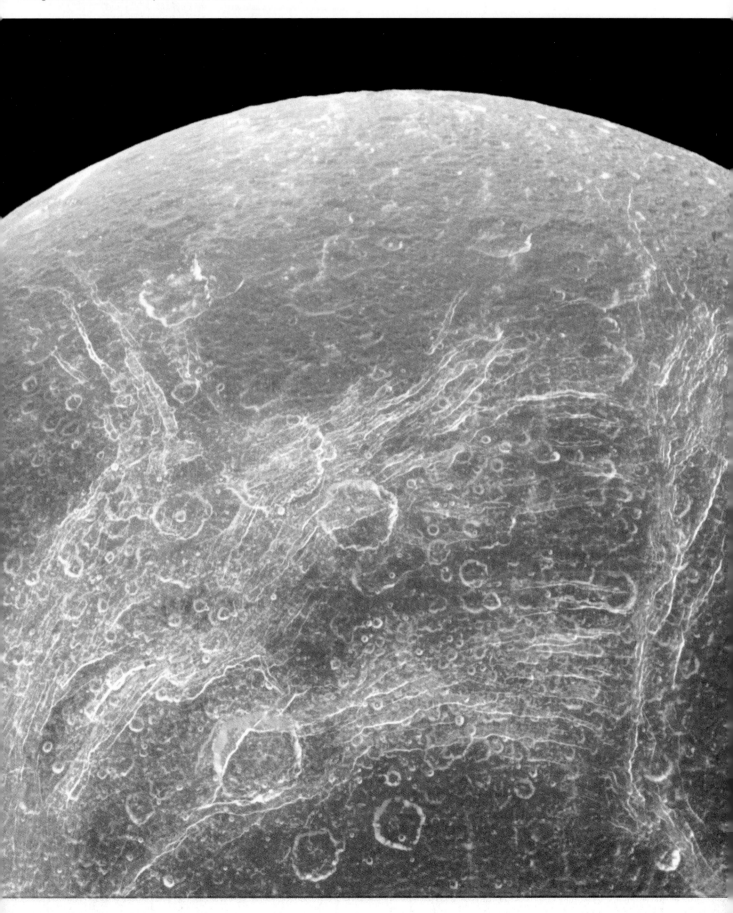

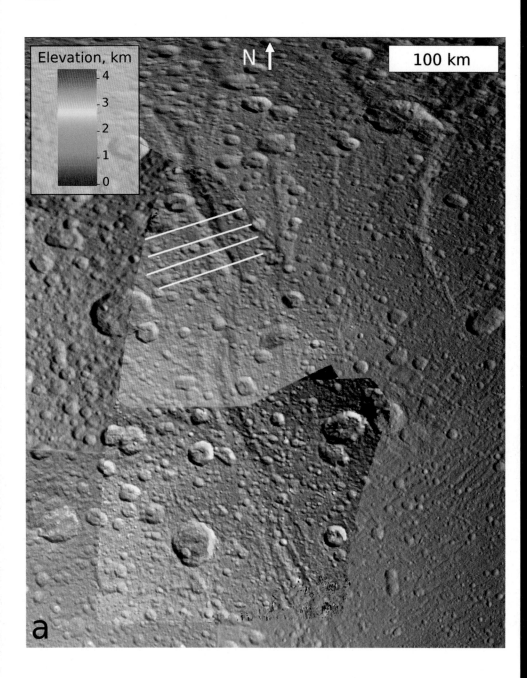

Elevation, km

4

3

2

1

0

N ↑

100 km

a

SAGGING UNDER THE WEIGHT

A ridge of mountains 800 kilometres long has caused the ground underneath it to buckle and sag by half a kilometre. This would only have been possible if the interior of Dione had been warm enough to make the ice pliable, which would have been the case had there been a sub-surface liquid ocean. In this image, colour denotes the elevation of the land, with red as the highest and blue as the lowest. Image: NASA/JPL–Caltech/ Space Science Institute/Brown University.

CURVING CANYONS

A closer view of Dione's wispy terrain streaking across the surface, seen by Cassini on 27 January 2010. Image: NASA/JPL/Space Science Institute.

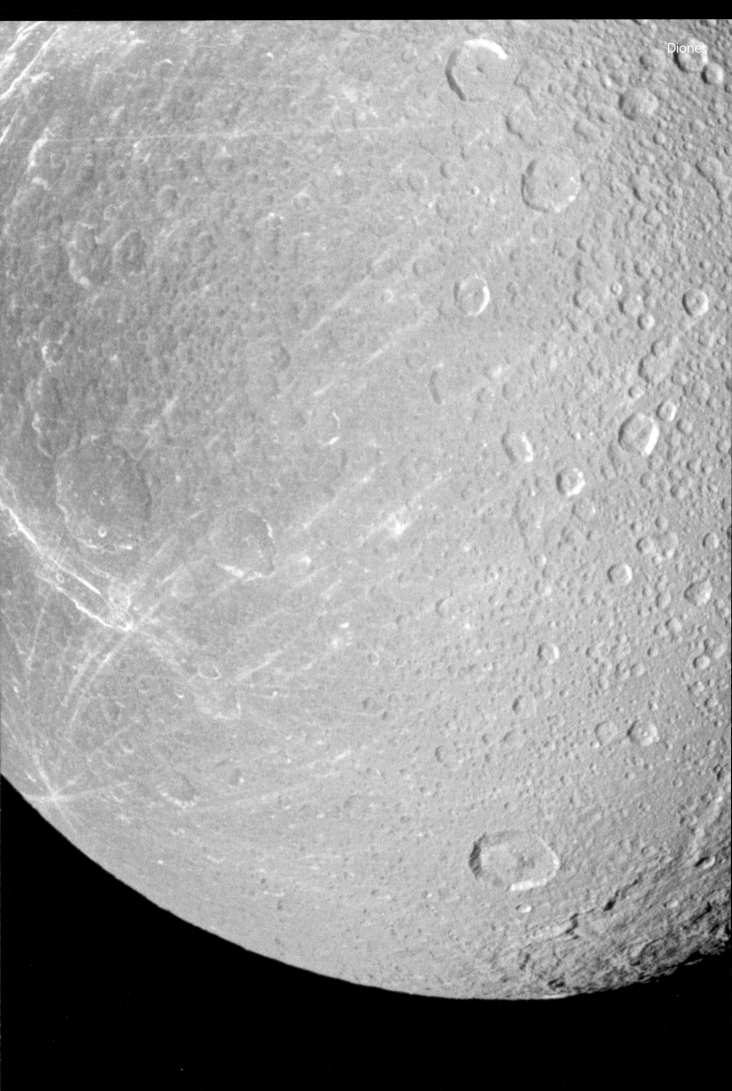

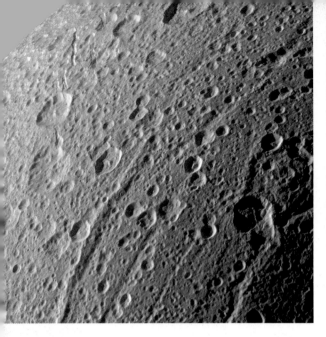

RAREFIED AIR

Cassini's plasma spectrometer has measured a tenuous atmosphere of oxygen molecules that are sputtering off water-ice on the surface. The atmosphere is five trillion times less dense than Earth's. Image: NASA/JPL/Space Science Institute.

A MOON OF TWO SIDES

The false-colour Mercator projection of Dione's terrain reveals the stark contrast between Dione's relatively clean leading hemisphere that is covered in icy particles from the E-ring and its dark trailing hemisphere, dirtied by radiation that alters the chemical composition of the ice, as seen on the other icy moons. However, Dione is different in that it sports canyons that criss-cross the dark zone. Image: NASA/JPL–Caltech/Space Science Institute/Lunar and Planetary Institute.

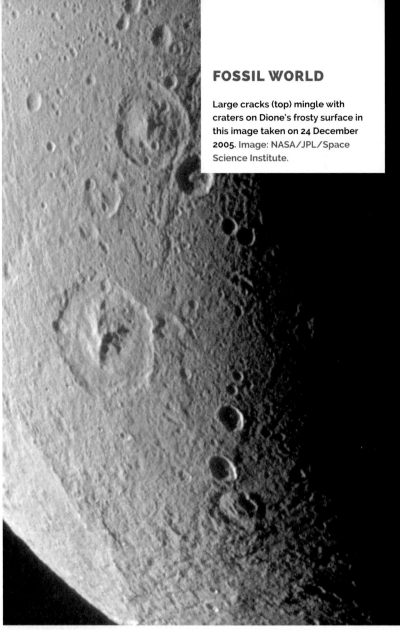

FOSSIL WORLD

Large cracks (top) mingle with craters on Dione's frosty surface in this image taken on 24 December 2005. Image: NASA/JPL/Space Science Institute.

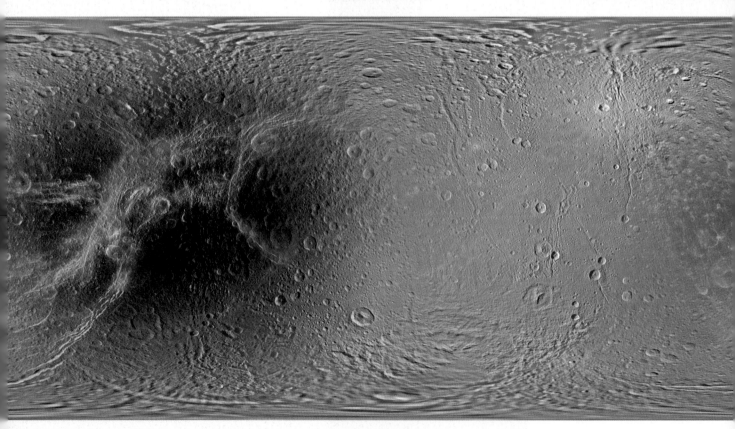

WISPY

A half-moon Dione displays deep craters on its terminator, and the wispy terrain on the moon's limb that is actually the bright walls of canyons. The large crater in the south of the moon is named Dido. Image: NASA/JPL/Space Science Institute.

PEEK-A-BOO

Mimas is caught peeking out from behind the dark cratered limb of Dione. Image: NASA/JPL–Caltech/Space Science Institute.

Rhea

As the ninth largest moon in the Solar System, Rhea is the standard bearer for icy, cratered moons.

Rhea at a glance

Diameter:	1,528km
Mass:	2.3×10^{21}kg
Density:	1.2g/cm^3
Orbital radius from Saturn:	527,108km
Orbital period:	4 days, 12 hours and 24 minutes
Discovered:	1672

Oxygen is one of the more common molecules in the Universe, but until recently we thought that oxygen atmospheres were quite rare, at least in our Solar System. Earth has an oxygen-rich atmosphere of course; we inhale it with every breath. Cassini's Plasma Spectrometer and Ion and Neutral Mass Spectrometer, however, have discovered two other locations in the Solar System where we can find an oxygen atmosphere: Dione and the subject of this chapter, namely Rhea. Of course the air on Rhea, which is Saturn's second largest moon, is far too thin to breathe, while the cold would freeze life and the radiation in Saturn's magnetosphere would fry life, but at least the air that is there is made of atoms and molecules of oxygen and carbon dioxide, only in quantities five trillion times less dense than on Earth.

When high-energy particles strike Rhea's icy surface, they liberate oxygen from the water-ice (the hydrogen in the water is light enough to quickly escape Rhea's feeble gravity), while the carbon dioxide either comes from dry ice buried amongst all the water-ice, or from dark carbon-rich material deposited on its trailing hemisphere, just like on the moons Tethys and Dione.

For a time, it looked as though Cassini's instruments had also detected something else rather unique about Rhea. In November 2005, while performing a fly-by of the moon, Cassini detected a drop in high-energy electrons on opposite sides of the Rhea's globe, as though something that was present around Rhea was shielding Cassini from the charged particles whizzing around Saturn's magnetosphere. Armed with this information, scientists at University College London's Mullard Space Science Laboratory inferred the presence of an unseen debris disc nearly six-thousand kilometres wide centred on Rhea, plus at least one distinct ring orbiting Rhea that was made from rubble ranging from pebbles to boulders.

This was extraordinary. "Seeing almost the same signatures on either side of Rhea was the clincher," said University College London's Geraint Jones at the time. "After ruling out many possibilities, we decided these were most likely rings. No one was expecting rings around a moon."

As it turned out, the discovery may have been too extraordinary. Subsequent fly-bys turned up no further evidence for rings: or debris disc, despite observing Rhea from a variety of angles. Whatever caused the drop in high-energy electron particles that Cassini measured in 2005 has not happened since, which brings those original observations into question. Given that Cassini made its final fly-by of Rhea in 2013, this is a mystery that only a future mission will be able to solve.

Liquid history

What we do know about Rhea for sure is what we can see on its surface. Heavily cratered, Rhea sports two large craters, named Tirawa, which is 360 kilometres across and five kilometres deep, and Mamaldi, which is even larger at 480 kilometres and even older, given that it is partly underneath Tirawa. On even larger scales, the geography of Rhea is split into two different types. One type sports many craters larger than 40 kilometres and is clearly very ancient terrain, while the other type that is common around the polar regions and in patches on the equator appears younger, with less craters and none over 40 kilometres in diameter. The inference is that the younger terrain has been resurfaced somehow at some point in Rhea's history. This resurfacing may have been possible by action from below; radioactive decay from rocky constituents of Rhea's interior could have kept the moon warm long enough for a liquid water sub-surface ocean to develop. On occasions this liquid may have reached the surface through fractures in the ice, which have since frozen over beneath giant ice cliffs called 'chasmata'. Further evidence for an ocean long ago comes in the form of uplifted blocks of terrain scattered amongst older landscapes and which could have been raised up by geological activity from beneath as convection currents warmed the ice, causing sections of the surface to shift.

Alas, unlike moons such as Tethys, there is not much that stands out on the surface of Rhea. That's not to say it does not have its own stark beauty, but what makes Rhea special lies above the icy ground.

FRACTURED

Rhea's surface sports bright wisps that can be seen in visible light (left) and which become clearer to see when viewed in false colour (right). The wisps are actually ridges with huge cliffs of ice. Image: NASA/JPL/Space Science Institute.

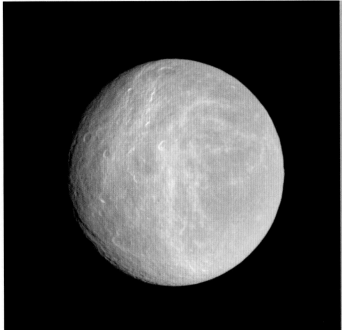
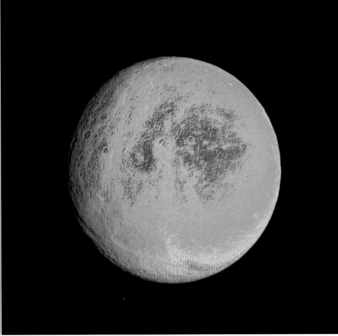

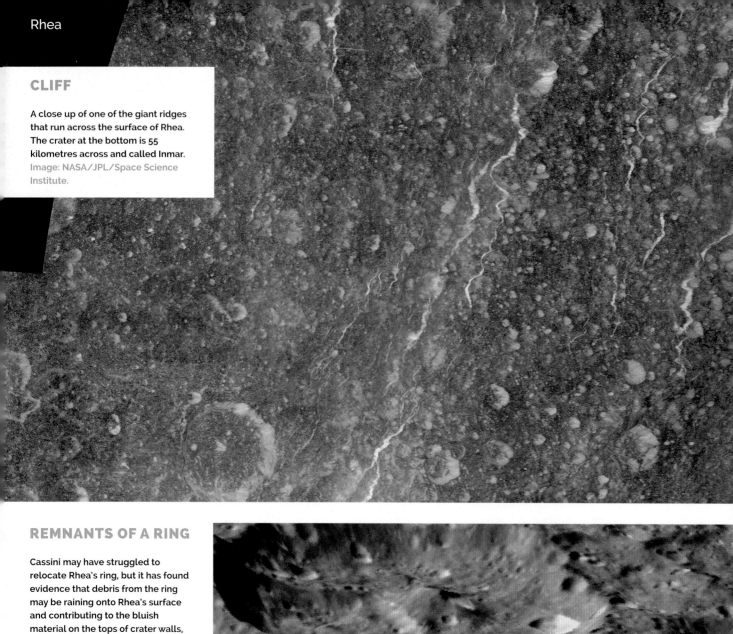

CLIFF

A close up of one of the giant ridges that run across the surface of Rhea. The crater at the bottom is 55 kilometres across and called Inmar.
Image: NASA/JPL/Space Science Institute.

REMNANTS OF A RING

Cassini may have struggled to relocate Rhea's ring, but it has found evidence that debris from the ring may be raining onto Rhea's surface and contributing to the bluish material on the tops of crater walls, forming a narrow band ten kilometres wide that encircles Rhea's equator.
Image: NASA/JPL/Space Science Institute/Universities Space Research Association/Lunar and Planetary Institute.

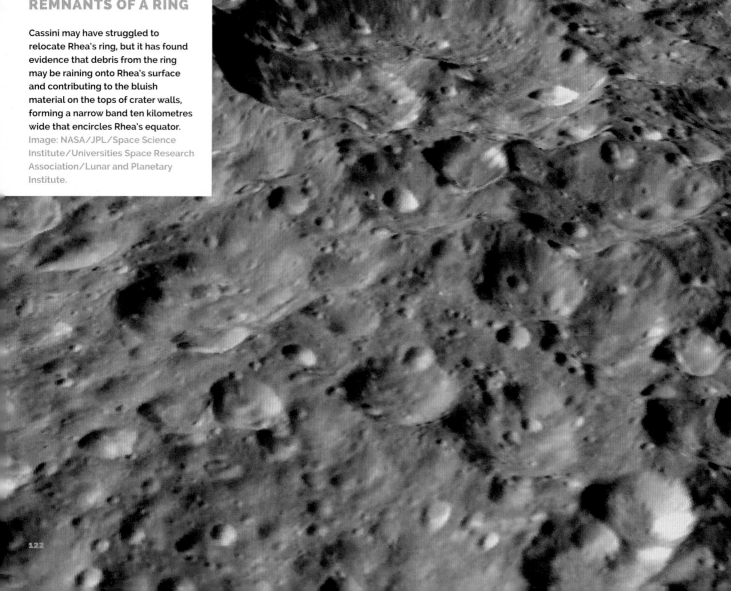

HEADING SOUTH

Cassini is looking straight down at Rhea's south polar region in this image. Rhea has two different types of terrain – an older terrain with more larger craters, and younger terrain, found in patches near the poles, which has fewer craters, especially large ones. Cassini took this image of Rhea on 12 April 2008. Image: NASA/JPL/ Space Science Institute.

BLACK STRIPE

Rhea passes in front of Saturn, the dark edge of the rings above and beyond it as seen on 17 July 2007. Image: NASA/JPL/Space Science Institute.

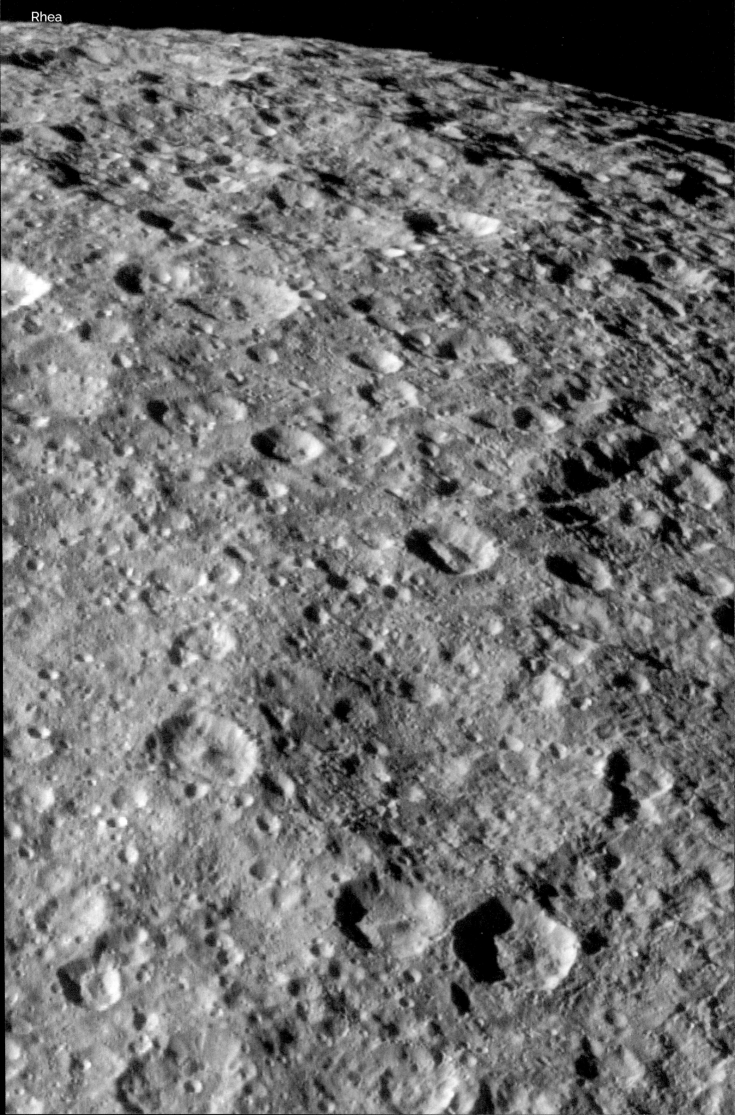
Rhea

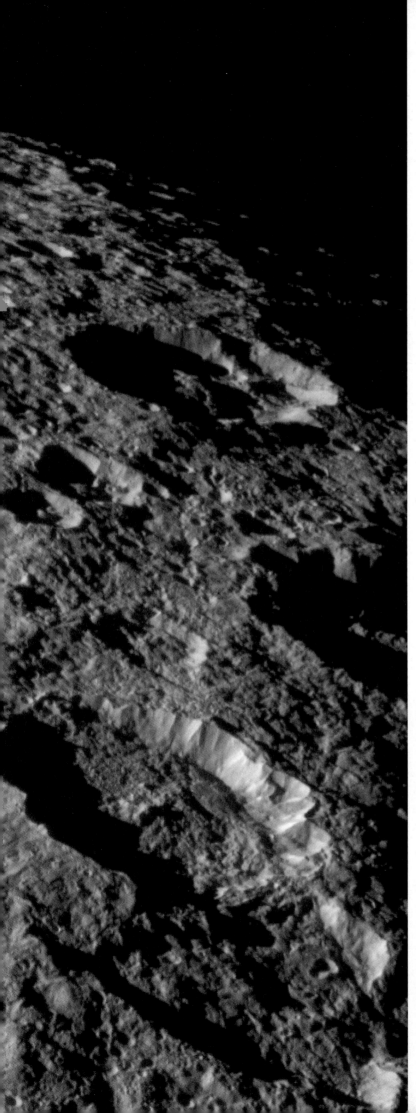

What's in a name?

Saturn's moons evoke the mythological memory of one of the oldest generations of Ancient Greek gods: the Titans. Among their number were Tethys, Phoebe, Atlas, Epimetheus, Prometheus, Hyperion, Iapetus and Rhea, who was an earth goddess. It was Rhea who gave birth to the Olympian gods including the mighty Zeus. Their father, the Titan Cronos, feared his offspring, driven by a prophecy that one of his sons would kill and usurp him. To avoid this fate Cronos would swallow each of his children, but when Zeus was born, Rhea smuggled him away. Once Zeus had grown to be an adult, he made his father throw up the children whom he had swallowed and alongside Zeus they became the Olympian gods. A war of the gods ignited, with the Olympians defeating Cronos and the Titans and casting them into the Underworld – all, that is, except for some of the Titans' other children, including Atlas, whom Zeus put to work holding up the sky on his shoulders, and Epimetheus and his brother Prometheus, who did a deal with Zeus. Like his father, Zeus feared one of his sons was plotting to usurp him. Prometheus knew who and ratted the perpetrator out in exchange for his own freedom.

LUNAR-LIKE LANDSCAPE

Rhea's craggy, cratered surface, as seen from a distance of 43,000 kilometres on 10 March 2012, looks reminiscent of the lunar landscape. Image: NASA/JPL–Caltech/Space Science Institute.

CLOAKED IN OXYGEN

Rhea is Saturn's second largest moon and is covered in an extremely thin oxygen atmosphere. Image: NASA/JPL/Space Science Institute.

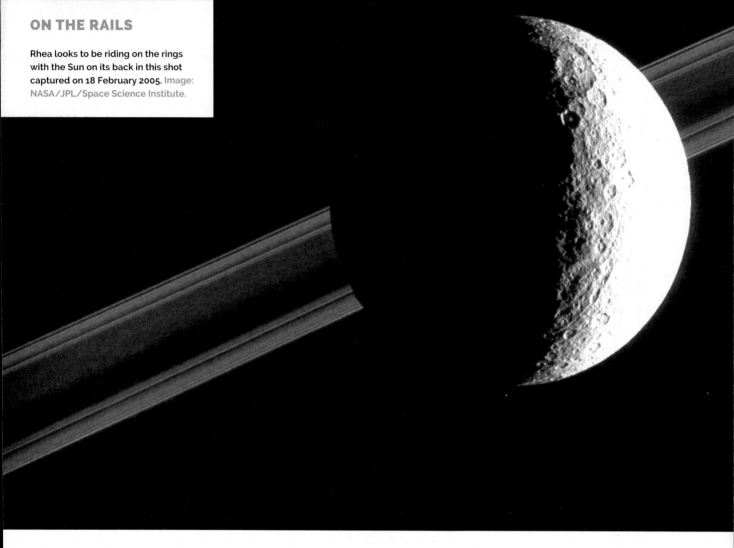

MISSING RING

An artist's impression of the hypothesised ring of rubble around Rhea, with the ringed planet in the background. However, evidence for at least one ring was only seen once, in the way something shielded Cassini from charged particles that swamp the Saturnian system. During every subsequent fly-by of Rhea, Cassini has been unable to detect the rings. Image: NASA/JPL/JHUAPL.

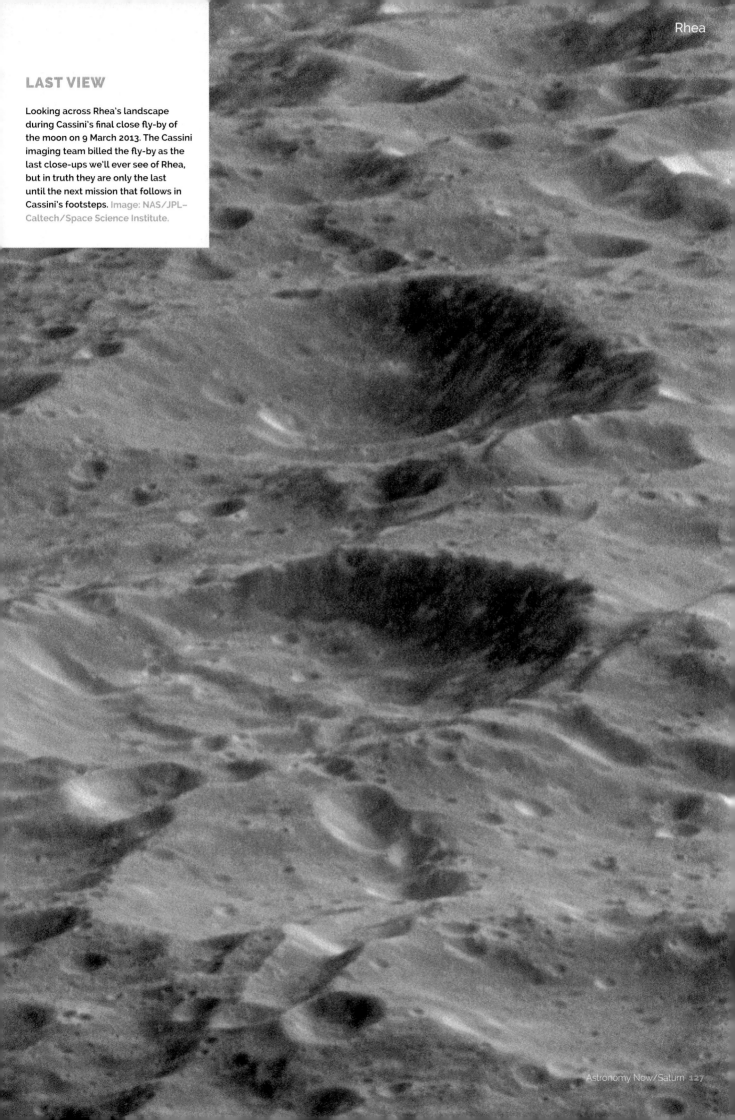

LAST VIEW

Looking across Rhea's landscape during Cassini's final close fly-by of the moon on 9 March 2013. The Cassini imaging team billed the fly-by as the last close-ups we'll ever see of Rhea, but in truth they are only the last until the next mission that follows in Cassini's footsteps. Image: NAS/JPL–Caltech/Space Science Institute.

The TITAN of

Alongside Jupiter's moon Europa and one of Saturn's other moons,
Enceladus, Titan is perhaps the most important moon in the Solar System.

It is the most enigmatic moon in the Solar System: hidden by a cloak of haze, Titan is the only moon known to have a significant atmosphere and liquid on its surface. The reason it can hang onto an atmosphere is its great size: at 5,152 kilometres across it is the second largest moon in the Solar System, just 116 kilometres smaller than Jupiter's moon Ganymede and both are larger than the planet Mercury. The primitive chemistry in its atmosphere, on its surface and in its seas could be the closest we know to conditions on the primordial Earth, before life began. Yet it is so cold on Titan, averaging around –179 degrees Celsius, that water is frozen as hard as stone and lakes and seas are filled with liquid petrochemicals instead.

Discovered by the Dutch astronomer Christiaan Huygens in 1655, his robotic namesake would venture to Titan riding on the back of the Cassini spacecraft and land on its bleak surface on 14 January 2005 in the most daring planetary touchdown ever attempted. Huygens landed on a world controlled by methane, but the presence of its methane-rich atmosphere was not known until it was confirmed spectroscopically from Earth by Gerard Kuiper in the 1940s. Maddeningly, chemical by-products of the breakdown of methane molecules by ultraviolet light from the Sun creates an opaque haze that acts to prevent efforts to view the moon's surface.

Knowing the chemistry of the atmosphere, speculation was rife as to what lay on the surface below. Was Titan covered in seas of black, oily liquid methane? Could there even be primitive life surviving off methane and hydrogen rather than water and oxygen? In the 1990s Earth-based radar hinted at the presence of a large 'continent', named Xanadu. Was Xanadu just a highland region, or a true island surrounded by sea?

It was only when Cassini–Huygens arrived in the Saturnian system in the summer of 2004 that answers began to be forthcoming. Cassini possessed instruments that could beat Titan's obscuring haze, while little Huygens would dare to go where no one – no thing – had gone before.

mystery

HALO

Titan, sporting a purple halo of light scattered from a detached layer of hydrocarbon particles in its stratosphere. This image was taken on 2 July 2004, just one day after Cassini's very first fly-by of the giant moon. Image: NASA/JPL/Space Science Institute.

Methane, methane, everywhere

Titan's chemistry, surface evolution and atmosphere is dominated by the methane cycle, replacing the familiar water cycle that we experience everyday on Earth.

HECK OF A VIEW

Giant Titan, which is the largest moon of Saturn, is utterly dwarfed by the ringed planet. Titan in turn dwarfs fellow moon Dione, seen next to it, while the rings of Saturn are caught edge on but their shadow cast against the planet. Titan and Dione may look like they are next to each other, but in reality they are 600,000 kilometres apart in this image. There is nowhere else in the known Universe where you can get views like this, which was captured by Cassini on 21 May 2011.
Image: NASA/JPL–Caltech/Space Science Institute.

When learning about Earth's water cycle at school, I was introduced to a cheery character in the textbook called Walter Droplet. In his own fictitious words, he would describe how he would fall from the sky as rain, hail, sleet or snow, percolate through the surface and find his way into the tributaries of rivers, running down towards the sea. Along the way, he and his fellow water droplets would sculpt the landscape through erosion before evaporating back into the atmosphere, where the cycle would begin again. On our planet water drives the weather, shapes the land and even allows life to flourish. It is essential to our environment. On Titan there is a cycle similar to Earth's water cycle, but Titan's is drastically more alien. On this frigid moon of Saturn, where surface temperatures plummet to −179 degrees Celsius and it is so cold that water–ice forms the bedrock, it is not a water cycle, but a methane cycle that drives the weather, erodes the landscape and shapes both the surface and the atmosphere.

Enveloping shroud
A concoction of predominantly nitrogen, with some methane and nitriles (molecules containing hydrogen, nitrogen and carbon), Titan's atmosphere is a misty yellow–orange. It looks like a cloudy world – after all you can't see down to the surface. There are actually few distinct clouds. Rather, it is a thick, noxious haze that obscures our view of Titan.

Both the haze and the methane cycle begin in the upper atmosphere. Up here, methane and nitrogen molecules come into contact with ultraviolet light from the distant Sun. This ultraviolet is energetic enough to break the molecules apart into lots of little molecular chunks that begin to drift downwards through the atmosphere, descending one to two millimetres per second.

"Methane is very effective in absorbing solar ultraviolet radiation and that breaks up the methane," says Ingo Mueller-Wodarg, an atmospheric scientist from Imperial College, London. "It is what drives the entire chemistry of Titan."

Many of the by-products of methane are called Polycyclic Aromatic Hydrocarbons (PAHs for short), which are able to bond into larger molecules on their way down down towards the surface. Methane is what is known as a hydrocarbon – a molecule made of carbon and hydrogen atoms, just like natural gas on Earth – and the PAHs recombine into more complex hydrocarbons

LAYER CAKE

All the haze in Titan's atmosphere produces as many as a dozen layers climbing several hundred kilometres above the frigid surface. This is a false-colour ultraviolet image taken by Cassini as the spacecraft looked back on the night-side of Titan with only a thin crescent at the limb of the moon illuminated by sunlight. Image: NASA/JPL/Space Science Institute.

A THICK, NOXIOUS HAZE OBSCURES OUR VIEW OF TITAN

such as ethane, propane, benzene, ethylene, cyanogens, hydrogen cyanide and so on. This fog of tiny hydrocarbon particles contributes to the smoggy haze that cloaks the surface and produces a purplish crown that adorns Titan as the largest moon of Saturn. The crown is a halo in the upper reaches of the atmosphere, produced by sunlight scattered off layers of haze.

The percolation of the various hydrocarbon compounds through the haze leads to them raining or even snowing out onto the surface. Just like on Earth, precipitation plays a major role in Titan's environment. It is astounding to think that there is another body in the Solar System where it rains, although Titan's rain is a far cry from the rain we are used to.

Despite its unhealthy (to Earth life, at least) constituents, Titan's atmosphere does have some striking similarities with that of our own planet. During its descent through the atmosphere, the European Space Agency's Huygens probe encountered regions similar to Earth's troposphere and stratosphere. The stratosphere on Earth is a region of increasing temperature with altitude, caused

by the ozone layer absorbing the Sun's radiation. There is no ozone on Titan, but all those tiny little aerosols are extremely efficient in absorbing sunlight and consequently they heat the atmosphere around them.

On the other hand, the lower atmosphere is much more sluggish. "It takes years for it to respond to any change in heating," says Mueller-Wodarg. "If the Sun stopped shining, Titan's lower atmosphere wouldn't react for a few years. Therefore you don't have any diurnal (day/night) changes [in temperature] like we do on Earth. What you do have is changes between hemispheres that have time to build up a seasonal temperature difference, enough to generate strong winds and turbulence."

Cloud appreciation

While the foul fumes that hang above many of Earth's big cities cannot hold a candle to Titan's smog, actual distinct clouds on Titan are rare beasts valued by the scientists. Not only do clouds play a large part in the methane cycle, producing the precipitation that runs-off into rivers and lakes, they are also the signal of switching seasons.

When Cassini arrived in the Saturnian system in 2004 and made the first of more than a hundred visits to Titan, it found that clouds were clustered in two main locations. The first was at latitude –40 degrees south where, all of a sudden, localised clouds would materialise. What's more, there appeared to be a chain of cloud-forming regions at this latitude, with methane clouds roiling in the atmosphere, climbing to a height of 40 kilometres in just a few hours before dissipating in a fraction of that time as a shower of methane rain. The gale-force winds at this altitude would drive the clouds westwards, creating huge cloudy tails stretching up to 1,000 kilometres in length. Beyond this line of latitude and moving farther south, a vast region of toxic smog capped Titan's south pole. This smog and the clouds at 40 degrees south are linked.

A WINDOW INTO TITAN

Titan's atmosphere becomes increasingly transparent the further Cassini delves into infrared wavelengths. On the left is a true colour image – this is what Titan would look like if you flew to Saturn in a spacecraft. You will notice that you cannot see any of the surface or indeed any details in the atmosphere – it is all just a featureless orange smog. The image on the right is more revealing. It was taken at the near-infrared wavelength of 0.94 microns, at which light can pass unhindered through the haze and reveals details of Titan's surface terrain, with the light and dark areas representing regions with materials of different reflectivity. North on Titan in this image is up and tilted 30 degrees to the right. Image: NASA/JPL/Space Science Institute.

The global circulation of Titan's atmosphere is the result of a giant Hadley cell. Atmospheric gas rises on convection currents in the southern hemisphere and moves into the opposite winter hemisphere, where it sinks through a large vortex at the winter pole, before being redistributed as part of a continuous cycle. Rising air at −40 degrees south was forming clouds and cutting off atmospheric circulation to the south polar region, causing smog to build up there. Meanwhile, Cassini saw a second and rather different set of clouds building up over Titan's north pole. Cassini's visual and infrared mapping spectrometer (VIMS) picked up the signal of a massive cloud of ethane, methane's by-product, which was actually snowing onto the north pole; large flakes of ethane would fall to the ground in a slow-moving blizzard under the pull of the low Titanian gravity (which is seven times weaker than Earth's gravitational force). VIMS detected the ethane cloud as a bright band between heights of 30 and 60 kilometres, between latitudes of 51 degrees north and 69 degrees north – Titan's arctic circle. For the first five years of Cassini's exploration of Titan, its north pole (like Saturn's) was in the grip of winter, where it was cold enough for the ethane to snow, rather than rain, out of the clouds. The chill of winter, however, meant that the north pole with its towering ethane cloud was not a particularly active place.

After the equinox, which was enjoyed by all Saturn's moons as well as the planet itself, things began to change on Titan. Winter departed from the north and plunged southwards. Three years after the equinox, Cassini observed the formation of a high-altitude haze and a swirling vortex at the south pole as the circulation on the moon reversed itself. Found above the vortex is a toxic cloud of frozen hydrogen cyanide. Six months after the equinox the upper atmosphere, 500 kilometres above the surface, responded to the change in seasons by heating up as gases began to sink and compress into the stratosphere. However, hydrogen cyanide gas freezes at −148 degrees Celsius, implying that the stratosphere had since cooled much faster than anyone had expected. This was backed up by observations of the temperature of the atmosphere with Cassini's Composite Infrared Spectrometer (CIRS).

Meanwhile the north was on the verge of a balmy summer. Before Huygens landed on Titan, planetary scientists speculated that large seas made from black, oily liquid hydrocarbons could cover vast swathes of the surface. This turned out not to be entirely correct – most of the surface is dry, but there are numerous lakes and rivers with tributaries branching off from them that look eerily like Earth's rivers, lakes and small seas. The majority of these lakes are located in Titan's northern

TECTONIC TITAN

Every time Cassini makes a fly-by of Titan, such as it did on 9 and 25 October 2006 when the individual images in this composite were taken, the spacecraft is provided with the opportunity to peer through the haze with the infrared eyes of the Visual and Infrared Mapping Spectrometer (VIMS) and see surface details. In the centre is a roughly circular feature – possibly an old impact crater. To its south are mountain ranges that may have been uplifted by tectonic forces that followed the violent impact. Image: NASA/ JPL/University of Arizona.

REFLECTIONS ON TITAN

So far from home, it is reassuring to see something so familiar: the glint of the Sun reflecting from a body of liquid partly hidden by clouds. This is not Earth, however, but Titan. On the odd occasions that the haze thins, sunlight reflects brightly off the lakes' dark waves.

The reflection seen here is from the giant Kraken Mare, which is seen emerging from the darkness of the terminator. The illumination angle of the Sun relative to the lake is 40 degrees. Kraken Mare is the largest of the seas on Titan and dominates the moon's northern hemisphere. With the end of Cassini's mission now in sight in 2017, the spacecraft's remaining fly-bys of Titan are limited; August 2014, when this image was snapped, was the final fly-by during which it would be able to see Kraken Mare.

With summer comes a change in weather patterns. Scientists were surprised by the slow onset of the cloudy weather that had been expected, but around the same time that this image was taken, clouds were seen beginning to gather. Indeed, the bright semi-circular object just above centre in the image is the infrared signature of a methane cloud, while the coastline of Kraken Mare also shines brightly, indicating that the ground there was previously wet, but that, as spring turns to summer, evaporation takes hold and leaves deposits behind, as one would find on salt flats on Earth. Image: NASA/JPL–Caltech/University of Arizona/University of Idaho/Greg Smye-Rumsby.

hemisphere and in July 2014 clouds were observed forming over Ligeia Mare, which is the second largest lake on Titan. These clouds, as they grow and evolve, ultimately result in precipitation, resupplying the lakes with fresh liquid. During its descent through the lower atmosphere, Huygens passed through a low-lying layer of methane cloud and took measurements of a persistent drizzle of methane rain. The precipitation is so fine and misty that the annual rainfall from this drizzle amounts to only 50 millimetres, but it is enough to keep the top-surface constantly damp. The main rain showers are thought to come in storms during summer – the clouds forming over Ligeia Mare were the first seen above the planet in four years since the previous southern storm wiped the atmosphere clear. The onset of cloud formation in the north is predicted to be a precursor to a new summer storm season.

Land of lakes

A large leap forward towards cracking the puzzle behind the mechanisms of the methane cycle is understanding the lakes. That they seem to cluster in the north more than the south is one of their many mysteries, although infrared maps of the northern surface show that the terrain there is somewhat different to the rest of the planet. The northern lakes tend to all have similar shapes with rounded edges and steep sides. This might mean they pool in regions where the landscape has collapsed following the eruption of a 'cryovolcano' that spews out ice instead of molten lava. Or perhaps the lakes create their own beds by dissolving soluble rock, which here on

The dune seas

Cassini has identified numerous equatorial and southern lowland regions on Titan, given names such as Shangri-La, Belet, Fensal, Aztlan and Senkyo. These lowlands are filled with endless rows of dunes, running from west to east. In total they cover 13 percent of Titan's surface, equating to more than ten million square kilometres. The dunes have been seen in the highlands too, but there they tend to be more widely separated. Rows of dunes can be a couple of kilometres wide and as much as 100 metres high. Although they look eerily like sand dunes in the Sahara Desert, Titan's dunes are another example of how the moon shares a phenomenon seen on Earth, but puts it at a metaphorical 'right angle'. In this case, Titan's dunes are not made of sand, but ice crystals instead, which makes sense when you consider how cold Titan is and the role that water-ice takes as the equivalent of bedrock on Earth.

The dunes have been a source of mystery for much of Cassini's mission, but now that mystery has been solved. The problem was that although the dunes point eastwards, the prevailing winds near the surface should be blowing westwards with the planet's rotation. The answer is found higher in the atmosphere where raging methane storms blow eastwards around the time of equinox. Occasional downdrafts blowing at ten metres per second can overcome the weaker westerly winds near the surface and pick up ice crystals. The surface westerlies, on the other hand cannot sculpt the dunes because they do not blow over the critical wind speed of 1.4 metres per second needed to start rearranging the grains. As the easterly downdrafts occur only at equinox, the tunes will be left relatively untouched for at least 15 years until the next equinox.

DUNES ON TITAN AND EARTH

A comparison between ice crystal dunes on Titan, in the lowland dune seas of Belet and Fensal, and similar dunes on Earth, in Oman and the Kalahari Desert. The differences in the dunes' appearances on Titan are a result of latitude and elevation. Fensal is north of the equator, in what tends to be the wettest hemisphere, and that makes it more difficult to build dry dunes. Hence Fensal's dunes appear more widely separated and smaller. In the radar images from Titan, the dunes appear as dark streaks. The spacing between the dune rows is apparent in the lightness or darkness of the images – Belet's dunes are spaced much more closely and hence the image appears darker.

Image: NASA/JPL–Caltech/GSFC/METI/ERSDAC/ JAROS/USA–Japan ASTER Science Team.

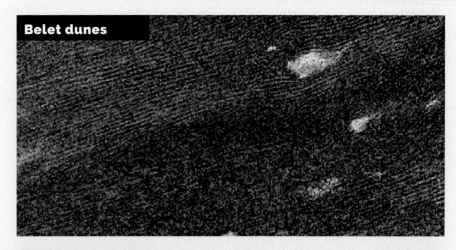

Belet dunes

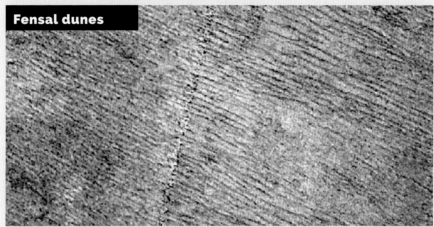

Fensal dunes

Oman dunes

Kalahari dunes

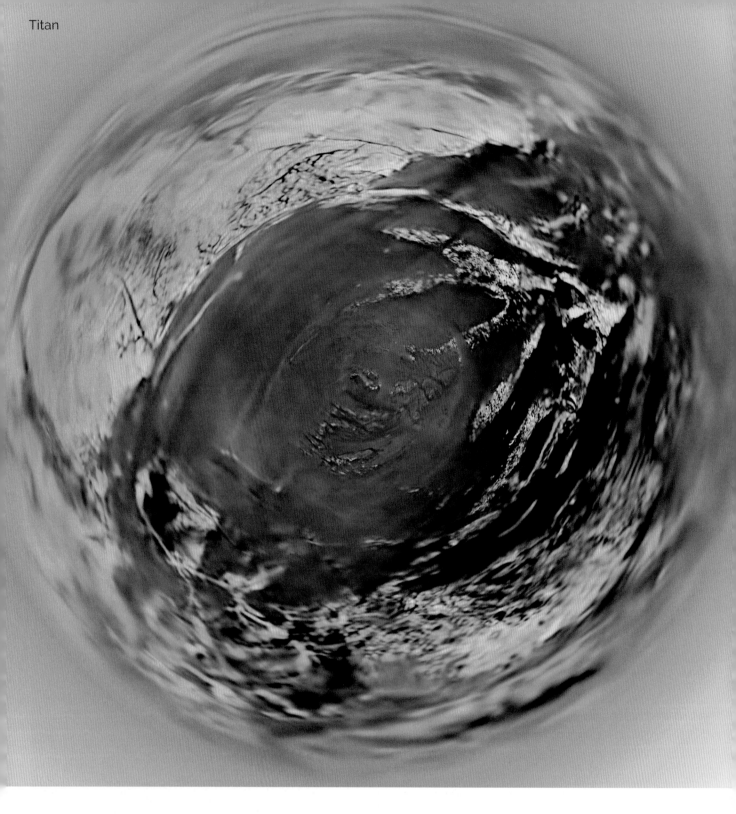

THE VIEW FROM ABOVE

While still dangling underneath its parachute five kilometres above the surface, the European Space Agency's Huygens probe captured this fish-eye view of Titan's surface. It shows hills with the dark tributaries of rivers and a large floodplain below that may have been drenched in liquid only a decade or so before Huygens' arrival. Image: ESA/NASA/JPL/University of Arizona.

THE PRECIPITATION IS SO FINE AND MISTY THAT THE ANNUAL HYDROCARBON RAINFALL AMOUNTS TO ONLY 50 MILLIMETRES

Earth we call 'karst' terrain. Either way, the lakes are not terribly deep. Radar sounding by Cassini has found that Ligeia Mare is 170 metres deep, while the largest lake, Kraken Mare, is deeper than 200 metres (Cassini's radar sounding does not function at depths greater than 200 metres). Ontario Lacus, the largest of the sparse southern lakes, is between 20 and 40 metres deep.

The lakes are a great way of keeping track of the climate on Titan. In recent years radar returns and infrared observations have shown strange features on the surface of the two largest lakes, Kraken Mare and Ligeia Mare. Planetary scientists have nicknamed them 'magic islands'. The exact nature of these features remains a mystery, but there are a couple of good possibilities. One is that they are bubbles caused by methane gas

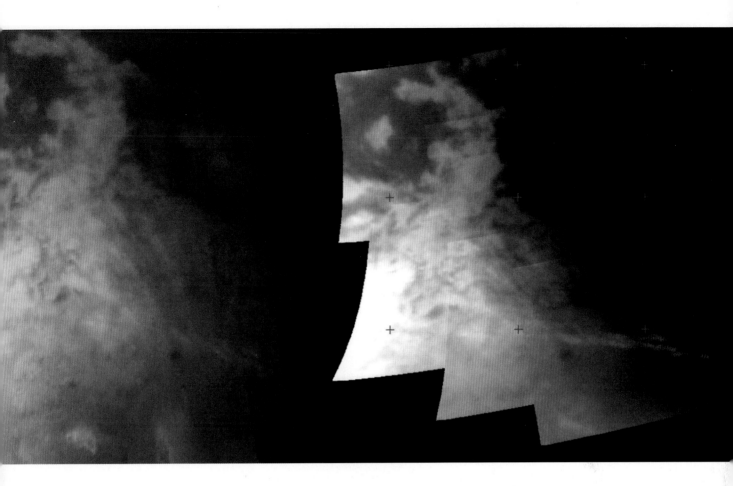

MOUNTAINS ON A MOON

Two views of mountain ranges that span large areas across Titan and tower above the surface at heights peaking at 1.5 kilometres. At the bottom of the image on the right is a band of blue cloud caused when methane in the atmosphere cools, descends and condense into fog before being driven over the mountains by the wind. Image: NASA/ JPL/University of Arizona.

rising up to the surface as ice melts on the lake bed. Another explanation is that they could be waves blown by winds growing stronger as the summer stormy season approaches. The third intriguing idea is that they are methane-icebergs, but for these to exist the temperature needs to be just right. Methane-ice is denser than liquid methane so normally it would sink, but summer temperatures might see the ice break away from the lake bed and bobble up to the surface. Cassini's Visible and Infrared Mapping Spectrometer has detected the magic islands at a specific infrared wavelength of five microns (millionths of a metre), which is what would be expected from specular reflection off a wet surface, or from waves. This would seem to rule out bubbles, but we may never know whether icebergs float on Titan's great lakes until we send a probe to sail on them.

The great lakes on Earth, such as Lake Superior or Lake Windermere, do not go through periods of drying up. That is because they are replenished through rainfall, if not directly onto the lakes themselves, then running off into rivers or seeping underground to make its way to the lakes. On Titan, however, there is a problem. The rainfall rate is not nearly high enough to keep the lakes stocked up and during summer they begin to evaporate. For the lakes not to dry up completely they must therefore be replenished, but the question is, from where?

There is a bigger problem lurking behind the scenes. A true methane cycle would see methane precipitate out of the atmosphere, pool onto the surface and then evaporate back into the atmosphere only to rain out again and so on, continuing the cycle. The trouble is, once in the atmosphere, not only is methane broken apart, but so is the cycle. Clearly it is not a closed cycle – there must be an input of methane from somewhere.

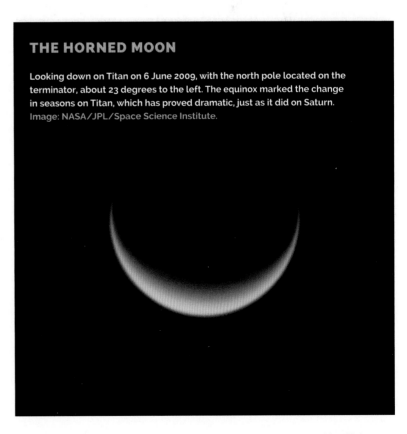

THE HORNED MOON

Looking down on Titan on 6 June 2009, with the north pole located on the terminator, about 23 degrees to the left. The equinox marked the change in seasons on Titan, which has proved dramatic, just as it did on Saturn. Image: NASA/JPL/Space Science Institute.

THE ONSET OF CLOUD FORMATION IN THE NORTH IS PREDICTED TO BE A PRECURSOR TO A NEW SUMMER STORM SEASON

The origin of Titan's methane

Once upon a time, Cassini scientists thought a dark feature on Titan's surface called Ganesa Macula was a volcanic dome that had spewed out a 'lava' of water-ice and ammonia that had formed pancake-shaped sediments around it. After closer examination, it turned out the Ganesa Macula was not dome-shaped at all. Regardless, scientists still expect that there are, or at least have been, 'cryovolcanoes' on Titan and that their icy explosions are the principal way that methane is brought to the surface from deep within, replenishing the stores of methane above ground.

Beneath the surface, floating in a briny liquid water ocean containing a healthy mix of ammonia that acts as an anti-freeze, are high-pressure pockets of water–ice called clathrates, inside which methane hides in gaps between the water molecules. As pressure forces the clathrates to rise to the surface, like magma beneath a volcano on Earth, they blast out through cryovolcanoes.

The clathrate structure is broken down, with ice floes covering the surface while the methane is released into the atmosphere.

At least that is one theory, but the origin of Titan's methane runs deeper than a few cryovolcanoes. Indeed, the consensus is that Titan has lived through three major methane releases over its history and that we are seeing the latter stages of the third release, which began 500 million years ago. The first release occurred just after Titan had formed, when heat from its genesis, plus heat from radioactive elements inside its rocky core, provided the energy for methane to be exhaled by the moon during Titan's first few hundred million years of existence. It is thought that the entirety of Titan's thick atmosphere resulted from this outgassing. The second methane event happened two billion years ago. The aforementioned heat from radioactive elements in the core had, by this time, softened Titan's rocky core enough for it to churn up as the moon rotated and release heat. This convective burst of heat sparked another round of outgassing.

The first two events could quite possibly have released enough methane for there to have been large oceans on the surface, as opposed to today's modest

GULLYWASHER IN THE VOLCANIC ARC

The aftermath of a ferocious rainstorm of methane droplets on the ground at Hotei Arcus, as depicted by the space artist Michael Carroll. Seeing the results of such rainstorms from orbit, using only infrared and radar vision, is difficult, but the vision of artists and scientists can bring it into focus. Hotei Arcus is an arc-shaped region that curves between a jagged mountain range and a broad plain. Brightness changes have been observed in Hotei Arcus, leading some scientists to suspect that it could be an area of cryovolcanism. This point of view is backed up by the presence of flow deposits between 100 and 200 metres thick, which could by frozen ice-lava that has vented from a volcano. However, the brightness changes could also be attributed to ammonia frosts that regularly appear before evaporating. From the mountains run gullies, carved out by methane rain and, in Michael Carroll's artwork, the hydrocarbon rain has washed out the gullies.
Image: NASA/JPL.

THE TITAN'S FOOTPRINT

The Greek titans after which Titan is named (among the titans were Rhea, Tethys, Phoebe, Hyperion, Iapetus, Atlas, Prometheus and Epimetheus, all of which give their names to moons of Saturn) were divine deities that walked like giants amongst mortal men. Fitting then that the largest lake in Titan's southern hemisphere, Ontario Lacus, should look like a giant's footprint. This image was built up from radar echoes. Bright areas are regions that reflect the radar strongly, meaning they are either sloped towards Cassini when it was beaming its radar at the surface, or they have rough, jumbled surfaces that can scatter radar. Black regions are smooth areas that can absorb radar, such as a hydrocarbon lake. You can clearly see the shoreline of Ontario Lacus in this image, with rounded bays and eroded outcroppings. Image: NASA/JPL–Caltech/ASI.

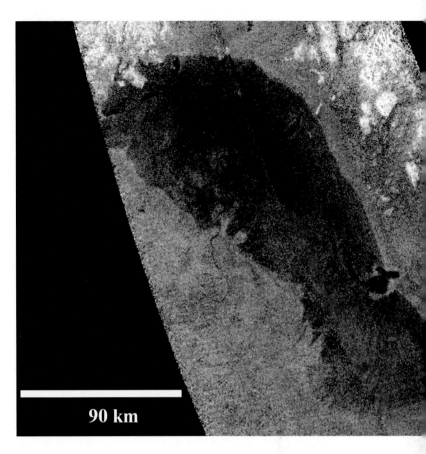

90 km

lakes. The third release, of which we are currently seeing the tail end, has supplied enough methane to enrich the atmosphere but not to create large seas. This third methane burst has been caused by the cooling, rather than heating, of Titan's interior. The cooling caused the underground ammonia–water ocean to crystallise, which has upset the thermal balance of the ocean, leading to widespread temperature variations that create the energy for the current outburst. It is expected that after the current outgassing has ceased, there will be no more until the deep future, when the ageing Sun grows more luminous near the end of its life and heats Titan sufficiently for outgassing to resume. We seem quite fortunate to be witnessing outgassing now because, once it has stopped, the atmospheric methane will disappear along with the rainfall, lakes and exotic carbon chemistry.

THE DEATH STAR HAS CLEARED THE PLANET

Looming over the shoulder of Titan like the malevolent Death Star from *Star Wars* is Titan's fellow moon Tethys with its large crater Odysseus. In this image Tethys was 1.2 million kilometres beyond Titan. Tethys actually passed behind Titan in what astronomers term an occultation, before reappearing on the opposite limb. Titan, at 5,150 kilometres across, is about five times bigger than 1,062-kilometre wide Tethys. Image: NASA/JPL/Space Science Institute.

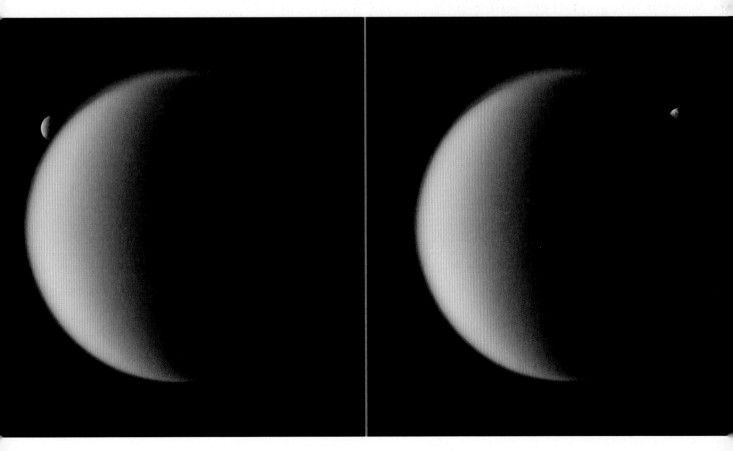

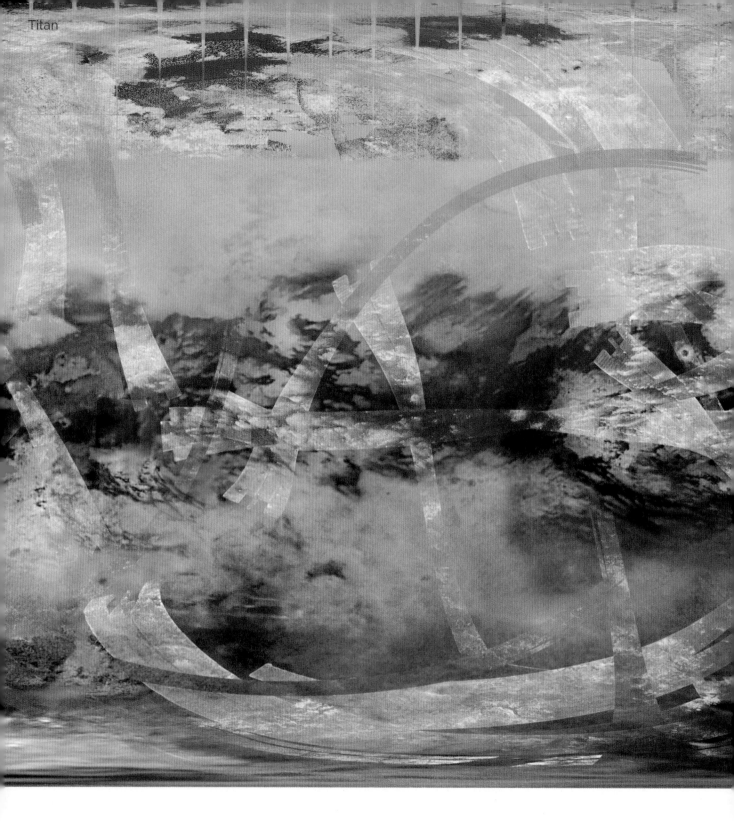

Titan

A MAP OF TITAN

A composite map of Titan incorporating infrared and radar data. Image: NASA/JPL/Greg Smye-Rumsby.

MAGIC ISLANDS

A sequence of radar images showing anomalous changes off the coastline of Ligeia Mare between different Cassini fly-bys of Titan in 2013 and 2014. In the radar images the dark area is the lake and the bright areas the jagged coastline. Something appeared off the tip of the coast in July 2013, only to have disappeared in October 2013 but then reappeared in August 2014. The unexplained feature is 160 square kilometres in size and is suspected to be either a particularly wavy region of the lake, or a methane iceberg. Image: NASA/JPL–Caltech/ASI/Cornell.

Titan

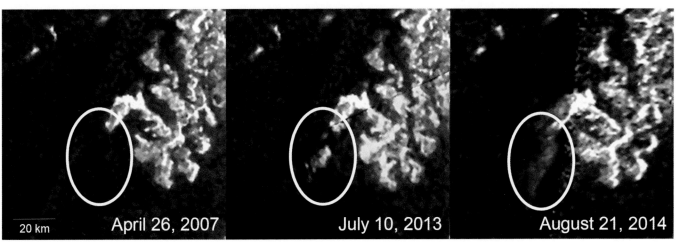

20 km
April 26, 2007
July 10, 2013
August 21, 2014

Interview:

Ingo Mueller-Wodarg

Three years after Cassini arrived in orbit around Saturn, *Astronomy Now* caught up with Ingo Mueller-Wodarg of Imperial College, London, who specialises in studying planetary atmospheres and is also a member of the science team for Cassini's Ion Neutral Mass Spectrometer. We asked him about his thoughts regarding Titan's atmosphere.

Why is Titan's atmosphere so thick?

That is a very good question and I wish I had the answer. I'm not sure anybody knows the answer to that. You can say that the more massive the body the more likely it is to have an atmosphere. Secondly, it is a function of what gases are available. Where does the gas come from? Was it there when the moon formed? In that case gravity might have been strong enough to keep it there. Or, was it just a piece of rock without an atmosphere and the atmosphere gradually outgassed from the inside? Those are two possible scenarios of how you get an atmosphere. Either the gas was there from the primordial material – and certainly the gas giants are a fine example of that, the hydrogen and helium that you find on Jupiter and Saturn was there when the Solar System formed – or like the Earth's atmosphere and [that of] the other terrestrial planets, and probably Titan as well I suspect, [the gas] came from inside, outgassing. Once you have an atmosphere then you need to be able to hold on to it. Gravity is one thing, but you'd think Ganymede, which is the largest moon in the Solar System, would also have an atmosphere. The problem with Ganymede is that it is probably too close to Jupiter. So you have a double-effect: a) that Jupiter's gravity is disturbing it, which may have stripped it of its atmosphere, and b) the magnetosphere of Jupiter may have contributed to it being stripped away. On Titan there seem to be ideal conditions where it is just massive enough to retain the atmosphere and cold enough so that the gas doesn't escape thermally. Plus, although it is being stripped by Saturn's magnetosphere, the rate at which it loses material to the magnetosphere is low enough for the atmosphere to still be around. So I think it is a combination of things.

Has Titan met your expectations?

It has certainly not been a disappointment. My speciality is the upper atmosphere and there we have found a lot of surprises. It was very different from what we expected and we still don't understand everything that is going on. I am working with the Ion and Neutral Mass Spectrometer Team,

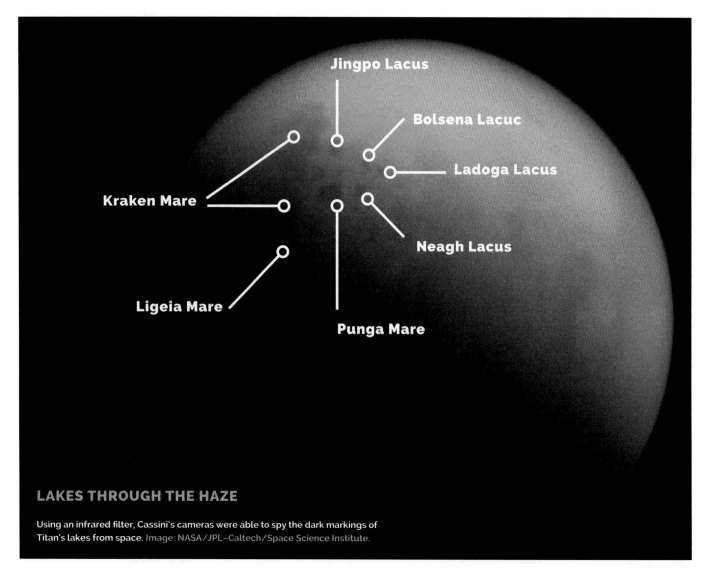

Jingpo Lacus

Bolsena Lacuc

Ladoga Lacus

Kraken Mare

Neagh Lacus

Ligeia Mare

Punga Mare

LAKES THROUGH THE HAZE

Using an infrared filter, Cassini's cameras were able to spy the dark markings of Titan's lakes from space. Image: NASA/JPL–Caltech/Space Science Institute.

which takes gas samples from Titan's upper atmosphere during every orbit in which Cassini flies close to Titan. So from that we found a lot of surprises. For example we found very heavy hydrocarbons in the upper atmosphere, above 1,000 kilometres, and that we did not expect at all. Being so heavy we would have expected them to be lower down in the atmosphere, but we found them all the way up to 1,400 kilometres, which is really high up. That suggests that either there is a lot of mixing going on that transports them up from below, or we don't quite understand the chemistry yet. We don't understand the horizontal structure [of pressures and temperatures] and global circulation of the winds, at least in the upper atmosphere. I've been working on theoretical models to predict what they would be like and when we actually looked at the data compared to the model there are some similarities but overall it is very, very different and that suggests that it is not as easy as the Sun doing the whole job, heating the dayside and building up the winds to transport the gases around. It is much more complicated than this.

Another surprise were atmospheric waves that Huygens detected. Huygens had this wonderful suite of instruments, HASI, the atmospheric structure instrument, and it measured densities from the top of the atmosphere all the way down to the surface. If you look at those profiles, they derived temperatures from those and those temperatures are full of little waves and wiggles and so on.

Does studying Titan's atmosphere help us understand our own atmosphere in any way?

I would think so, definitely. Some parallels have been drawn between Titan and primordial Earth. We have a nitrogen atmosphere and a very similar structure and so on. I think we can learn about how the Earth's atmosphere may have started off, we get to learn a lot about the very complicated chemistry that happens on Titan but which doesn't really occur here on Earth. I think it is basically just looking at another body under different conditions and of a different size and a different distance from the Sun, but once you understand a body like that, the better you understand the basic physical laws that also apply to Earth. I'm a theoretician, I build models and to start with we use these models as Earth atmosphere models. We then export them to Titan and that completely challenges that we've known so far, but it isn't so easy [on Titan], it is usually much more complicated. Then you begin to appreciate what actually is different about Earth. So you don't just learn facts about Titan that you can apply to Earth, but rather it is about appreciating Earth in its uniqueness, why the Earth is the way it is. You can only appreciate that if you look at another body that is kind of similar, but not quite. I think that just appreciating things by looking at another planet is very, very important. The same applies to looking at Venus, for example; you can look at any other planet and always seem to learn something about Earth. I mean, on Titan you have interesting cloud formation processes that may be important for Earth as well. The Cassini spacecraft now measures things on Titan that have never been measured on Earth, so actually we have better instruments looking at Titan than we have looking at Earth!

LAKE SUPERIOR'S SUPERIOR

The craggy shape of Ligeia Mare, the second largest hydrocarbon lake on Titan, presented here in a false-colour RADAR image. The lake, which has a surface area of 126,000 square kilometres, is bigger than Lake Superior and appears to contain several islands, while river channels feeding the lake can be seen towards the bottom and top. The coastline sports two main types of terrain: eroded and hummocky 'crenulated' terrain and 'subdued' terrain with smooth slopes and long channels. Image: NASA/ JPL–Caltech/ASI/ Cornell.

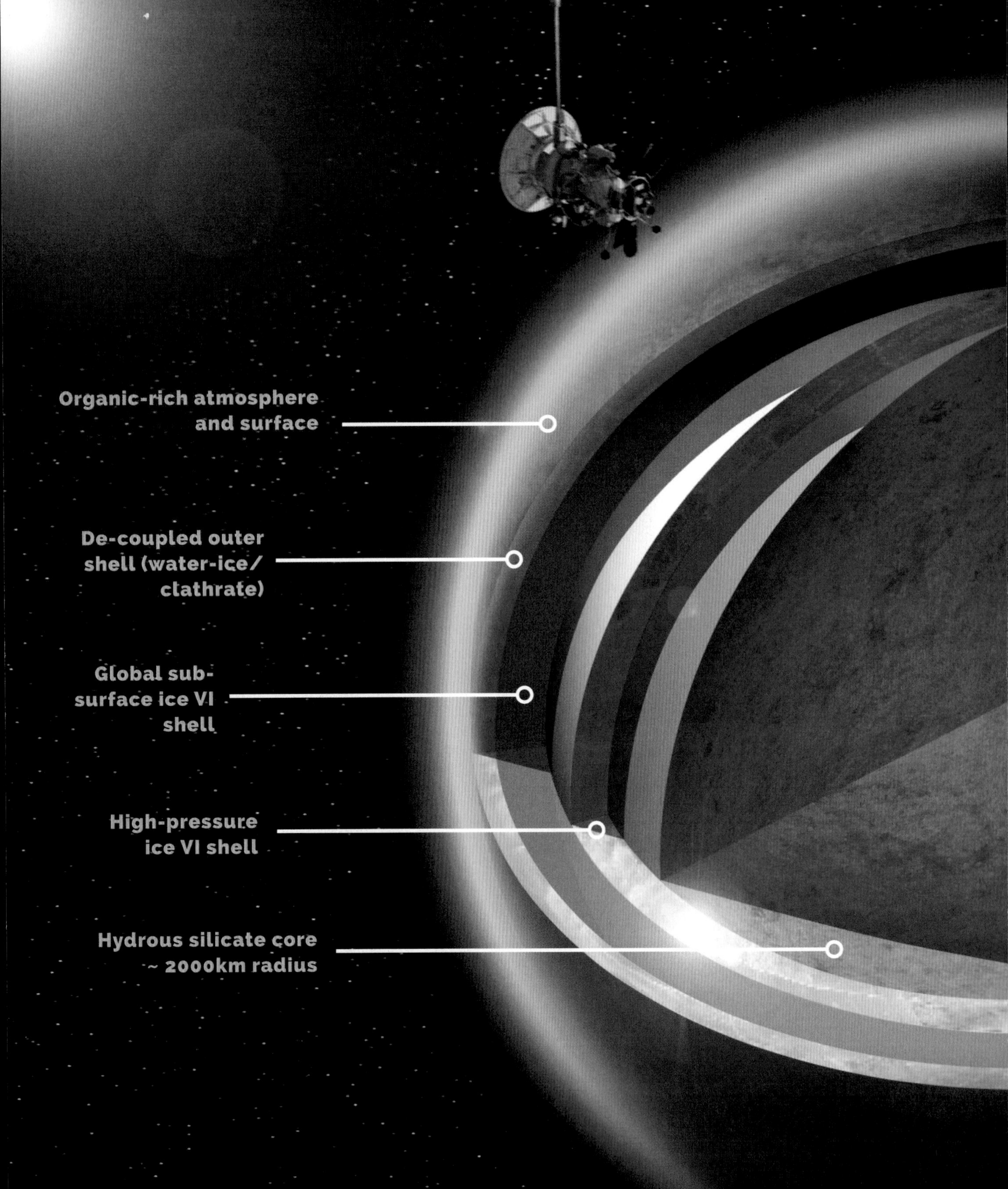

Titan

Organic-rich atmosphere
and surface

De-coupled outer
shell (water-ice/
clathrate)

Global sub-
surface ice VI
shell

High-pressure
ice VI shell

Hydrous silicate core
~ 2000km radius

Titan's underground ocean

Like many other icy moons, such as Europa and Ganymede around Jupiter, Titan probably has a vast global ocean of water buried deep beneath its icy crust. Although Titan's surface is far too cold to support liquid water, Titan's core is kneaded by Saturn's gravity and this generates heat. Titan orbits Saturn in an elliptical orbit, which means that sometimes it is close to the planet and feels Saturn's gravity more strongly and at other times is further from Saturn and feels its gravity less. This results in Titan's interior being stretched and squeezed as it orbits Saturn, heating it up to the point that water – with a dose of anti-freeze in the form of ammonia – can exist underground at an undetermined depth. The ocean is thought to be vast: a global layer of water beneath the clathrate shell and above a layer of exotic ice called ice X, which is able to exist in high temperatures because of the intense pressure that it is under. Ice X exists because of the versatility of the hydrogen bonds that connect the hydrogen and oxygen atoms in the crystalline lattice of a water molecule. There are 16 different ways in which these bonds can arrange the atoms, with ice X being the tenth variation, and some of these variations are able to withstand a lot of pressure – ice X forms at pressures 600,000 times Earth's surface pressure.

Back to the ocean, though, and we can see telltale signs of its presence in Titan's shape. All this squeezing and stretching of Titan causes solid tides, or a bulge, in Titan's surface pointed towards Saturn. If Titan were solid all the way through to the core, the bulge would only be a metre high as the solid rock and ice would be too stiff to stretch too much. Titan's bulge, however, is ten metres high, indicating a more flexible interior such as a water ocean.

More evidence for the ocean is in the seemingly paradoxical measurements by Cassini of Titan's gravity field. Normally when flying over mountains one would expect slightly more gravity, yet when Cassini flies above Titan's mountain ranges, the pull of gravity decreases, almost as though there should be a void rather than a massive lump of solid ice. This can be explained if the mountains are literally just the tip of the iceberg, with huge roots that stretch right into the underground ocean and are lodged in huge icebergs that act as effective counterweights, pressed up against the ocean's ceiling by buoyancy factors.

A third factor is the rotation of the Titan's surface. Features appear to have moved relative to the spin of Titan – it is like taking off from Manchester and flying into space and back in exactly 24 hours, only to find that when you return to the exact same location that you blasted off from, that the city has moved and you find yourself in the middle of the North Atlantic instead. This could happen if the outer shell of Titan was not attached to the inner core but instead was floating detached on an ocean.

Wherever we find liquid water in the Solar System, we wonder about life and Titan's ocean is no different. The answer is, we have no idea whether the subsurface ocean could potentially be habitable. We do expect it to be very salty – as salty as the Dead Sea. We know this because to explain Titan's overall gravity requires a briny ocean that is dense with salts such as sodium, potassium and sulphur.

Unlike Titan's hydrocarbon lakes, we may never swim through the underground ocean, but knowing that it is there adds another layer of complexity to this beguiling moon.

How to land on an alien moon

In January 2005, a little probe called Huygens made history by landing on Saturn's largest moon, Titan.

DAREDEVIL PLUNGE

Huygens thunders into Titan's atmosphere at 22,000 kilometres per hour in this artist's impression. The spacecraft's heat shield reached 1,800 degrees Celsius. Image: ESA/D Ducros

It is a record not likely to be broken any time soon. On 14 January 2005 a compact, flattened cylinder, chock-full of sensors, cameras and scientific experiments, went hurtling through the orange skies of the mysterious moon Titan. The surface of the moon was still largely unknown, hidden behind a veil of dense smog produced by a haze of hydrocarbon aerosols, but all was about to be revealed. Parachutes unfurling, the probe, named Huygens, was buffeted by winds, swaying on its ropes as the surface loomed up, sporting a terrain of craggy ice-rocks and the dark tributaries belonging to rivers formed from a black, oily chemical mix of liquid ethane, methane and other hydrocarbon molecules. Then came touchdown, the 318 kilogram probe reduced to a relative featherweight in Titan's light gravitational touch. On the surface, Huygens fired pictures of its new surroundings, relayed by way of its mothership Cassini, back home to Earth and the eagerly awaiting throng of scientists and press, to confirm that the European Space Agency (ESA) had successfully accomplished the most distant landing ever achieved. Until we send something to land on one of the moons of Uranus or Neptune, or a body in the Kuiper Belt, this record will not be broken.

Of course, Huygens was not just about setting records. Titan is a moon that fascinates us even more now that we have landed on it and mapped it from orbit. The more we see of it, the more we want to understand it. What Huygens discovered for the 72 minutes it spent transmitting data from Titan's surface before the relaying station – Cassini – disappeared over the horizon (Huygens' batteries died soon thereafter) has played a crucial role in providing a more personal insight into the environment of the moon.

The importance of Huygens' achievement in landing on Titan is more apparent once one understands why scientists view Titan to be so important. Discovered by the Dutch astronomer Christiaan Huygens in 1655, Titan is the second largest moon in the Solar System; at a diameter of 5,152 kilometres, it is just 116 kilometres smaller than Jupiter's moon Ganymede. Its significant mass means it has enough gravity to hold onto a frigid and thick atmosphere that many scientists suspect resembles a version of Earth's primordial atmosphere, stuck in deep freeze and filled with all manner of chemically interesting molecules rich in hydrocarbons such as methane, ethane, propane and so on that are important for some of the chemistry of life. The presence of a methane-rich atmosphere had been confirmed spectroscopically from Earth by Gerard Kuiper in the

HUYGENS SUCCESSFULLY ACCOMPLISHED THE MOST DISTANT LANDING EVER ACHIEVED

TOUCHDOWN ON TITAN

An artist's impression of the Huygens probe sat at its landing site on the surface of Titan. The pebble that it is believed to have broken lies in front of Huygens. Image: ESA/C Carreau.

1940s, but maddeningly the atmosphere proved opaque to any efforts to view the moon's surface.

Knowing the chemistry of the atmosphere, speculation was rife as to what lay on the surface below. In the 1990s Earth-based radar had hinted at the presence of a large continent, named Xanadu, but the prevailing models of Titan's environment at the time suggested that the moon could be covered in an immense sea of liquid hydrocarbons. When NASA's Cassini spacecraft arrived in the Saturnian system in the summer of 2004, with little Huygens piggybacking along with it, it was afforded a few opportunities to scan Titan in haze-beating infrared and radar wavelengths. Yet these scans were only across narrow strips of the moon and Cassini would take years to build up a close-to-complete map. Huygens did not have years; six months after arrival, on Christmas Day 2004, Huygens said goodbye to Cassini, its partner since launch in 1997, and headed for Titan where it would encounter who knows what.

The unknown moon

The uncertainty about what Huygens was headed into led to some doubts about how to define the mission. "I used to get into awful trouble with ESA whenever I called it a lander," says the Open University's Professor John Zarnecki, who was lead scientist on the Surface Science Package, one of six instrument suites on board Huygens. "Formally, it was an atmospheric probe."

Looking back, this seems strange given its famous landing, but when designing Huygens, ESA had a problem. Without knowing what the environment that Huygens would be entering would be, they could not ask the probe's builders to design something for an unknown surface and expect it to survive.

"We didn't know what we would land on, whether it would be solid ice as hard as granite or a liquid sea," says Zarnecki. "So for ESA the primary mission was to make measurements of the atmosphere. Survival on the surface was always going to be an added bonus."

Huygens plunged into Titan's atmosphere at 6.8 kilometres per second, opening its main parachute at an altitude of 150 kilometres as it ejected its heat shield, slowing its descent to around 160 metres per second. At 30 kilometres high, the temperature was –201 degrees Celsius, with westerly winds blowing at 34 kilometres

SAYING GOODBYE

Huygens – Cassini's companion for eight years – departs to dive into Titan's atmosphere. The separation had to be delayed until Christmas 2004 because of a fault with the communication system between the two craft. By saying goodbye at Christmas instead of three months earlier, Cassini would be able to approach Titan from a different angle that would be better to hear Huygen's radio calls. Image: ESA/D Ducros.

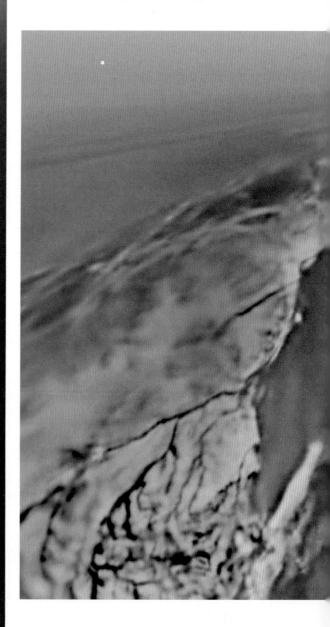

per hour. Huygens passed into the stratospheric haze at a height of 21 kilometres, then at seven kilometres high the wind suddenly changed direction to blow easterly, having slowed to a gentle one kilometre per hour. Then the wind switched direction yet again just a kilometre above the icy surface and the temperature warmed slightly. Huygens was even able to record the sound of the wind howling during its descent.

As the ground loomed up from below, craggy hills riven with channels that looked just like rivers came into view. When Huygens gently dropped down onto the surface amidst freezing temperatures of –179 degrees Celsius, it was to relief and perhaps a little surprise that the diminutive probe had survived and found itself in a completely alien landscape.

A soft landing

What are we to make of Titan's surface? An image returned by Huygens showed a desolate landscape, strewn with pebbles of ice, as hard as rock in the chilly environment. One of the round pebbles in front of Huygens appeared broken, split into two pieces. An orange, overcast hue swamped everything.

It certainly was not an ocean of liquid methane, but nor was it a terrain of pure ice. The signals from the sensors onboard the Science Surface Package were also complicated. The onboard penetrometer that measured the force of the impact suggested that Huygens had hit something hard, then entered deeper into softer ground. The science team had to report this to a press conference, just six hours after the most ambitious space touchdown ever attempted.

"We had to quickly find something to say about data that was very complex and in fact would take years to analyse," says Zarnecki. "We still argue about who it was who said it, but someone suggested that the hard signal to begin with and then softer as you go into the surface was a bit like crème brûlée, with a crust and then soft underneath."

When Zarnecki relayed this analogy at the press conference, it ended up on the front page of newspapers across the world. "Anyone who took any notice of the landing will remember crème brûlée and even now people remind me of it," says Zarnecki. "It wouldn't have surprised me if they served crème brûlée at the tenth anniversary dinner at ESOC (the European Space Operations Centre in Germany)!"

Ironically, given how famous the crème brûlée comment was, later analysis indicated that it was, in fact, incorrect. Remember the broken pebble in front of

LOOKING DOWN

As Cassini plunged through Titan's atmosphere, it captured this view of the ground, showing mountains and valleys, river channels and floodplains. Image: ESA/NASA/JPL/University of Arizona.

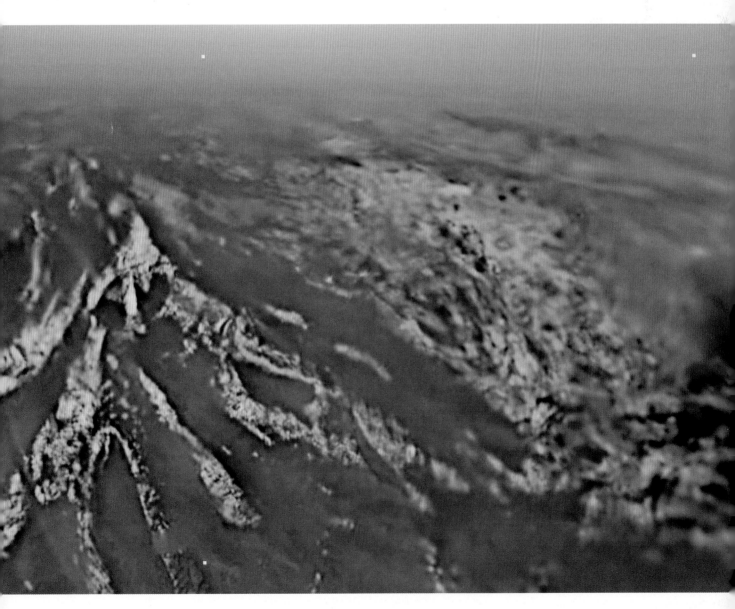

Descending to Titan 2005

Having passed through a layer of haze at an altitude of 21km, Huygens now has its landing site locked in its sights. At 7km up, the wind changes direction, causing Huygens to begin to drift westwards but still falling at 19kph.

- Wind speed **34kph**
- Air pressure **277mb**
- Temperature **−201°C**

- Wind speed **1kph**
- Air pressure **985mb**
- Temperature **−188°C**

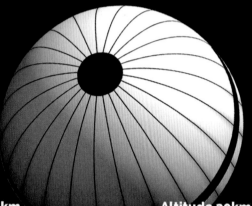

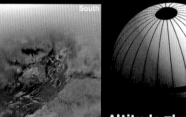

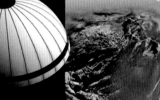

South

Sou

Altitude 150km

Having raced towards Titan at a free-fall velocity of over 21,000 kilometres per hour (kph), Huygens' heat shield began to dramatically slow its approach as it entered the upper atmosphere. By the time the main parachute opened at an altitude of 150km, Huygens had slowed to a velocity of 600kph.

Altitude 30km

Altitude 7km

West

North

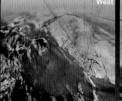

West

Nor

30°N

180°E 0°

150°E

UT

Time of signal
received on Earth

UT

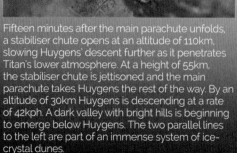

UT

Landing sequence looking East

At an altitude of 150km, the contrast in colours between the blue of the upper atmosphere above and the orange smog below is apparent. The small circle indicates the eventual landing site, only mere hints of the surface terrain peeking through the haze.

Fifteen minutes after the main parachute unfolds, a stabiliser chute opens at an altitude of 110km, slowing Huygens' descent further as it penetrates Titan's lower atmosphere. At a height of 55km, the stabiliser chute is jettisoned and the main parachute takes Huygens the rest of the way. By an altitude of 30km Huygens is descending at a rate of 42kph. A dark valley with bright hills is beginning to emerge below Huygens. The two parallel lines to the left are part of an immense system of ice-crystal dunes.

The channels on the surface are carved by methane rain running away in rivers that quickly dry up after the rainstorm has ended. The channels are hundreds of metres wide and many kilometres long. The hills to the left are a few hundred metres tall.

On 14 January 2005, the European Space Agency's intrepid little Huygens probe plunged through Titan's thick nitrogen and methane atmosphere. Let loose from its mother ship, Cassini, three weeks earlier, Huygens went where no other probe has ever gone before, landing on the surface of this intriguing moon and revealing a landscape never before seen by human eyes. In doing so, Huygens entered the record books as the most distant human-built object on the surface of another Solar System body. It was a tremendous achievement of science and engineering. This is the story of Huygens' adventure.

Again, the wind changes direction and Huygens begins moving towards the south-east. In the last few hundred metres to the surface the wind picks up very slightly into a breeze that helps sculpt the aforementioned dunes. The temperature has settled at around −180 degrees Celsius, the moon's average global temperature.

- Wind speed **2kph**
- Air pressure **1373mb**
- Temperature **−181°C**

Altitude 1km

South

West

North

Huygens' landing site is a ridge of icy bedrock. This outcropping ridge is a piece of transitional terrain indicating the change from highlands to lowlands, similar to the geography found near Earth's coasts. Huygens drifted to the ground at a leisurely 17kph. Its instruments and sensors, active the entire journey, carefully study the surface. And then, impact! The surface is damp and muddy, littered with water-ice pebbles. Huygens continues to communicate with Cassini for a further two hours.

- Wind speed **3kph**
- Air pressure **1456mb**
- Temperature **−180°C**

Altitude 0.3km

South

West

North

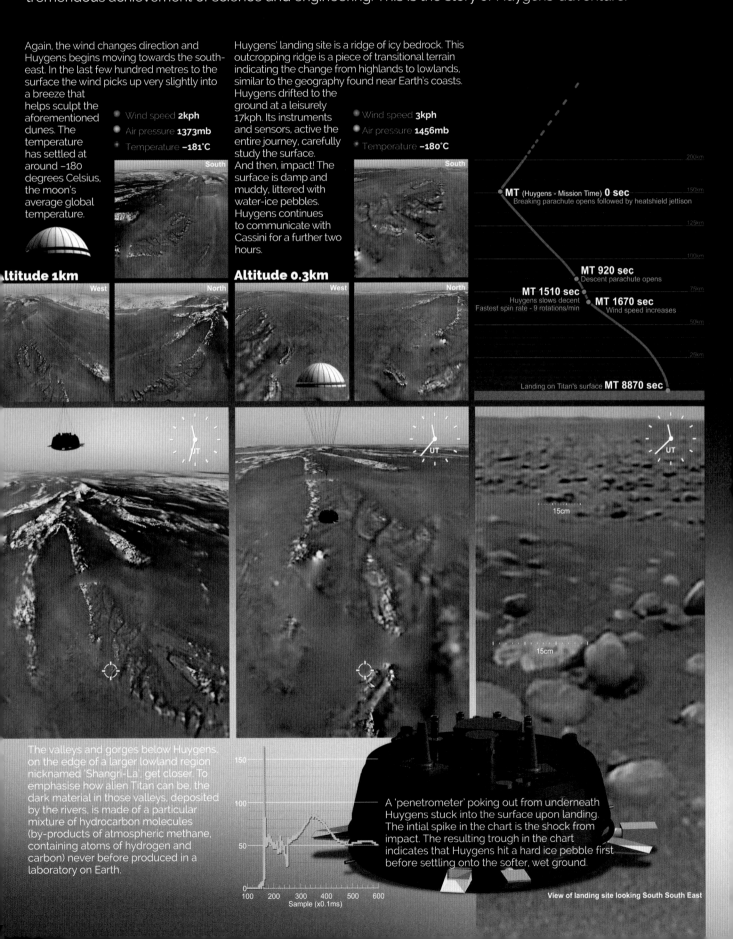

200km

150km

MT (Huygens - Mission Time) **0 sec**
Breaking parachute opens followed by heatshield jettison

125km

100km

MT 920 sec
Descent parachute opens

75km

MT 1510 sec
Huygens slows decent
Fastest spin rate - 9 rotations/min

MT 1670 sec
Wind speed increases

50km

25km

Landing on Titan's surface **MT 8870 sec**

UT

UT

UT

15cm

15cm

The valleys and gorges below Huygens, on the edge of a larger lowland region nicknamed 'Shangri-La', get closer. To emphasise how alien Titan can be, the dark material in those valleys, deposited by the rivers, is made of a particular mixture of hydrocarbon molecules (by-products of atmospheric methane, containing atoms of hydrogen and carbon) never before produced in a laboratory on Earth.

150

100

50

0

100   200   300   400   500   600
Sample (x0.1ms)

A 'penetrometer' poking out from underneath Huygens stuck into the surface upon landing. The intial spike in the chart is the shock from impact. The resulting trough in the chart indicates that Huygens hit a hard ice pebble first before settling onto the softer, wet ground.

View of landing site looking South South East

FIRST LOOK AT TITAN

After Huygens had landed on the surface of Titan on 14 January 2005, it took tis image of what lay in front of it – a pebble-strewn floodplain under an oppressive orange fog. Notice the pebble at bottom left – the theory is that Huygens struck that pebble and broke it as it landed. The 'rocks' just below the centre are about 85 centimetres from the probe and are about 15 centimetres in size. Image: ESA/NASA/JPL/University of Arizona.

Huygens? Zarnecki's team now suspect that Huygens hit that, or another pebble, first, which provided the hard surface signal, before touching the softer, icy gravel that littered the muddy ground. Round pebbles are formed by the action of liquid flowing over rocks (or rock-hard chunks of ice, in this case), smoothing their edges through abrasion – hence you find pebbles at the seaside. Clearly liquid had flowed over Huygens' landing site at some point. "If we had landed maybe 15 to 20 years earlier, we might have landed on a lake," says Zarnecki. "I suspect if you put your hand into that gravel, it would be moist underneath – there is all sorts of indirect evidence that it was damp where we landed."

Evidence for this included how heat was rapidly drained from Huygens once on the surface by the wet, heat-leeching ground. These findings were incredible. Until then, Earth was the only body in the Solar System with liquid flowing across its surface. Now, Huygens had come down in either a floodplain or a dried-up seasonal lake. Although the lake has not yet returned, it could well do so in the next decade as the seasons change, clouds form, and methane rains from the orange sky and collects as liquid running down through tributaries into rivers that open into a lake, ultimately washing Huygens away.

Ahead of its time

Huygens was, at that time, probably the most significant scientific event managed by the European Space Agency. While the Cassini mothership is purely a NASA mission, Huygens was Europe's time to shine and do something nobody had ever achieved before. In many ways it was just as big as the event it was a precursor to, the recent landing of the little triple-legged probe Philae onto comet 67P/ Churyumov–Gerasimenko. However, whereas Philae and its mothership Rosetta received plenty of attention in the news and online social media, Huygens made its historic landing just before such media had become the phenomena that they are today. It was also a learning experience for ESA about how popular such events can be amongst the press and the public.

"I remember talking to the PR person at ESOC three weeks before the landing," says Zarnecki. "She asked whether I thought anyone would be interested in the landing and turn up for a press event. Three weeks later there were 300 members of the press there. I think that was when it dawned on the agency that what they are doing, aside from being great science and great technology, is really cool stuff that is newsworthy and the public worldwide have a real interest in."

And how does the tension and the drama of Philae's eventful landing compare to Huygens? "I have been very privileged to have been at ESOC for all four of ESA's major encounters," Zarnecki reminisces. "I was project manager for one of the instruments on Giotto as it flew past comet Halley in 1986, and then a second comet in 1992. I was at ESOC for the Philae landing, on which I was just a bit-part player, and obviously I was there for Huygens. Although Philae was dramatic and exciting, it couldn't compare for me with Huygens, because that was a project I had lived and breathed every day from 1990 to 2005. I'm not a poet or a writer who can put into words the emotions and the tension and the drama of ten years ago, but that was quite some day I can tell you, one that will never to be repeated, at least, I suspect, not for me."

A RETURN TO TITAN?

Huygens was hermetically sealed to protect against the cold in such a way that it could probably have floated had it splashed down rather than touched down, and that is what John Zarnecki wants to do next. He has his sights on one day launching a mission to one of the two largest lakes, or seas, in Titan's northern hemisphere, named Ligeia Mare and Kraken Mare (they are huge, 126,000 and 400,000 square kilometres in size respectively). Tantalisingly, Zarnecki has already once came close to fulfilling this dream.

"A few years ago a bunch of us put in a proposal to NASA for a floating probe called TIME, the Titan Mare Explorer," he explains. In 2009, TIME was pitted against around 30 other proposals for missions to other planets, moons and asteroids in the Solar System. "I thought we were a long shot, but then when the proposals were down-selected to three, we were among them. In the end they got cold feet and selected INSIGHT, a Mars geophysics probe, which is a perfectly good mission."

TIME would have spent at least weeks, and possibly months, floating on one of the large northern seas, taking samples of the lake liquid, imaging the distant shoreline with a panoramic camera, studying waves on the seas and going down in the record books as the first

extra-planetary boat. Yet there is more to Titan than just lakes, which make up around ten percent of the surface. There are also dunes of ice crystals blown by the gentle winds that Huygens detected on the way down, as well as the presence of cryovolcanoes.

A balloon-mission, in contrast to TIME, would be able to circumnavigate Titan from the air and take in all the different types of scenery, hovering over areas of interest, dropping down to take samples and perhaps even deploying landers or mini-rovers.

"Titan is actually quite good for this sort of thing, with its thick atmosphere and low gravity," says Zarnecki. "A balloon could do a complete circuit of Titan in about two weeks."

Unfortunately, both TIME and the balloon mission are stuck in development hell. Powering these missions is a serious technical challenge, particularly as the type of radioisotopic thermoelectric generator that TIME would have used has been discontinued by NASA. Still the concepts remain, and one day it is hoped a space agency will get around to turning them into a reality.

"They are technically very challenging, but we can do them," says Zarnecki. "The trouble is there is so much good stuff to do in the Solar System."

DRIFTING

An artist's impression of a future Titan probe sent to sail on the hydrocarbon waves of Kraken Mare. Image: JHUAPL/ Lockheed-Martin.

Is there life on Titan?

Could the answer to the ultimate question – is there life beyond Earth? – be found on Titan? Some scientists suspect that it is a possibility.

ALIEN DIET

Beneath the haze, is there hydrogen-guzzling life at work replenishing Titan's methane?

Image: NASA/JPL–Caltech/Space Science Institute.

To answer the question in the title: well, why not? Of course, it is not going to be like any kind of life on Earth – the conditions on Titan are just too 'alien', if you will pardon the pun – but there is no physical law that states life can only follow the set of rules laid down on Earth. Having said that, it is a huge leap to go from saying that it is feasible that life could exist on Titan, and expecting to actually find such life there.

If there is life, it is unlikely to be more complex than microbes. One of the things that would potentially hold back life on Titan is that it is darned cold. With so little heat energy available, metabolic processes would be slow, so if there is life on Titan, it is likely to be quite sluggish.

Aside from the temperature, Titan's conditions are actually quite similar to the early Earth's. It is the only body in the Solar System besides Earth to have an atmosphere of predominantly nitrogen and the atmospheric pressure on the surface is 1.5 times Earth's surface pressure. The constituents of Titan's atmosphere besides nitrogen – all those exotic hydrocarbons – are believed to have been found on the early Earth too and those hydrocarbons are the building blocks of many of the raw materials that life uses. Again, we must be careful here: just because they can be used by life does not mean that they inevitably will be used by life.

Okay, so we have come to the conclusion that it is possible, albeit unlikely, that Titan could support simple life of some form. Now, is there any evidence, any at all, that could support this claim? Actually, yes there is. It is very circumstantial, but intriguing nonetheless. Curious minds such as ours would be remiss not to at least follow it up, even if it is just to rule it out.

Any life on Titan must be methane-based, rather than being dependent on water and oxygen, says Dr Chris McKay of NASA's Ames Research Center. "We only know of two worlds that have liquids on their surface, which are Earth with water and Titan with a liquid methane–ethane mixture," he says. "If life does indeed make do with what's available, then maybe life on Titan is making do with liquid methane."

The diet of Titanian life

Such life forms would be described as 'methanogens' and would consume hydrogen and two kinds of hydrocarbon, namely acetylene and ethane that are by-products of methane, and catalyse them together to generate energy. For example, each gram of acetylene consumed could provide a life form with 3.85 kilojoules of energy, which is the equivalent of 920 calories. This chemical reaction

ANY LIFE ON TITAN MUST BE METHANE-BASED, RATHER THAN BEING DEPENDENT ON WATER AND OXYGEN

LIFE ON THE ICE

An artist's impression of ice on one of Titan's lakes. The boundary between liquid and solid could be the perfect place to find Titanian life sheltering. Image: NASA/JPL– Caltech/USGS.

would cause the microbes to release or exhale methane the way we breath out carbon dioxide and this would be a very neat solution to the mystery of how Titan's methane is replenished.

So there is the first piece of circumstantial evidence: an anomalous replenishment of methane in Titan's atmosphere. However, if Titanian beings really do take advantage of this chemical reaction, then there should be a notable depletion of hydrogen, acetylene and ethane on Titan.

Amazingly that is exactly what inputting observations by Cassini into models of Titan's atmosphere built by scientists, has found. Using data from Cassini's Composite Infrared Spectrometer and the Ion and Neutral Mass Spectrometer, Darrell Strobel of Johns Hopkins University discovered that molecular hydrogen, which makes up some of the debris when methane molecules are broken apart by sunlight and flows downwards through Titan's atmosphere, seems to be disappearing at the surface. Meanwhile, Roger Clark of the US Geological Survey

has used data from Cassini's Visible and Infrared Mapping Spectrometer to search for acetylene on the surface of Titan. Acetylene should be produced when solar ultraviolet breaks apart methane, but no acetylene could be found, as though it were being gobbled up as soon as it reaches the ground. A similar depletion of ethane has also been known about for some time.

However, in situations like this, Occam's razor – the notion that the simplest explanation is more often than not the correct one – must be applied. The lack of acetylene could be the result of solar ultraviolet or even cosmic rays acting upon the acetylene molecules in the atmosphere before they reach the ground and transforming them into more complex molecules. Regarding the hydrogen, it is possible that the atmospheric models that predict that it should be evenly spread throughout the atmosphere and on the surface are incorrect, or that the hydrogen molecules are being absorbed into more complex molecules before reaching the ground. Or there could be some unknown non-biological surface catalyst that is reacting with the hydrogen, causing it to disappear.

This is not a puzzle that Cassini will be able to solve. Future missions must return to Titan carrying the kit required to make the measurements and try to sample any life, if it is there, just as future missions to Mars will seek to do. Until then, life on Titan is going to be limited to ifs, buts and maybes.

TITANIAN LIFE COULD CONSUME HYDROGEN, ACETYLENE AND ETHANE AND CATALYSE THEM TO GENERATE ENERGY

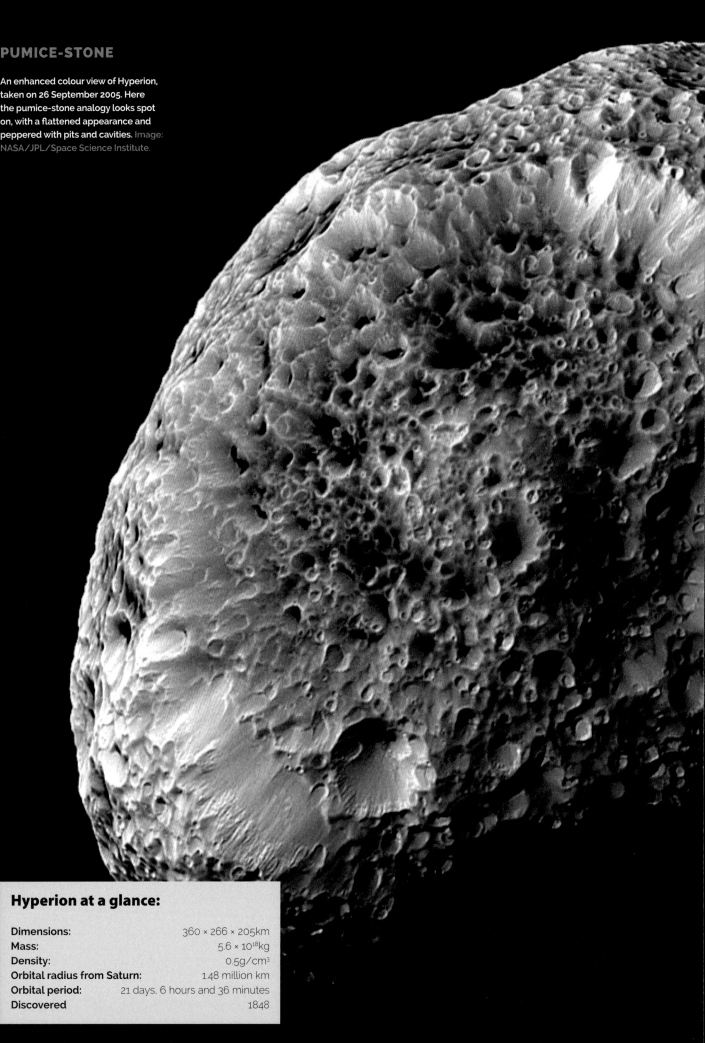

PUMICE-STONE

An enhanced colour view of Hyperion,
taken on 26 September 2005. Here
the pumice-stone analogy looks spot
on, with a flattened appearance and
peppered with pits and cavities. Image:
NASA/JPL/Space Science Institute.

Hyperion at a glance:

Dimensions:	360 × 266 × 205km
Mass:	5.6 × 10^{18}kg
Density:	0.5g/cm³
Orbital radius from Saturn:	1.48 million km
Orbital period:	21 days, 6 hours and 36 minutes
Discovered	1848

Hyperion

Battered and smashed, Hyperion is the weirdest looking moon out of Saturn's retinue of natural satellites.

In our Saturnian adventure, we have already met the lucky moons, Mimas and Tethys, which bore the full brunt of a massive whack from an impactor and lived to tell the tale. Now meet the moon that was not so lucky: Hyperion.

It looks like a grey pumice-stone in space, peppered with deep pits, irregularly shaped, and tumbling chaotically along its orbit around Saturn. Hyperion is one of the largest moons in the Solar System to not be spherical – only Neptune's moon Proteus is larger and still potato-shaped. Its low density implies that it is very nearly all ice, possibly even just loosely accreted rubble with large cavities inside and given a frosty coating. The evidence all seems to point to Hyperion literally being a chip off the block, a large fragment from a shattered moon that was struck by an impactor an undetermined amount of time ago. However, not everybody agrees.

"I think Hyperion's low density and sponge-like appearance link it to a comet-like origin, probably from the Kuiper Belt," says Dale Cruikshank, a veteran planetary scientist at NASA's Ames Research Center. "How it could have found its way into an orbit around Saturn is unknown, but not impossible, I think." Indeed, Phoebe seems to also be a cometary body that has manoeuvred itself into orbit around Saturn. To counter this theory, you might point to Hyperion's tumbling rotation as a sign of it being sent spinning after it shattered in an impact, but its chaotic rotation is actually believed to be a consequence of a 3:4 gravitational resonance with Titan that pulls Hyperion's rotational axis all over the place.

Part of what makes Hyperion so unique are its unusual craters. Rather than featuring the usual mix of terraced walls, bowl-shapes, central peaks and central pits, Hyperion's craters are deep pits filled with a dark material that includes hydrocarbons that have been detected by Cassini's Ultraviolet Imaging Spectrograph (UVIS) and the Visual and Infrared Mapping Spectrometer (VIMS). The material is reddish in colour, but it becomes so concentrated in the deep-pit craters that it looks much darker. It is the same stuff that paints one hemisphere of Iapetus black and so presumably it also comes from the same source, namely outer moon Phoebe's dark ring. However,

THE EVIDENCE POINTS TO HYPERION BEING A LARGE FRAGMENT FROM A SHATTERED MOON THAT WAS STRUCK BY AN IMPACTOR

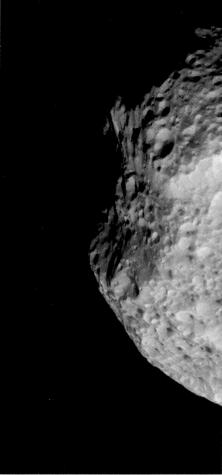

SATURN'S SPONGE

Another view of Hyperion captured from a different angle, as imaged on 16 September 2011. Image: NASA/JPL–Caltech/ Space Science Institute.

ODDLY-SHAPED

Hyperion cuts a different figure in each camera shot as it tumbles chaotically along its orbit. This image was taken on 25 August 2011. Image: NASA/JPL–Caltech/Space Science Institute.

exactly which hydrocarbons are involved is uncertain, says Cruikshank.

"The kind of spectroscopy that we do is sensitive to basic types of hydrocarbons, but not individual molecular identifications," he says. "If these were in the form of ices, we could be quite sure of the specific molecules, but when they are components of this tar-like, or soot-like, opaque solid material, we are lucky to be able to identify the fundamental types of organic compounds. That's the situation we're in with Iapetus, Phoebe and Hyperion."

All of the craters on the various moons in the Saturnian system illustrate the 'impact' (pun intended) that the type of surface being slammed into has on the shape of the crater. In general there are two different types of crater: simple, small bowl-shapes and larger, more complex craters. The bowls result from small impactors simply excavating material in the ground where they crash. In complex craters, one shock wave from the impact compresses the ground, while a shock wave also moves in the opposite direction, back up into the asteroid or comet doing the impacting, reverberating off the back of that and shattering it. The reflected shock wave then travels back down into the crater and excavates large amounts of already compressed material from the ground. This splashes back down outside the crater forming an 'ejecta

blanket', while larger chunks are thrown out further to form secondary craters. Gravity causes the crater walls to collapse, which forms terracing around the inner rime of the crater. The melted crater floor rebounds under the stress, forming a central peak on rocky worlds, but these do not form on icy moons. Instead, when the impact is into ice rather than rock, the centre of the crater collapses into a pit as impact melt drains away through cracks, leaving a void behind. A ring of hills or mountains can still surround this 'central pit' and, sometimes, a frozen dome of thin ice can form over the pit, as warmer material from below rises up like a bubble. Meanwhile, shock waves that ripple through the ground can create a secondary ring around the main crater. A look at the large craters on Mimas and Tethys shows many of these features associated with large impacts into ice.

Hyperion, however, is different, but again environment plays a part. The appearance of Hyperion's craters is a result of the moon' porous, low-density structure. Impacts sink into the moon rather than blasting material out, while the low gravity means that any debris ejected by the impact has a good chance of escaping from Hyperion completely, rather than falling back onto the moon, leaving craters with sharp edges rather than blanketed in icy debris.

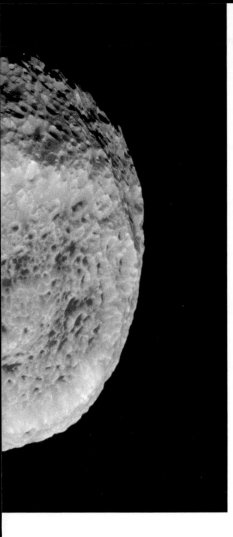

FOR THE LAST TIME

Cassini made its final close approach to Hyperion on 31 May 2015, when its narrow-angle camera snapped this image of a crater-strewn surface. Image: NASA/JPL–Caltech/Space Science Institute.

LIGHT AND SHADOW

Hyperion's odd shape means that under differing illumination it can look very different. Here the lighting puts the focus on the bumpy limb of the moon. Image: NASA/JPL/Space Science Institute.

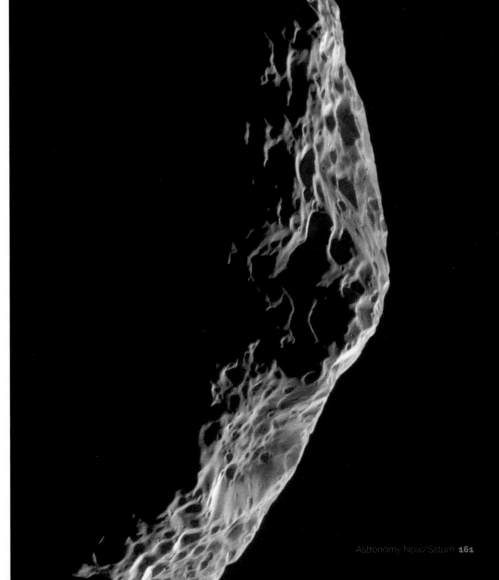

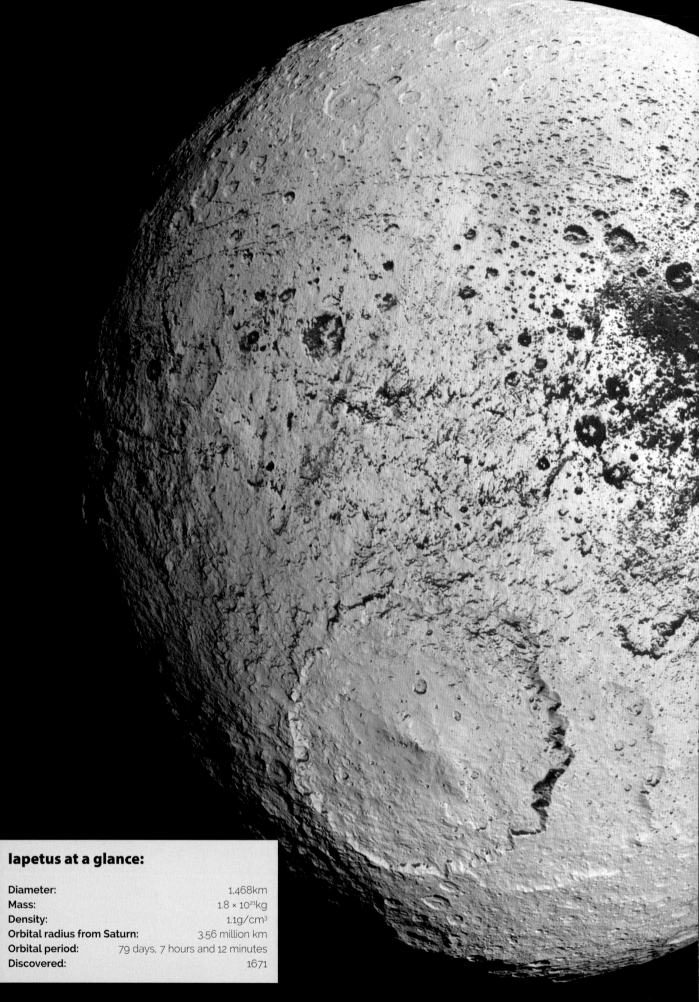

Iapetus at a glance:

Diameter:	1,468km
Mass:	1.8×10^{21}kg
Density:	1.1g/cm³
Orbital radius from Saturn:	3.56 million km
Orbital period:	79 days, 7 hours and 12 minutes
Discovered:	1671

Iapetus
the yin- yang moon

The tallest mountains in the Saturnian system are to be found on distant Iapetus, but these mountains are merely the start of the moon's odd features.

There is one moon that is more enigmatic, bizarre and downright dumbfounding than all the others orbiting Saturn: Iapetus. Pronounced eye-APP-eh-tus, it sports a veritable assortment of strange features. One hemisphere is an icy white; the other tainted black. It is oddly misshapen, with a bulging equator and squashed poles. A huge ridge of mountains that runs around the moon's equator has been nicknamed the 'great wall of Iapetus'. The moon's orbit is also unusual, being highly-inclined with respect to most of the other moons of Saturn.

Cassini's first, distant encounter with Iapetus on New Year's Eve 2004, merely raised more questions than it answered. Two-and-a-half years later came the spacecraft's only close fly-by of the moon, when Cassini flew within 1,640 kilometres of its surface on 10 September 2007. This close encounter answered some of the outstanding questions about Iapetus, but left many more open-ended.

Giant ice mountains
When Cassini flew within 123,400 kilometres of Iapetus towards the end of 2004, it found a stunning sight: a massive ridge or chain of continuous mountains that runs around nearly three-quarters of the moon. Nobody had ever seen anything as astonishing as this on any moon or planet before. The ridge, or great wall, averages 12 to 13 kilometres in height, although some sections tower almost as tall as the record-breaking 24-kilometre volcanic mountain called Olympus Mons on Mars. Where craters have formed over the wall, their exposed rims reveal ice, which suggests that the entire great wall is composed of giant ice mountains. Curiously, the great wall does not extend around the complete circumference of Iapetus, but ends when the bright terrain begins, with only a few isolated mountains here and there, and there

JEKYLL...

The bright trailing hemisphere of the moon Iapetus. Because it is tidally locked to Saturn, its trailing and leading hemispheres do not change. On the right of the moon is the transition zone between the icy-white hemisphere and the dark side.
Image: NASA/JPL/Space Science Institute.

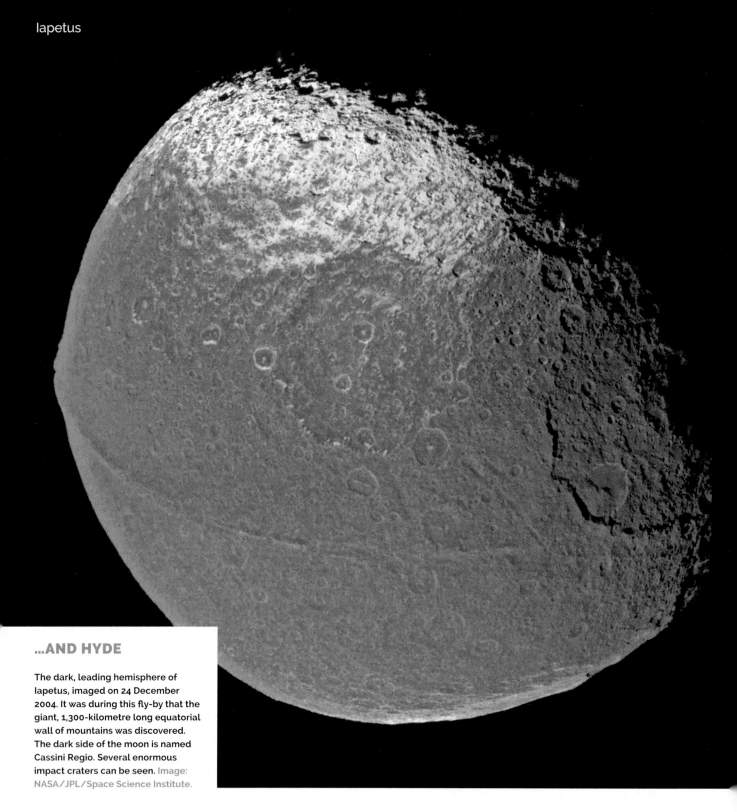

...AND HYDE

The dark, leading hemisphere of Iapetus, imaged on 24 December 2004. It was during this fly-by that the giant, 1,300-kilometre long equatorial wall of mountains was discovered. The dark side of the moon is named Cassini Regio. Several enormous impact craters can be seen. Image: NASA/JPL/Space Science Institute.

is no obvious reason for why this should be so. Still, it has not stopped scientists speculating about the wall's origin. One hypothesis from scientists working on the Cassini mission at the Jet Propulsion Laboratory (JPL) is that Iapetus is a moon frozen in time, captured forever in a still moment from its youth. However, whereas we seek eternal youth, in Iapetus' case it has left the moon in a bit of an unsightly, yet fascinating, mess.

The Cassini team's idea stems from Iapetus' rather slow rotation – a day on this icy moon lasts 79 Earth days! Surely it must have been spinning faster in the past. A combination of a relatively fast rotation – between five and sixteen hours – and a warm heart powered by the radioactive decay of the isotopes aluminium-26 and iron-60 (isotopes are variations of elements that are

not stable and like to decay into other elements, giving out radiation) could have produced Iapetus' distinctive flattened, bulging shape. As it span, its malleable interior began to bulge outwards, stretching its surface area in the process. When the radioactive decay dropped below a sufficient level to keep Iapetus' interior warm, the moon froze solid in this oblate shape and contracted. The extra, stretched surface area had nowhere else to go other than to fold up into the equatorial ridge that we see today.

"Iapetus span fast, froze young and left a body with lasting curves," said JPL's Julie Castillo. "Its development literally stopped in its tracks."

This is not a perfect theory. A similar process occurred on other icy moons such as Jupiter's moon Ganymede, but it left a complex pattern of ridges all over those moons,

rather than just at the equator. The great wall's absence in the bright section of Iapetus is also perplexing. Incidentally, Iapetus' crust must be very thick and rigid to hold all the weight of the giant ridge without deforming, and some scientists think this means that the great wall must have been deposited onto Iapetus' surface, rather than having folded up as part of its crust or risen up from within the moon. Andrew Dombard of the University of Illinois and colleagues have suggested that a giant impact into the surface of Iapetus long ago sent enough debris into orbit around it to form a small moon of Iapetus, the same way that Earth's Moon is thought to have resulted from the debris of an ancient collision. This small satellite's orbit, however, was not a steady one and gravitational tidal forces from Iapetus caused its orbit to decay and the moon eventually broke up. As it orbited around Iapetus' midriff, this debris would then have fallen neatly onto the equator to form the great wall.

Alas, it is unclear how this puzzle can be resolved in the near future, as there is nothing else in the Solar System similar to the great wall and none of the ideas out forward so far appears to fit the facts perfectly. As such, Iapetus' equatorial ridge will remain fertile ground for our imaginations to run riot.

Not so black and white

Nothing explains why the great wall can be found only on the dark terrain. This practically black landscape is named

AVALANCHE!

The rubble of a landslide that has fallen down the 15-kilometre-high scarp that runs around the rim of a giant impact crater called Turgis, which is 580 kilometres across. The debris from the landslide has flowed halfway across a smaller, 120-kilometre wide crater that lies within Turgis.
Image: NASA/JPL/ Space Science Institute.

Cassini Regio, not for the spacecraft but for Giovanni Cassini, who discovered Iapetus in 1671 and immediately noticed its two-faced nature. Indeed, this startling yin-yang likeness is obvious even to amateur astronomers viewing Saturn's moons telescopically from their back garden. As Iapetus orbits Saturn, we see the trailing hemisphere from Earth when it is west of Saturn, appearing 1.7 magnitudes brighter in the night sky than the darker leading hemisphere does when we see that east of the ringed planet. Through Giovanni Cassini's somewhat limited seventeenth-century telescope, Iapetus seemed to simply disappear! Because we know that Iapetus is an ice moon and ice is bright, it might seem logical to suggest that the mysterious dark material that covers one hemisphere is not native to the moon. It is as though Iapetus flew through some kind of dark cloud or plume and got dirt on its face in the process.

Perhaps it did. In 2009 NASA's Spitzer infrared space telescope discovered a dim ring of material around Saturn that was centred on Phoebe, the outermost moon. Now, this ring may be dim, visible only in infrared light, but it is also enormous, covering 10,000 times the area that Saturn's main rings do, with a thickness of 2.3 million kilometres. As it absorbs sunlight, it slowly re-emits it as heat that is detectable as the infrared light that Spitzer saw. The release of infrared photons removes angular momentum from the ring particles, causing their orbits to spiral inwards. The particles encounter several moons along the way, including Iapetus, which

MOUNTAINS AND VALLEYS

Looking along the great wall of Iapetus, at mountains that climb ten kilometres tall, or higher, with cratered valleys between them. The number of craters that pepper the equatorial ridge tells us that the mountains are very old. Image: NASA/JPL/Space Science Institute.

shares an inclined orbit with Phoebe and its ring of dust, which is presumably sputtered from the surface by micrometeoroid impacts. So Iapetus ploughs through the dirt that is infalling from this ring and the ice on its leading hemisphere becomes coated in a thin veil of dust. Infrared observations of Iapetus by Cassini's Composite Infrared Spectrometer (CIRS) during the 2007 fly-by showed that this coating grows 'warm' enough (–146 degrees Celsius) to allow the slow release of water vapour. Over time, the ice sublimates (turns directly into a gas from a solid) and Iapetus' low gravity allows the water molecules to hop across the moon to the clean poles and trailing hemisphere where they accumulate. The constant transport of ice to these 'cold traps' keeps

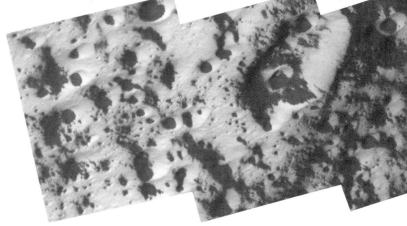

them looking fresh, while the leading hemisphere looks black in contrast – there are barely any shades of grey to be found on Iapetus. The concept is called thermal segregation and although the evidence for it occurring on Iapetus is relatively new, it is actually an old idea: the theory was first proposed back in 1974 by Asoka Mendis and Ian Axford.

"We haven't seen the water–ice evaporating – the process would be too slow to watch in real time," says John Spencer, a CIRS team member from the South-West Research Institute in Boulder, Colorado. "But we see lots of evidence for it, in the form of the bright frost patches on the shady side of craters and the shape of the bright/dark boundary on Iapetus, plus the thermal segregation seen in close-up images."

Tilmann Denk, a Cassini imaging scientist based at the Free University in Berlin, is even more confident that this transport of ice is the solution to Iapetus' two faces.

"I'm pretty confident that the 350-year old riddle about the bright/dark dichotomy has been solved," he tells *Astronomy Now*.

Planning for a fly-by

Denk was involved in organising the imaging schedule for the 2007 fly-by of Cassini, something he had been planning for seven years, and he gives an insight on the work that goes into planning the observations during a spacecraft fly-by.

"By 2003/2004, we already had a good selection of the surface targets and what we wanted to look for," he says. "These included the 'Voyager mountains', the equatorial transition zone, the dark terrain at ultra-high resolution, the dark-floored crater Harmon near the centre of the trailing side, the western terminator area and a global trailing side mosaic. Final detailed planning started in early 2007 when the fly-by ground-track 'tweak' had been adopted by the project management [a trajectory change had been worked out in autumn 2006, which improved the data quality for almost all the

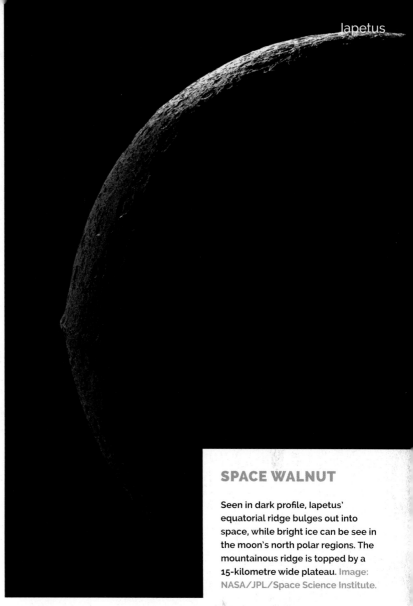

SPACE WALNUT

Seen in dark profile, Iapetus' equatorial ridge bulges out into space, while bright ice can be see in the moon's north polar regions. The mountainous ridge is topped by a 15-kilometre wide plateau. Image: NASA/JPL/Space Science Institute.

TRANSITIONS

A scan of images taken across Iapetus' transition zone between the dark Cassini Regio and the bright white ice of its trailing hemisphere. As one moves into Cassini Regio we find that what remains of the visible ice there resides on slopes and crater walls that are facing away from the Sun and towards the south pole of the trailing hemisphere, so they are less likely to receive sunlight and sublimate. Image: NASA/JPL/Space Science Institute.

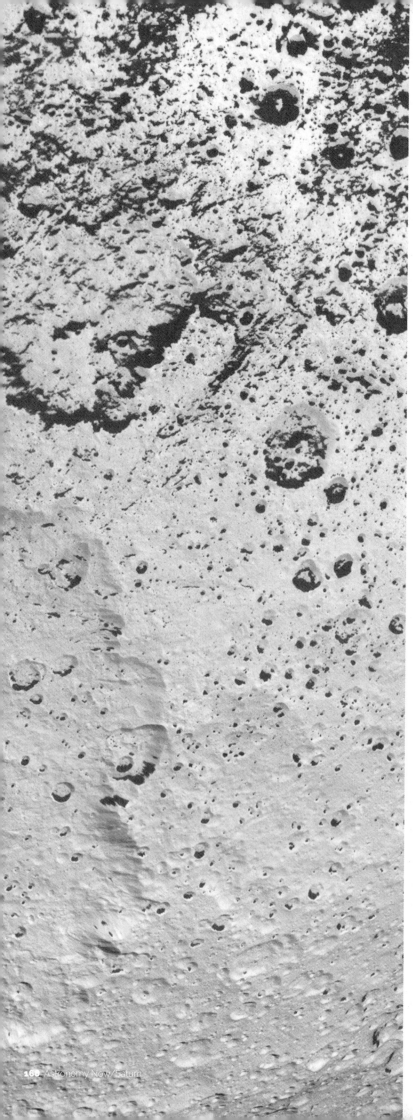

instructions]. Final planning included attitude control of the spacecraft and shutter planning for the Imaging Science Subsystem (ISS). This ended about mid-July, when it was all set in stone."

When 'talking' to Cassini, scientists do not give the spacecraft commands in real time, because the time delay in sending signals from Earth to Saturn and back again (it takes around one hour and twenty minutes for a signal to reach Saturn) makes it impossible. Instead, each month scientists upload a 'background sequence' to the spacecraft that details all Cassini's activities for the coming month. The Iapetus fly-by was uploaded to the spacecraft on 12 August 2007 as part of background sequence 's33'. After that, all scientists could do was sit back and see what happened.

The plan was for 662 frames of Iapetus to be taken on 10 September; 592 were actually 'shuttered' and 463 images were ultimately downloaded to Earth. It was always the intention to take more pictures than could be included on the spacecraft's recorders, because the volume of each image on the recorders was unknown and the aim was to compensate to make sure that all the recorder space was used up. While sending the images back to Earth, a few were lost because of poor compression.

It was not just the imaging subsystem that was returning data: CIRS, the Visible and Infrared Mapping Spectrometer (VIMS) the Ultraviolet Imaging Spectrograph (UVIS) and the RADAR equipment all needed to get a look in too. "The spacecraft attitude [during the fly-by] was designed by our team in Berlin, and we iterated our work with the other instrument teams and included their wishes for scans (CIRS, UVIS), longer stares (VIMS) and mosaics (ISS)," says Denk. "For RADAR, we had to include special time windows that only RADAR could use."

Then Cassini hit a hitch in returning the data to Earth. Just as it began to transmit, the spacecraft was struck by a rogue cosmic ray (a charged particle such as a proton travelling at close to the speed of light). This shut Cassini down for a few hours as it entered a precautionary safe-mode until the spacecraft ran diagnostics to check that it was still healthy. The following day normal service was resumed and the recorded data was received on Earth for scientists to immediately begin pouring over.

Free-flowing

The equatorial ridge, coupled with several large craters (there are five craters on Iapetus wider than 350 kilometres) with steep sides, provide ample slopes for landslides to tumble down. Indeed, an analysis of Cassini's close-ups of the moon in 2007 found evidence of 30 massive avalanches, 17 down crater walls and the remaining 13 down the mountainsides of the great wall.

SNOW WHITE

A close-up slice of Iapetus' bright hemisphere, leading into the transition region with Cassini Regio. Imaging this transition region to better understand the differences between the bright and dark sides of Iapetus was a key part of Cassini's mission during its fly-by of the moon in 2007. Image: NASA/JPL/Space Science Institute.

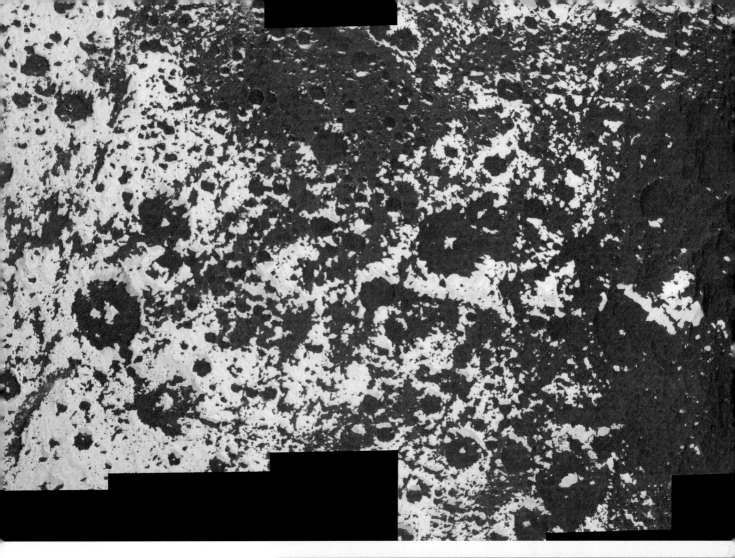

ICE TO DUST

Another view of Iapetus' transition region. The dark material is a coating of dust, which has probably fallen towards the moon from the giant dust ring associated with outermost moon Phoebe. Image: NASA/JPL/ Space Science Institute.

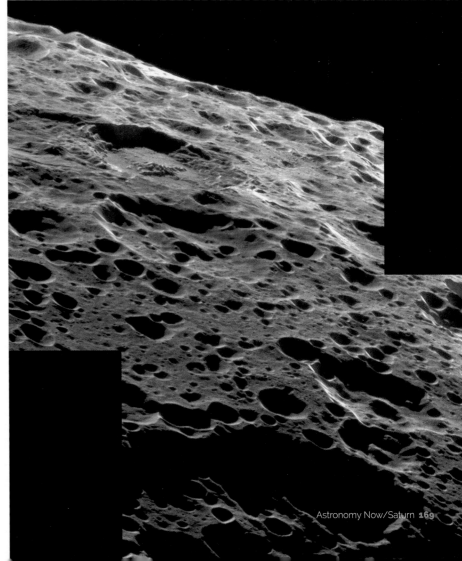

RUGGED MOON

Mountains, craters and pits are the order of the day on Iapetus in this image, taken as Cassini cruised 13,500 kilometres above the surface. Towards the upper left we see a crater that is a little sharper than the rest, with complex terraced walls sporting landslides and a central peak of hills. Its sharpness compared to its neighbouring craters implies it is one of the younger craters on Iapetus – but still billions of years old. Image: NASA/JPL/Space Science Institute.

BLACK AND WHITE

The surface of Iapetus rolled out flat in a Mercator projection. Here the difference between the dark leading hemisphere and the poles and the bright trailing hemisphere is startling. Image: NASA/JPL/Space Science Institute/Lunar and Planetary Institute.

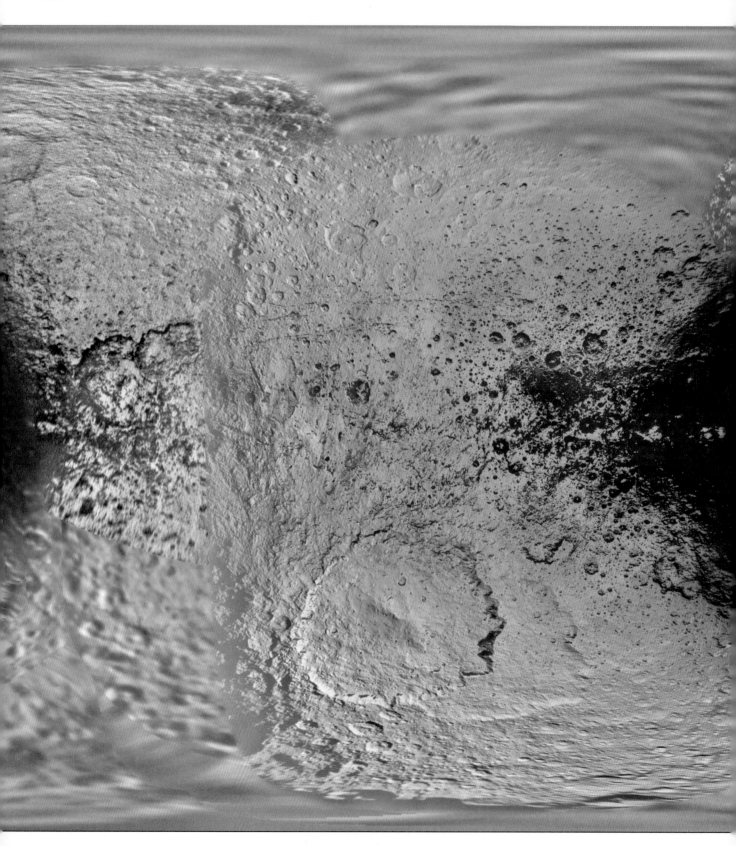

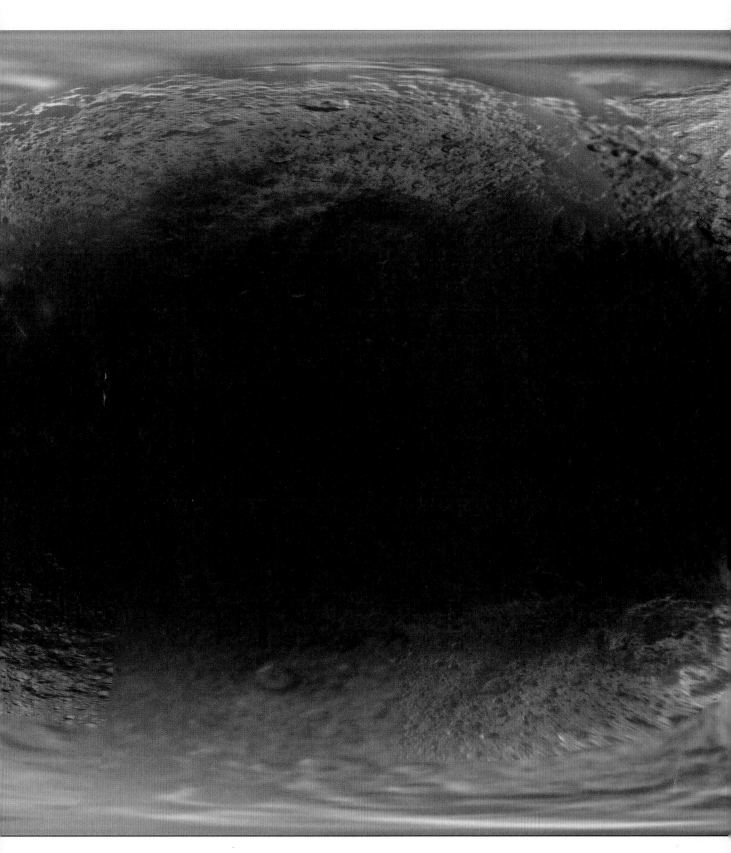

In fact, Iapetus seems to suffer more major avalanches as the ice gradually sublimates away than any other planet or moon in the Solar System with the exception of Mars. The mystery behind the landslides is that they seem to move phenomenally quickly – rather than tumbling helter-skelter down mountainsides, the falling ice seems to flow as friction becomes negligible. Understanding why the friction all but disappears is testing geophysicists to the limit. However, a similar phenomenon occurs when a tectonic fault-line on Earth suddenly slips and the level of friction between the rocks drops. Again, geologists are unsure why this happens, but one possibility is that tiny contact points between the two rock faces are flash-heated so quickly that the heat doesn't get chance to escape, but melts the rock instead, which makes it 'slippery'. Something similar could be occurring on Iapetus, allowing landslides to flow for many, many kilometres. Suffice to say, future space tourists to Iapetus may not find its mountainsides the safest slopes for skiing – particularly when operating in three percent of Earth's gravity!

THE GREAT WALL

The giant wall of mountains that splits Iapetus' northern and southern hemispheres rides into the distance in this image taken on 10 September 2007, as Cassini looked down on the moon. The tallest mountains are over 20 kilometres high. Image: NASA/JPL/Space Science Institute.

CASSINI REGIO

This view of Iapetus' dark side shows the moon's squashed shape and equatorial ridge running around it like a giant seam holding two halves of the moon together. Iapetus may have gained this walnut-shape from when it was young and spinning fast. Its interior, warmed by the radioactive decay of elements, would have begun to bulge outward at the equator. When Iapetus grew too cold and froze inside, its surface contracted and folded up into the great wall. Interestingly, we can work out Iapetus' age based on the half life – the time it takes for half of the atoms to decay – of the radioactive elements involved, namely aluminium-26 and iron-60. This puts Iapetus at 4.564 billion years old, which is as old as Saturn itself. Image: NASA/JPL/Space Science Institute.

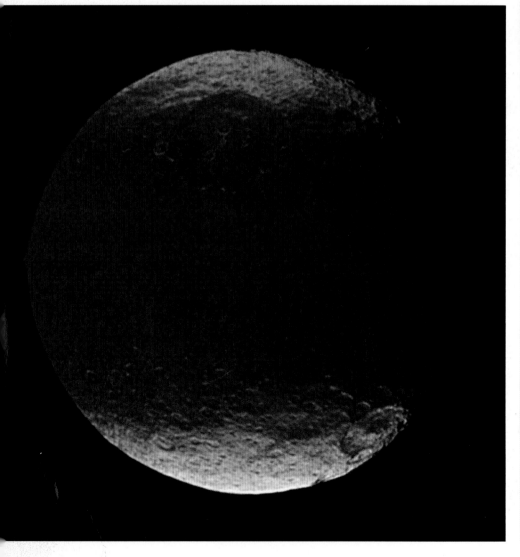

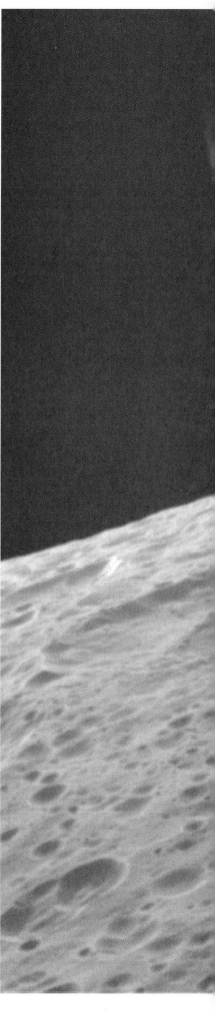

Phoebe

Saturn's last major moon is an object from another place and another time.

Phoebe at a glance

Dimensions:	218 × 217 × 203km
Mass:	8.3 × 10^{18}kg
Density:	1.6g/cm^3
Orbital radius from Saturn:	12.96 million km
Orbital period:	1 year, 185 days, 13 hours and 30 minutes
Discovered:	1899

A BLAST FROM THE PAST

Saturn's moon Phoebe is a relic protoplanet from the very dawn of the Solar System. Phoebe also has a place in the record books from the dawn of astronomical photography – it was the first moon to be discovered by photography, by William Pickering in 1899. Image: NASA/JPL/Space Science Institute.

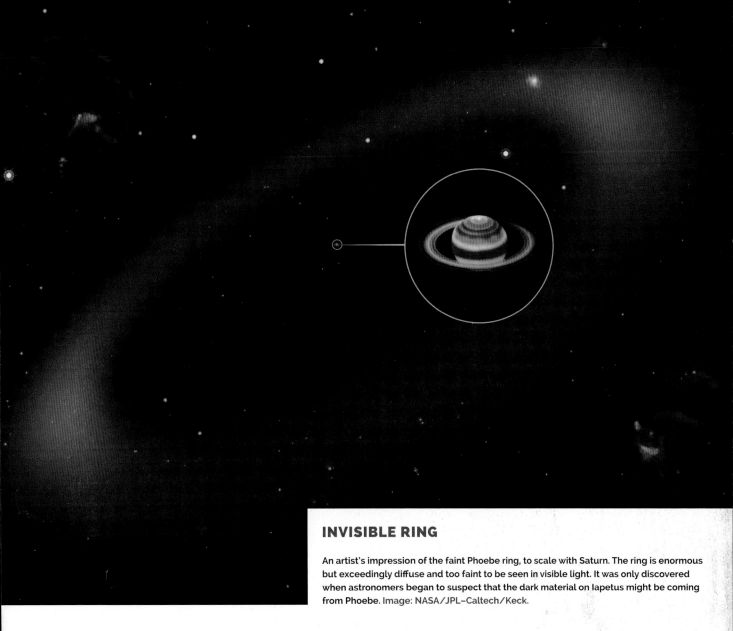

INVISIBLE RING

An artist's impression of the faint Phoebe ring, to scale with Saturn. The ring is enormous but exceedingly diffuse and too faint to be seen in visible light. It was only discovered when astronomers began to suspect that the dark material on Iapetus might be coming from Phoebe. Image: NASA/JPL–Caltech/Keck.

It is ironic that the last moon that we come to was actually the first to be visited by Cassini, back in 2004, prior to the spacecraft's entering into orbit around Saturn. Phoebe is not Saturn's outermost moon – a few tiny, scattered moons lie beyond it – but to all intents and purposes Phoebe is the sentinel at the gate. Its orbit is weird – moving around Saturn backwards compared to the other moons and inclined at an angle of 27 degrees, Phoebe is a law unto itself. Little wonder: it was not even born around Saturn.

Phoebe is an interloper, an object that drifted too close to Saturn and was caught in its gravitational web. Scientists used to think that it was a captured asteroid, but Cassini's one and only visit to Phoebe threw that idea out of the window. Instead, Phoebe is something far more profound: an ancient planetary seed from the distant Kuiper Belt, which is a band of icy objects beyond the orbit of Neptune, which count Pluto amongst their number. Objects like Phoebe were the first large bodies to form in the Solar System. There were countless numbers of them. Some were successful and grew into fully fledged planets like Earth and Saturn, frequently by merging with each other. Others were destroyed, smashed by impacts. And some were left homeless, destined to wander the depths of the Solar System stillborn. Phoebe is one of

those, which makes it a tremendously important object to study because its material is pristine, dating back to the first few million years in the life of the Solar System, which means it can tell us much about the conditions back then and how they resulted in the planets we see today.

"Unlike primitive bodies such as comets, Phoebe appears to have actively evolved for a time before it stalled out," says Julie Castillo of the Jet Propulsion Laboratory. When it was born from the 'solar nebula' of gas and dust that the Solar System was gradually condensing out of, Phoebe was warm inside, warm enough for liquid water and also warm enough to settle into a nearly spherical shape. In the 4.54 billion years since then, it has been battered and bruised by impacts and is now more irregular than spherical. It gives an indication of how violent the early days of the Solar System were – another 'protoplanet' that we know of, the asteroid Vesta, seems to have evolved in similar fashion and been wounded by the same ferocious types of impacts.

PHOEBE IS AN INTERLOPER FROM THE KUIPER BELT THAT DRIFTED TOO CLOSE TO SATURN AND WAS CAUGHT IN ITS GRAVITATIONAL WEB

The ice below

Phoebe is a fairly dark object, but this comes from a layer of tar-like material several hundred metres thick that overlie a brighter, icy crust. The ice can be seen in crater walls, which appear brighter than the surrounding surface. An example of this can be seen in the largish crater at the top of the picture. Image: NASA/JPL/Space Science Institute.

The heat that Phoebe was born with allowed a variety of chemical reactions that resulted in the most diverse mineral composition seen anywhere in the Solar System other than on Earth. Cassini's Visual and Infrared Mapping Spectrometer detected hydrocarbons, ferrous iron-bearing minerals, trapped carbon dioxide, phyllosilicates (silicate minerals including clay and serpentine), nitriles, organics, and cyanide compounds, the latter two of which are not seen in such quantities anywhere else in the realm of the planets.

Phoebe is coloured a dark red (organic minerals often create a red cast on a planetary surface) from a 500-metre thick layer of these minerals and molecules mixed together into a tar-like substance. This leads to Phoebe having a low reflectivity, and both its colour and brightness are typical of other Kuiper Belt objects, while its density is similar to Pluto and Neptune's moon Triton, which is also thought to be a captured protoplanet from the Kuiper Belt. A few hundred

million years after the birth of the Solar System, the planets were in the process of migrating inwards and outwards from the Sun before they settled down into their current locations. All this upheaval in the Solar System succeeded in scattering many Kuiper Belt objects, including Phoebe and Triton.

The great ring

Phoebe has had a huge influence on some of the other moons orbiting Saturn. As micrometeorites pepper Phoebe's surface, they smash off tiny pieces of dusty debris that forms an immense ring, so big that it is the largest structure in the Solar System besides the Sun's magnetic bubble, the heliosphere. Yet so big is this ring that its particles are spread thinly. In fact, if you were in the middle of the ring, you would not even notice it. It took the infrared vision of NASA's Spitzer Space Telescope to discover the ring's cool infrared glow, which radiates at a measly −190 degrees Celsius.

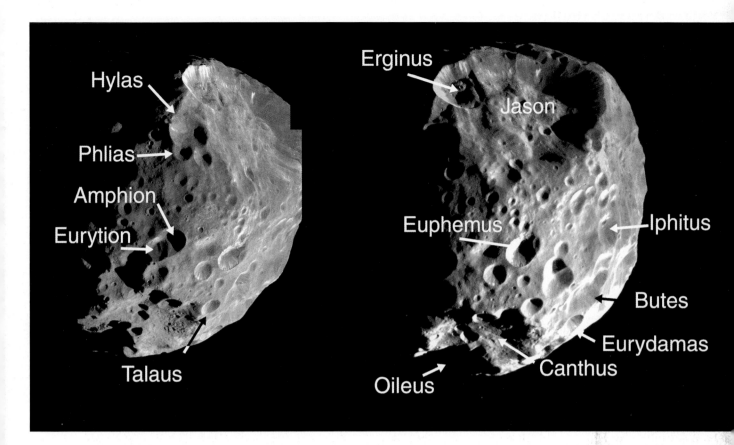

The ring starts at about six million kilometres from Saturn, and extends another 12 million kilometres, or about 300 times the diameter of Saturn. Its vertical thickness is immense too, equivalent to 20 times the diameter of Saturn. So huge is this volume of space that you could fit around a billion Earths into it.

The particles of this ring are tiny grains of ice and dust, rotating retrograde (backwards) along with Phoebe but in the opposite direction to the other moons, including its nearest neighbour, Iapetus. The ring particles migrate inwards towards Saturn, crossing Iapetus' orbit, where Iapetus' leading hemisphere ploughs into them, staining it a dark black. It is the rain of Phoebe ring particles that has sparked the thermal segregation that we see on Iapetus, resulting in one bright hemisphere and on dark hemisphere. The ring dust may also supply the dark material found at the bottom of Hyperion's pit craters, and even some of the dark stains on some of the inner icy moons. Phoebe has certainly made its mark, both literally and figuratively.

In many ways, Cassini has been extremely fortunate to have been able to study Phoebe up close, even if it were only briefly. Phoebe itself could have justified a space mission to investigate this relic from the dawn of the Solar System; for it to be an addition to Cassini's prime mission was just all the more fortunate.

CRATER ON ICE

A 13-kilometre wide crater on the surface of Phoebe. The trails that seem to run down this simple basin-shaped impact site are where loose material has tumbled down the slopes. The bright spots that are seen in this image are exposed ice. Image: NASA/ JPL/Space Science Institute.

THE ARGONAUTS

Above: Befitting a very ancient object such as Phoebe, its many craters are named after the mythical crew of the Argo from *Jason and the Argonauts*. The largest crater is Jason, at around 100 kilometres across and with walls 16 kilometres high. Image: NASA/JPL/ Space Science Institute.

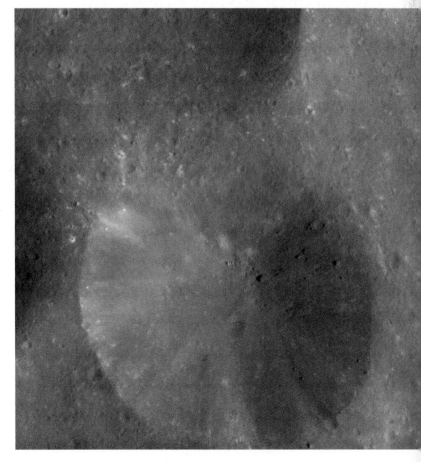

The view from

the gallery

Saturn and its moons put on a cosmic show for Cassini, doing a dance around each other as the spacecraft watches on. Some of the scenes look so fantastic that they could have almost come out of a science fiction film, but they are real, with the moons as actors and Saturn the director working on the cosmic stage.

TITAN AND EPIMETHEUS

The arc of Saturn's rings cuts between tiny Epimetheus (above the rings) and the huge sphere of Titan in the background. The dark gap in the rings is the Encke Gap and the tiny dot of the moonlet called Pan is also visible within it. Cassini was 667,000 kilometres from Epimetheus when it snapped this alignment, while Titan was 1.8 million kilometres from Cassini when it took this image on 28 April 2006. Image: NASA/ JPL/Space Science Institute.

RHEA AND DIONE

Above: Rhea looms above and Dione lies in the distance in this image taken on 11 January 2011. About 863,000 kilometres lies between the two moons, while Cassini was 61,000 kilometres from Rhea when it caught this scene on its narrow-angle camera. Image: NASA/JPL/Space Science Institute.

LITTLE AND LARGE

Right: Cassini saw Rhea passing in front of giant Saturn on 4 February 2007 with its wide-angle camera, at a distance of 1.2 million kilometres from Saturn. Rhea is much closer at 679,000 kilometres. Image: NASA/JPL/Space Science Institute.

TITAN AND DIONE

Above: what's this? Has Dione suddenly grown larger than Titan? Despite being 599,000 kilometres apart, the two moons look almost the same size, although in reality Titan is around five times larger than its cratered counterpart. Both moons are shown here, in this image taken on 6 November 2011, in contrasting true colour. Image: NASA/JPL/Space Science Institute.

BELOW LOOPING RINGS

Right: Saturn's glorious rings are seen looping above Mimas, which looks a little lost next to the gargantuan gas giant planet in this image captured on 4 September 2007, with Cassini 2.8 million kilometres from Mimas and 2.7 million kilometres from Saturn. Image: NASA/ JPL/Space Science Institute.

TITAN AND RHEA

Rhea is the second largest moon orbiting Saturn, but you would never guess it looking at this image. Rhea is absolutely dwarfed by Titan, and Rhea was 400,000 kilometres closer to Cassini than Titan was when this image was taken on 16 June 2011! Image: NASA/JPL/Space Science Institute.

RHEA AND DIONE, TAKE 2

Taken across the northern trailing hemisphere of Dione at a distance of 110,000 kilometres from Cassini on 11 April 2015, Rhea moves from left to right in the background, a further 390,000 kilometres away. Image: NASA/JPL/Space Science Institute.

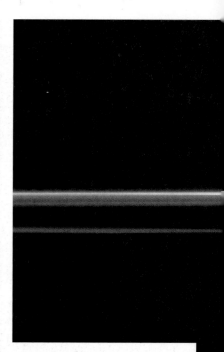

ENCELADUS AND RHEA

The two crescents of small Enceladus and large Rhea come into contact beneath the plane of Saturn's rings. Cassini was two million kilometres from Enceladus on 2 March 2006 when it caught this transit across Rhea, which is a further 800,000 kilometres beyond Enceladus. Image: NASA/JPL/Space Science Institute.

ENCELADUS

The velvety dark background of Saturn's night-side, lined by the dim shadows of the rings, is the wondrous backdrop for Enceladus in this image taken on 28 June 2007. Cassini was 291,000 kilometres from Enceladus. Image: NASA/JPL/Space Science Institute.

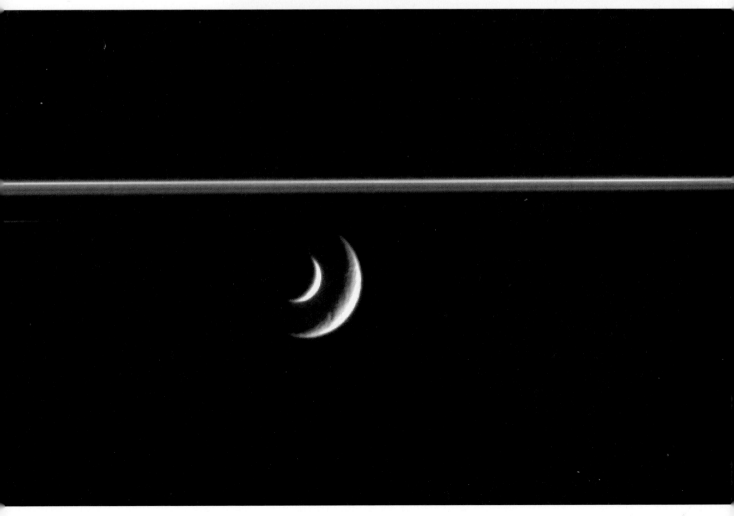

SHADOWS AND RINGS

Stunning geometry and colour between the curve of the rings and the straight line of Saturn's shadow is captured in this image, which looks down onto the north side of the rings as seen on 20 March 2009. Image: NASA/JPL/Space Science Institute.

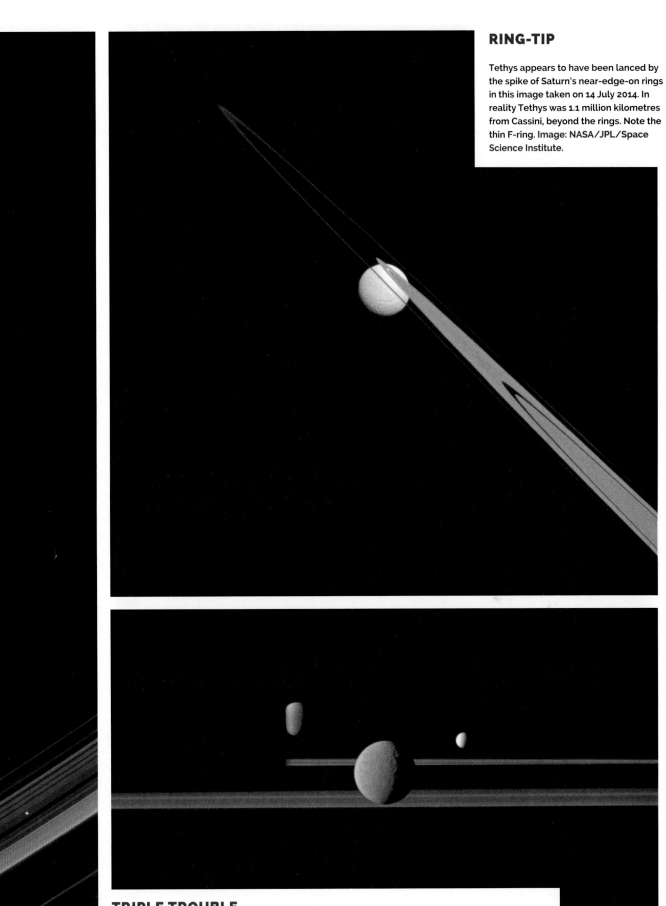

RING-TIP

Tethys appears to have been lanced by the spike of Saturn's near-edge-on rings in this image taken on 14 July 2014. In reality Tethys was 1.1 million kilometres from Cassini, beyond the rings. Note the thin F-ring. Image: NASA/JPL/Space Science Institute.

TRIPLE TROUBLE

From left to right we can see Dione, Rhea and Enceladus while they moved along their orbits around Saturn on 25 April 2011. Dione is just emerging from behind Saturn's dark limb. Enceladus is closer to Saturn, while Rhea in the middle is in the foreground, on the same side of the rings as Cassini and 2.2 million kilometres from the spacecraft. Enceladus is three million kilometres from Cassini and Dione is 3.1 million kilometres away – the scales on show here are just vast. Image: NASA/JPL/Space Science Institute.

Cassini's
curtain call

Buckle yourself in, as the Cassini spacecraft prepares to undertake a series of perilous dives into the rings and the upper atmosphere of Saturn, where the intrepid robotic explorer will meet its ultimate fate in 2017..

WHERE NO PROBE HAS GONE BEFORE

Cassini will spend its final months in an orbit in which it will swoop down between Saturn's inner C- and D-rings and the upper cloud layer of the planet, before finally taking the plunge into Saturn on 15 September 2017. Image: NASA/JPL/Space Science Institute/Greg Smye-Rumsby.

t was in 2004 that Cassini first stepped foot (or should that be antenna?) into the domain ruled by majestic Saturn, resplendent with its crown of rings and retinue of dutifully orbiting moons. Since then, Cassini has discovered astonishing geysers on Enceladus, hydrocarbon lakes on Titan and an enormous equatorial wall of twenty-kilometre tall mountains on Iapetus. It has seen up close a storm that threatened to engulf the ringed planet, watched fresh satellites emerge from the rings and witnessed views of the moons and planet aligned with one another in scenes that appear to have come straight from science fiction. All good things, however, must come to an end.

Plans have now been drawn up for Cassini's 'Grand Finale', which will see the space probe raise itself into a series of highly inclined orbits, starting in April 2017. Swooping down from high above the poles of Saturn, Cassini will pass inside the rings and get a taste of Saturn's upper atmosphere.

"We'll have great views of the poles," says Linda Spilker, Cassini's Project Scientist, who is excited at the potential for scientific discoveries that the new orbits could provide. The poles of Saturn in particular have beguiled us with their dramatic atmospheric vortices (see pages 36 to 47). They are not particularly mysterious in themselves – similar vortices are observed at the poles of Titan, Venus and indeed Earth – but seeing more of Saturn's north polar hexagon and understanding how the it interacts with the rest of the atmosphere is high on the list of things that Cassini scientists want to tick off on their 'to-do' list before the end of the mission.

Then, of course, there are the rings, which are magnificent and mysterious at the same time and, despite Cassini having a constant view of them, we are still struggling to find a definitive answer as to their origin. By moving inside the rings – between the inner C-ring and the planet itself – Cassini will get a more intimate view of the rings that could prove quite revealing.

"When we jump inside we'll be able to measure the mass of the rings, which right now is 100 percent uncertain," says Spilker. "If the rings are more massive than we expect then perhaps they formed at the same time as Saturn, but if they are less massive then they would probably be younger,

POLES

Cassini's final orbits will take the spacecraft looping over Saturn's poles, allowing excellent views of the atmospheric vortices and storms systems present there, as seen in this image taken on 12 August 2014. Image: NASA/JPL–Caltech/ Space Science Institute.

ORBITAL VECTORS

Cassini's daring end-of-mission will begin in late 2016, when it embarks on a series of orbits that take it just beyond the F-ring and which will push it up into a polar orbit that will eventually take it down between the rings and the planet. It will end its mission impacting into the atmosphere of Saturn. AN graphic by Greg Smye-Rumsby.

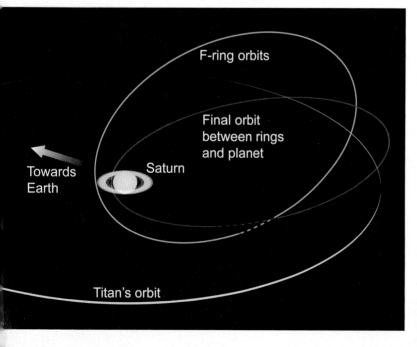

fuel and simply drift. On board are the three radioisotope thermoelectric generators, or RTGs, which produce electricity from the heat of radioactive decay of plutonium. Ensuring that we do not mess up Saturn's backyard with this nuclear material is paramount.

"Enceladus and Titan have liquid water oceans underneath their icy crusts," says Spilker. "We want to make sure that we do not accidentally crash into them and melt through the ice from the heat of the RTGs."

So as soon as the summer solstice has passed, Cassini will raise itself into its final orbits. The end of the mission is the only time Cassini could do this, as it would have required too much fuel to enter such an orbit and then return to an equatorial orbit. Once there, Cassini will be stuck there.

The spacecraft will make 22 of these orbits, each one taking seven days. "As the orbits go on we will walk closer and closer to the atmosphere of Saturn," says Spilker. "Then, in the final orbit, Cassini will get a little nudge from Titan that will send us deep into Saturn."

On 15 September 2017 Cassini will plummet through the creamy-hued atmosphere, tumbling to its fiery doom to become a part of Saturn itself in a rather fitting demise. Twenty years after its launch from Earth, Cassini's mission will be over.

All good things must come to an end, but often that is just to make way for the next good thing. Already there are discussions about the next mission to Saturn, with ideas and speculations about spacecraft that will hover closely over the rings using electric propulsion, a probe designed to enter Saturn's atmosphere in a controlled fashion and return valuable information, balloons or floating devices to explore Titan and even a mission designed to go and look for evidence of life inside Enceladus. Cassini's end may be in sight, but our exploration of Saturn is only just beginning.

formed by a comet or moon that got too close to Saturn and broke apart."

The weight of evidence is beginning to lean towards an origin as old as Saturn itself (see pages 48 to 65), but Cassini may be able to solve the puzzle once and for all.

Jumping inside the rings will also tell us more about the planet itself, getting close enough for Cassini to make the most sensitive readings of Saturn's magnetic and gravitational fields yet, which will inform us about the planet's interior. For instance, being unable to penetrate very far down into Saturn's atmosphere with its cameras, Cassini has not been able to deduce the interior structure of the planet. By measuring the precise gravity field, Cassini scientists will be able to infer details about the size of Saturn's core and its possible composition. Furthermore, getting a more accurate measurement of the magnetic field will hopefully be sufficient to distinguish it from the planet's rotation, with which the magnetic axis is almost perfectly aligned with. Finally, we may learn the exact length of Saturn's day, which is somewhere around ten hours and forty minutes.

Between now and then

There is still much work for Cassini to do before 2017, including monitoring seasonal changes on both Saturn and Titan. Saturn is now moving into northern summer, with the summer solstice in April 2017, while on Titan, says Spilker, some global circulation models predict that strong winds could blow up, driving waves on the northern lakes. Cassini will also complete mapping Titan at near-infrared wavelengths and get as much coverage as possible with the on board radar experiment. Away from Titan, Cassini still has two fly-bys of Enceladus where it will pass through the icy spray of its geysers, while it will also get close-up views of the likes of Tethys, plus some of the smaller moons that skirt the outer F-ring, such as Janus, Prometheus and Atlas.

Yet Cassini cannot carry on for ever. Its fuel is becoming depleted and Cassini will not be allowed to run out of

INSIDE THE RINGS

Cassini will fly inside the rings and above the planet's atmosphere, putting the spacecraft in a prime position to sample both gaseous molecules from the atmosphere and particles from the rings. Image: NASA/JPL/Space Science Institute.

FINAL DESTINATION

Saturn looms ominously as the final resting place for Cassini. Image: NASA/JPL–Caltech/Space Science Institute.

ONE LAST VISIT

Tethys is one of the last moons that Cassini will fly close to, in autumn 2015.
Image: NASA/JPL/Space Science Institute.

STEERING CLEAR

To avoid crashing into Titan, Cassini will send itself on a kamikaze flight into
the bowels of Saturn. Image: NASA/JPL–Caltech/Space Science Institute.

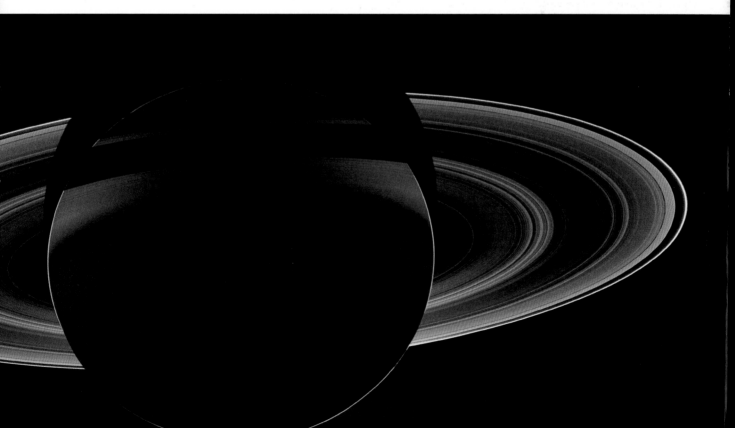

Meet the Cassini–Huygens family

None of this book would have been possible without the excellence and dedication of the scientists who have worked on the Cassini mission since its inception in the early 1980s up through to the present day. It is impossible to list everyone on this single page, but we would be remiss if not to at least mention some of the men and women who have made Cassini's amazing mission possible.

Cassini Programme Manager
Robert Mitchell

Cassini Deputy Programme Manager
Earl Maize

Cassini Project Scientists
Dennis Matson (until 2008)
Bob Pappalardo (2008–2010)
Linda Spilker (2010–end of mission)

Cassini Deputy Project Scientist
Scott Edgington

Cassini Project Science System Engineer
Nora Alonge

Huygens Project Scientist/Mission Manager
Jean-Pierre Lebreton

Huygens Mission Operations Manager
Claudio Sollazzo

Huygens Probe Operations Engineer
Shaun Standley

Huygens Mission Analyst
Artemio Castillo

Huygens Systems Engineering Manager
Thierry Blancquaert

Huygens Operations Scientist
Olivier Witasse

Huygens Science Operations Engineer
Miguel Perez-Ayucar

Interdisciplinary Scientists
Jeffrey Cuzzi
Tamas Gombosi
Jonathan Lunine
Tobias Owen
Laurence Soderblom
Darrell Strobel
Michel Blanc
Daniel Gautier
Francois Raulin

Cassini Principal Investigators
David Young (Cassini Plasma Spectrometer)
Hunter Waite (Ion and Neutral Mass Spectrometer)
Ralf Srama (Cosmic Dust Analyser)
Mike Flasar (Composite Infrared Spectrometer)
Carolyn Porco (Imaging Science Subsystem)
Michele Dougherty (Magnetometer)
Stamatios Krimigis (Magnetospheric Imaging Instrument)
Charles Elachi (RADAR)
Don Gurnett (Radio and Plasma Wave Science)
Richard French (Radio Science)
Larry Esposito (Ultraviolet Imaging Spectrograph)
Bob Brown (Visible and Infrared mapping Spectrometer)

Huygens Principal Investigators
Guy Israel (Aerosol Collector Pyrolyser)
Martin Tomasko (Descent Imager/Spectral Radiometer)
Michael Bird (Doppler Wind Experiment)
Hasso Niemann (Gas Chromatograph Mass Spectrometer)
Marcello Fulchignoni (Huygens Atmospheric Structure Instrument)
John Zarnecki (Surface Science Package)

CLASS PHOTO

Cassini scientists meeting at the Jet Propulsion Laboratory in 2010.
Image: NASA/JPL.